THE HUMANITIES IN PRECOLLEGIATE EDUCATION

THE HUMANITIES IN PRECOLLEGIATE EDUCATION

Eighty-third Yearbook of the National Society for the Study of Education

PART II

Edited by

BENJAMIN LADNER

Editor for the Society

KENNETH J. REHAGE

19 NSSE 84

Distributed by THE UNIVERSITY OF CHICAGO PRESS • CHICAGO, ILLINOIS

The National Society for the Study of Education

Founded in 1901 as successor to the National Herbart Society, the National Society for the Study of Education has provided a means by which the results of serious study of educational issues could become a basis for informed discussion of those issues. The Society's two-volume yearbooks, now in their eighty-third year of publication, reflect the thoughtful attention given to a wide range of educational problems during those years. A recently inaugurated series on Contemporary Educational Issues includes substantial publications in paperback that supplement the yearbooks. Each year, the Society's publications contain contributions to the literature of education from more than a hundred scholars and practitioners who are doing significant work in their respective fields.

An elected Board of Directors selects the subjects with which volumes in the yearbook series are to deal, appropriates funds to meet necessary expenses in the preparation of a given volume, and appoints a committee to oversee the preparation of manuscripts for that volume. A special committee created by the Board performs similar functions for the Society's paperback series.

The Society's publications are distributed each year without charge to more than 3,000 members in the United States, Canada, and elsewhere throughout the world. The Society welcomes as members all individuals who desire to receive its publications. For information about membership and current dues, see the back page of this volume or write to the Secretary-Treasurer, 5835 Kimbark Avenue, Chicago, Illinois 60637.

The Eighty-third Yearbook includes the following two volumes:

Part I: *Becoming Readers in a Complex Society*
Part II: *The Humanities in Precollegiate Education*

A complete listing of the Society's previous publications, together with information as to how earlier publications still in print may be obtained, is found in the back pages of this volume.

Library of Congress Catalog Number: 83-062345
ISSN: 0077-5762

Published 1984 by
THE NATIONAL SOCIETY FOR THE STUDY OF EDUCATION

5835 Kimbark Avenue, Chicago, Illinois 60637

First Printing, 6,000 Copies

Printed in the United States of America

Officers of the Society
1983-84

(Term of office expires March 1 of the year indicated.)

HARRY S. BROUDY

(1985)
University of Illinois, Champaign, Illinois

LUVERN L. CUNNINGHAM

(1984)
Ohio State University, Columbus, Ohio

MARGARET EARLY

(1986)
Syracuse University, Syracuse, New York

ELLIOT W. EISNER

(1986)
Stanford University, Stanford, California

A. HARRY PASSOW

(1985)
Teachers College, Columbia University, New York, New York

RALPH W. TYLER

(1984)
Director Emeritus, Center for Advanced Study in the Behavioral Sciences
Stanford, California

KENNETH J. REHAGE

(Ex-officio)
University of Chicago, Chicago, Illinois

Secretary-Treasurer

KENNETH J. REHAGE

5835 Kimbark Avenue, Chicago, Illinois 60637

Contributors to the Yearbook

BENJAMIN LADNER

(Editor)
President, National Humanities Faculty
Atlanta, Georgia

ABRAHAM ASCHER

Professor of History
Brooklyn College, City University of New York
Brooklyn, New York

JAMES A. BANKS

Professor and Chairman, Curriculum and Instruction
University of Washington
Seattle, Washington

GERMAINE BRÈE

Professor of Romance Languages
Wake Forest University
Winston-Salem, North Carolina

ROBERT COLES

Professor of Psychiatry
Harvard University
Cambridge, Massachusetts

EDWIN J. DELATTRE

President, St. John's College
Annapolis, Maryland and Santa Fe, New Mexico

BENJAMIN DEMOTT

Andrew W. Mellon Professor of Humanities
Amherst College
Amherst, Massachusetts

ELLIOT W. EISNER

Professor of Education and Art
School of Education, Stanford University
Stanford, California

HERBERT M. KLIEBARD

Professor of Education
School of Education, University of Wisconsin
Madison, Wisconsin

JOHN J. MCDERMOTT

Distinguished Professor of Philosophy and of the Humanities in Medicine
Texas A and M University
College Station, Texas

FRANCIS ROBERTS

Superintendent of Schools
Cold Spring Harbor, New York

Acknowledgment

Early in 1980, Dr. John Goodlad, a member of the Board of Directors of the Society, reported to the Board his conversations with Dr. Edwin J. Delattre, then Director of the National Humanities Faculty, about the possibility of a yearbook on the humanities in precollegiate education. The Board expressed great interest in having such a publication in its yearbook series. An invitation was extended to Dr. Delattre to prepare a proposal for the consideration of the Board.

A draft of a proposal, including abstracts of some of the projected chapters, was subsequently submitted by Dr. Benjamin Ladner, who had become Executive Director of the National Humanities Faculty. With the endorsement of the Board of Trustees of that organization, the proposal was presented to the Board of Directors of the Society at its meeting in the fall of 1980. The Society's interest in this publication was reaffirmed and a final decision to proceed was made at the Board meeting in February, 1981, at which time the full proposal was in hand together with an expression of the continuing commitment of the Board of Trustees of the National Humanities Faculty to the project.

As Executive Director and later President of the National Humanities Faculty, Dr. Ladner kindly agreed to assume editorial responsibility for the projected volume and to prepare the introduction and concluding chapter. His diligence and his extraordinarily competent editing have helped immeasurably to keep us on schedule in the processing of the manuscripts that comprise the yearbook.

We are extremely grateful to all who have participated in the preparation of this volume. The several authors provide a variety of viewpoints regarding the role of the humanities in precollegiate education. They also make interesting suggestions for enhancing the meaningfulness of instruction in the subjects that comprise that field.

The Society is especially indebted to the Board of Trustees of the National Humanities Faculty, whose endorsement of this enterprise and commitment to it is further evidence of the continuing interest of that organization in working for the improvement of instruction in the humanities in our elementary and secondary schools.

KENNETH J. REHAGE
Editor for the Society

Table of Contents

PAGE

Part Three

Humanities and School Programs

INTRODUCTION

The Humanities and the Schools

BENJAMIN LADNER

The primary issues for those areas of study called the humanities are also the central concerns of both education and contemporary culture in the last part of the twentieth century. Put simply, what are our efforts to educate (*educere*) "leading" from and toward? What image of *humanitas*, of the human condition and its possibilities, are we espousing by arranging the relations of adults and children under the rubric of education? What kind of world do we adults understand ourselves to inhabit; and what world do we imagine we are fashioning by introducing its forms and meanings to our children, even as we introduce new beings into the world as it presently is? Does the long tradition of knowledge in the humanities, with the assumptions it makes about the value and integrity of persons, of reflection, and of the world, necessarily become less meaningful or less plausible as an increasingly sophisticated technology fabricates a new material environment?

Well-intentioned apologists who have sought to tie the humanities to certain educational theories, political causes, or metaphysical systems have often succeeded only in blurring the humanities, thus making them even more inaccessible. In the process these spokesmen have offered little consistent, clear, common understanding of what the humanities are about, why they are needed, or how they fit into the larger context of vocational, technological, scientific, economic, or other academic enterprises. Attempts have been made to explain and justify the humanities by equating them with aesthetics, with almost any interdisciplinary activity, and with "subjective" or "affective" approaches to learning. As a result, they have been set in opposition to science, to facts, to practicality, and to answers.

And yet, the overriding dilemmas of our contemporary culture still cluster around what traditionally have been the central concerns of the humanities. When we know *how* to do something, how can we decide what we *ought* to do? Does what we know relate to what really is? What expressions of meaning, truth, and beauty should be taught to each new generation? Are there ideas and formulations of meaning on which we can base our lives? How do being born and dying make sense? Who is my neighbor and what are my responsibilities for her or for him? These are not merely abstract dilemmas for idle speculation. They are questions which appear in the concrete situations of Three Mile Island on the one hand, and in a second-grade classroom on an ordinary Wednesday in Philadelphia on the other.

The primary task of those who teach the humanities is now to identify the common ground on which persons can gather in order to make responsible judgments about the quality of life in our world in light of the traditions of the past and the competing demands of the future. The fundamental challenge for education in contemporary culture is to make vital, coherent connections and to identify patterns and structures of meaning which hold together otherwise disparate claims and idiosyncratic insights.

The persistent fragmentation of academic disciplines has placed the traditional work of the humanities in seeming isolation from other areas of inquiry. This has led to the popular view that issues in the humanities—the central questions and formulations of human experience—are unsuited to systematic study and teaching. In fact, however, it is precisely the act of making judgments about interrelationships and integral meanings which has always characterized the work of the humanities and which can give renewed significance to classroom teaching of humanities subjects. And there is a history of events, of modes of reflection, and of profound ideas that has informed this work. The issue now is not whether we have properly included this or that discipline in a curriculum called "the humanities"; it is whether we can recover the vitality and plausibility of the centuries-old commitment of human beings to the acts of thinking, reading, valuing, talking, and writing which have been the basis of our best efforts to educate ourselves and our children.

Formulating in general terms the relation of the humanities to our personal and collective lives is a task that will (and should) continue to occupy humanities educators. Parallel in importance, however, is the specific task of clarifying the role of the humanities in the schools, in precollegiate education. To deal with this question it is necessary to take a fresh look not only at the humanities themselves but also at the educational structures and cultural patterns of which they are a part. The problems of the humanities have increasingly become intertwined with the urgent problems of culture. The implications of this fact, however, do not necessarily require the development of more precise methodologies inside the disciplines of literature, history, or philosophy. There is now also a question of where these traditions of human inquiry intersect with the cultural patterns, historical conditions, and individual experiences so that these traditions can once again become accessible and plausible.

We are faced with the possibility that the traditional humanities disciplines themselves may hold no *clear-cut* solutions to our problems and, indeed, that they may even mislead in certain fundamental ways our present efforts to understand ourselves and our world. If this is so, we must respond to the need for developing modes of reflection, images of persons and culture, and approaches to teaching which can enable us to work more directly at the thresholds of institutions and individuals, professions and constituencies, communities and bureaucracies. These new efforts, of course, must be based upon the recovery and reconception of what is already known in the legacy of texts, ideas, religions, and art forms.

Reports which have recently been released on the quality of education in American elementary and secondary schools suggest that the task may not be an easy one. The report of the National Commission on Excellence in Education claims that "the educational foundations of our society are presently being eroded by a rising tide of mediocrity that threatens our very future as a nation and a people." The National Task Force on Education for Economic Growth calls for "a deep and lasting change in American education" to counter the low expectations and performance in public schools. The Twentieth Century Fund's Task Force on Federal Elementary and Secondary Education Policy declares that "the nation's public schools are in trouble" and proposes that salary bonuses be given to a new group of "master teachers." These reports reflect a widespread consensus in our culture that the nation's elementary and secondary schools are providing only mediocre education for our children.

The humanities are and have always been an antidote to such mediocrity. The schools, however, are a reflection and an extension of our culture. If there is something wrong with our educational institutions, then there is something wrong with the ways in which we have structured those things that matter most to us in our collective lives. The humanities in the schools cannot be talked about apart from the relation of schools to our culture. Unfortunately, the experience of and responsibility for "collective lives" have become less compelling for us just when they are most needed. The deterioration of a larger sense of community is directly tied to individual views of public institutions as mere structures for private self-interest. More pointedly, it is we educators who have created a public that is now skeptical of education generally and of humanities education in particular. The decision makers and image makers in our society are, after all, persons who were educated inside our academic structures. The crisis in the schools has not befallen us or been imposed upon us; we professional educators have helped significantly to bring it about.

Nonetheless, the humanities in particular will emerge with increasing importance in the years ahead because of the pressing need to make sense of our sophisticated instruments and scientific/technical information, as well as of our collective and individual lives in a complicated, dangerous, and problematic world. Furthermore, the primary work of the humanities must and will take place in the elementary and secondary schools. A part of the reason for this is that our children most immediately embody the realities of both the past and future of our culture. Another reason is surely that they almost never postpone for very long the joys of discovering, imagining, and creating which are characteristic of humanities education.

The humanities must continue to have three very clear concerns, namely those of language, values, and civility. They can make no sense apart from the central role of language. Walker Percy has observed that the most characteristic feature of human beings is that we are "symbol-mongers." Language is at once our most ordinary and most profound wedding of individual vitality and collective order. The unique work of the humanities in the schools is based upon the fact that in the schools, by and large, there still exist commonly acknowledged traditions of language which, despite the raid of educational jargon, still hold the possibility of making sense.

It is the special task of the humanities to sustain a community of discourse that fosters thinking not only as an isolated, private activity but also as convivial, collective, public deliberation. This is the concern for civility—those cooperative efforts which insure the care of the public realm in which we all exist. In cultivating an educated citizenry, which is the foundation of civility, the humanities not only foster a common language that *enables* us to speak and make decisions together, but they hold in focus what it is *important* to be talking about and deciding. Therefore, they bridge gaps between schools and colleges, between arts and sciences, between institutions and individuals, and formulate and interpret those things that matter uniquely to human experience.

This is why the humanities—especially as they are studied and taught in the schools—have particular responsibility for addressing questions of value and for placing in high relief those things which we have found to be worthy of human life. In the range and variety of their formulations, the humanities cut into the dailiness, the predicament, the yearning that lie close to the root of our being. The challenge of humanities education in the schools is now not so much a matter of dealing with what we do not yet know. It is having the courage to say plainly what the humanities have taught us. It is time for us to expose the error of those who characterize the humanities as vague, as mere opinion, or as dealing always with what no one knows or could ever know. After several thousand years of humanistic inquiry we have learned a great deal about the difference between the trivial and the profound, the difference between the humane and the inhumane, and about what things debase and what things ennoble our human existence. We know that it is better to learn than to be ignorant; that we share a common world that ought to be taken care of; that there are beautiful structures and forms worth protecting and preserving; that thoughtful action is better than random, impulsive behavior; that ideas do and ought to matter in human experience. We know, too, that there are unavoidable experiences in human life shared by all persons, experiences which teachers and students hold in common. These unavoidable conditions—birth, sexuality, breathing, hurting, dying, having a past, expecting a future, promising, lying, forgiving, remembering, dreaming—are as provocative as they are mysterious. And they have led to the configurations of writing, speaking, drawing, singing, figuring, testing, counting, remembering, and reading which have become the content of our school curriculum. We know all of these things in the humanities not as mere opinions but as genuine knowledge which has been discovered by persons much like ourselves who freely chose to fashion their lives to the demands of truth, beauty, and goodness.

The writers for this volume have not only made significant contributions to areas of knowledge within the humanities. They have also given themselves to the patient but rewarding task of making that knowledge available in interesting and challenging ways to teachers, administrators, and students in elementary and secondary schools. Through National Humanities Faculty programs and other projects they have worked in school settings across the country to improve the quality of teaching and learning in the humanities. What they have to say about the meaning of the humanities will undoubtedly lead to a better understanding of their significance. Beyond that, however, should their proposals for improvement and reform be taken seriously by teachers and administrators who are responsible for humanities education, we could nurture the next generation of inquiring minds with ideas and insights that are commensurate with the mystery of human experience and the prospect of human fulfillment.

Part One
RESHAPING HUMANITIES INQUIRY

CHAPTER I

The Decline of Humanistic Studies in the American School Curriculum

HERBERT M. KLIEBARD

"Humanism," John Dewey once remarked, "is a portmanteau word."[1] It packs together a variety of meanings, some drawn from its origins in fifteenth- and sixteenth-century Italy, some from its association with literature, particularly classical literature, some from its alleged opposition to theology, and, in more recent times, from its antiromantic and antinaturalistic temper. On its education side, it has come to be associated with a set of subjects, a segment of the school curriculum, believed to have the power to stir the imagination, enhance the appreciation of beauty, and disclose motives that actuate human behavior. From its early association with the study of Latin and Greek, humanism has gradually been expanded to the study of language generally as a distinctive possession of human beings, and with the arts—music, painting, sculpture, poetry—as the highest forms of expression by which human beings convey their experience and their aspirations. These, it turns out, are the very subjects that have suffered the steepest decline in the American school curriculum during the course of the twentieth century, a decline which, if continued, will at best make artistic expression and appreciation the province of a handful of sensitive souls whose mission it will be to preserve the higher culture and to protect it from degradation by the mob. In fact, the most persistent problem that humanism has had to face in the twentieth century is its inability to reconcile its central doctrine with the realities of mass public education. In some sense, that problem is a legacy dating back to the origins of humanism itself.

Humanistic Studies in the Curriculum

It is commonplace to refer to the Renaissance as a period characterized by a rebirth of learning. Actually, however, it would be difficult to argue that that period saw the spread of education to a significantly larger segment of the European world. Instead, when compared to the scholasticism that preceded it, there emerged from the Renaissance, not the spread of learning, but a redefinition of what it meant to be learned. The Renaissance was not only a time where learning was revered; it was a period when educational theory flourished and where education itself was being reconstructed. Many of the great works of that period are treatises making the case for one or another combination of studies including their order and sequence. Desiridua Erasmus's *De Ratione Studii*, Francois Rabelais's *Gargantua* and *Pantagruel*, Joannes Ludovicus Vives's *De Tradendis Disciplinis*, and various works issuing from the school founded by Vittorino da Feltre are pedagogical tracts and, more directly, arguments for a particular curriculum. It is hard to imagine another period in which the scholars of the time dedicated themselves so assiduously to the central curriculum question, "What should we teach?"

From the way the leading scholars of the Renaissance framed their answer to that question, we have derived our basic conceptions of what constitutes a humanistic education. As Emile Durkheim has pointed out, however, there were actually two, not unrelated but nevertheless distinctive, streams of thought in educational theory that emerged from that great body of pedagogical scholarship.[2] In the first, as represented mainly by Rabelais, the curriculum was conceived of as a vast and actually unending feast, a banquet so vast that it could only be consumed by giants. Nothing is omitted, not the casting of artillery, physical strength and manual dexterity, skill in every musical instrument, the work of apothecaries, geometry, Greek, Latin, Chaldean, Hebrew, Arabic, the dialogues of Plato, agriculture, metals, and precious stones. In short, Rabelais's curriculum is hardly a selection from what was known in the Western world; it is practically a comprehensive catalog of everything known. His selection of authors places Vergil alongside obscure writers of the fifteenth century and lumps together Plato and Pausanias. The special association of humanism with literary style and linguistic elegance is not basically derived from Rabelais. It is difficult if not impossible to distill from his curriculum catalog any body of studies that could be deemed more valuable than any other. The sciences of the day along with the practical arts enjoyed equal status with literary and linguistic studies. Durkheim interprets his contribution to educational theory as turning the direction in educational thinking from the purely formal to a curriculum that was designed to feed the mind. As Durkheim put it, in Rabelais we find a "curriculum whose object will be not to train the mind in formal intellectual acrobatics, but rather to nourish it, to enrich it, and to give it some substance."[3] A human being's intellectual appetite was seen by Rabelais as insatiable, and essentially all knowledge should be consumed. If nothing else, Rabelais helped break through the narrow constraints that had characterized the curriculum of the earlier period.

The second humanistic strain derived from the Renaissance is represented principally by the work of Erasmus. There is much in Erasmus that at least superficially resembles the unbridled appetite for learning that characterizes Rabelais's curriculum; but the list of authors to be studied that Erasmus drew up is not nearly as long nor as eclectic as is Rabelais's. Here one is not simply gobbling up everything in sight, but selecting certain delicacies with a purpose in mind beyond the mere satisfaction of the intellectual appetite. That purpose is expressed in the development of the *orationis facultas*, the ability to use language elegantly and expressively. "There is nothing," says Erasmus, "more magnificent and more worthy to be admired than discourse (*oratio*) which, when it contains a wealth of words and phrases, flows in abundance like a river of gold."[4] Unlike Rabelais, then, there is for Erasmus as well as for other educational theorists of the Renaissance, such as Vives, a hierarchy of studies with language in its several manifestations clearly at the top. The way of achieving the great purpose of education, elegance and precision in the use of language, was accomplished mainly by immersing the student in those masterpieces of literature that can serve as models. To humanist educators of the Renaissance, this meant intensive study of the classics of Greece and Rome, and hence the persistent legacy linking humanism to the study of Greek and Latin. As Durkheim expressed it, education in the Middle Ages was an intellectual fencing match; for Rabelais, it was a vast luxurious banquet, and for Erasmus it was the supreme development of the literary faculty.[5] For Erasmus, literature was not simply one of an array of subjects. It was the vehicle *par excellence* for shaping mind and character. Contemporary versions of what constitutes the humanistic studies are traceable to that vision; the Rabelais tradition seems to have become submerged.

With all the appeal that that vision held and continues to hold today, it also contained the seeds of the decline of humanism in educational practice. The rise of humanism as an educational ideal coincided, not accidentally, with the rise of a highly restricted class of cultivated aristocracy, a class capable of rarified tastes which were completely removed from the world in which the vast majority of Europeans lived. Humanistic education had its origins in a world where education served mainly as an adornment to courtly life. Without denying the value of that adornment to those privileged to enjoy it, humanistic education was never an education for power or even, for that matter, for survival. Individual feats of learning during the Renaissance are indeed astounding, but given the course of political and social events over the next three or four centuries, humanism as an educational ideal restricted to an elite class had to adapt or die. It did a little of both.

The Humanistic Curriculum in Nineteenth-Century America

The challenge of Rousseau and the romantic movement notwithstanding, humanism continued its firm hold on the American curriculum through most of the nineteenth century. The Yale College course of study in the early nineteenth century, more than any other in this country, embodied the curriculum orthodoxy that had evolved over the previous two hundred years. The first three years of study were devoted mostly to Latin, Greek, and mathematics, the traditional classical subjects, but with a smattering of such other subjects as astronomy, history, geography, and English grammar and rhetoric. The final year was devoted primarily to moral philosophy, metaphysics, English composition, and belles lettres.[6] The only options that existed were noncredit ones, but even these were sometimes alarming to college authorities. When Anglo-Saxon, for example, was introduced as a noncredit option, the outraged President Jeremiah Day announced: "It might soon be necessary to appoint an instructor in *whittling*."[7]

By contrast, other American colleges of the period were beginning to experiment with modifications of the traditional humanistic curriculum. After some mainly unsuccessful attempts to modify the course of study at the College of William and Mary, Thomas Jefferson was able to introduce a certain measure of choice for students in electing departments of study in the University of Virginia. In 1827, at the urging of George Ticknor, the Harvard College curriculum was revised to permit students to substitute work in a modern foreign language for up to half of the requirement in Greek and Latin (although, in practice, such substitutions were rare.) Three years earlier, in 1824, Hobart College was established as the first college in the United States (or England for that matter) with no instruction in Greek or Latin. There appeared to be a modest but decided movement among some of America's leading colleges away from rigidly prescribed curricula with Latin, Greek, and mathematics at the core. A minor rebellion among Yale undergraduates in 1825 led, ultimately, to what became the first coherent attempt to justify the time-honored curriculum of Yale College and hence the mainstream of curriculum theory in early nineteenth-century America.

Two years following the rebellion, at the 1827 commencement, State Senator Noyes Darling, a former student at Yale College, proposed the elimination of the "dead languages" and the substitution of modern languages. At almost the same time, the Connecticut legislature, taking into account the apparent dissatisfaction of students with the Yale program of studies, called for similar reforms along practical lines. President Day sensed the danger, and on September 11, 1827, the President and Fellows of Yale College passed a resolution that a committee "inquire into the expediency of so altering the regular course of instruction in this college as to leave out of said course the study of the *dead languages*, substituting other studies therefor."[8] Also to be considered was the possibility of eliminating those "dead languages" as a basis for admission to Yale.

Published originally in 1828 under the title, *Reports on the Course of Instruction in Yale College: By a Committee of the Corporation and the Academic Faculty*, and a year later as "Original Papers in Relation to a Course of Liberal Education," the Report is at once the most comprehensive account of the conventional wisdom on curriculum in the early nineteenth century and the most spirited defense in its time of the humanistic curriculum against the onslaught of modernity. The

Report was divided into two sections with President Day himself mainly responsible for Part I, a general defense of Yale's course of study, and with Professor James K. Kingsley, probably America's leading classical scholar, undertaking the defense of the study of Latin and Greek in Part II. By the nineteenth century, humanistic education had become closely associated with faculty psychology, and much of President Day's defense was based on the idea that certain subjects of study had the power to invigorate the various faculties of the mind, such as memory, imagination, and reasoning. (President Day himself had earlier published two books on faculty psychology.)

Day began his defense by admitting that Yale's "present plan of education admits of improvement."[9] He also expressed surprise that there were reports to the effect that the program of studies was "unalterable" and alluded to the fact that many alumni have remarked upon return visits that the college had changed considerably. Day thus established that he was not opposed to change per se. What concerned him particularly was the persistent cry that "our colleges must be new-modeled; that they are not adapted to the spirit of age; that they will soon be deserted, unless they are better accommodated to the business character of the nation."[10] What he seemed to fear most was an abandonment of the humanist ideal in favor of the immediately practical.

After asserting that the chief purpose of any college is to "Lay the Foundation of a Superior Education," Day presented, in what has become the most famous passage of the Report, the chief defense for the continued validity of the humanist curriculum.

> The two great points to be gained in intellectual culture, are the *discipline* and the *furniture* of the mind; expanding its powers, and storing it with knowledge. The former of these is, perhaps, the more important of the two. A commanding object, therefore, in a collegiate course, should be to call into daily and vigorous exercise the faculties of the student. Those branches of study should be prescribed and those modes of instruction adopted, which are best calculated to teaching the art of fixing the attention, directing the train of thought, analyzing a subject proposed for investigation; following with accurate discrimination, the course of argument; balancing nicely the evidence presented to the judgment; awakening, elevating, and controlling the imagination; arranging with skill, the treasure which memory gathers; and guiding the powers of genius.[11]

Thus, by using the standard mental disciplinarian argument, Day was able to deflect the persistent concern expressed by educational reformers and students regarding the usefulness of certain of the traditional subjects. Their usefulness lay not in any immediate practicality but in their ability to develop certain highly valued habits of thought, habits of thought that, in the long run, were the foundation of what we mean by education.

The notion that the mind was composed of a discrete set of identifiable faculties waiting there to be exercised constituted the most powerful justification for a curriculum that incorporated the traditional disciplines of knowledge. Almost miraculously, there appeared for each of the identified faculties a subject perfectly suited to its development. As Day put it:

> From the pure mathematics, he learns the art of demonstrable reasoning. In attending to the physical sciences, he becomes familiar with facts, with the process of induction, and the varieties of probable evidence. In ancient literature, he finds some of the most finished models of taste, by English reading he learns the powers of the language in which he is to speak and write. By logic and mental philosophy, he is taught the art of thinking; by rhetoric and oratory, the art of speaking. By frequent exercise on written composition, he acquires copiousness and accuracy of expression. By extemporaneous discussion, he becomes prompt, fluent, and animated.[12]

Along with the development of the individual faculties, mental discipline theory placed great emphasis on the harmonious development of all faculties leaving none to wither or atrophy. "The mind," Day declared, "never attains its full perfection, unless its various powers are so trained as to give them the fair proportions which nature designed."[13] The traditional branches of learning and faculties of the mind not only presented a certain correspondence, they also exhibited a certain "symmetry and balance" which ought to be brought to the fullest perfection. The root metaphor in mental discipline theory is, of course, mind and body, and Day expressed in those metaphorical terms his ideal education: "As the bodily frame is brought to its highest perfection, not by one simple and uniform motion, but by a variety of exercises; so the mental faculties are expanded, and invigorated, and adapted to each other with the different departments of science."[14] By departments of science, Day was referring not specifically to the natural sciences but to what today we would call the disciplines of knowledge. His appeal was for balance and against a high degree of specialization, an argument for what later became known as general education.

Professor Kingsley's defense of Latin and Greek in Part II of the Report was equally impassioned and also infused with mental discipline as the chief object of higher education. He began his section of the Report, for example, by defining liberal education as "such a course of discipline in the arts and sciences, as is best calculated, at the same time, both to strengthen and enlarge the faculties of the mind, and to familiarize it with the leading principles of the great objects of human investigation and knowledge,"[15] almost a paraphrase of Day's famous *discipline* and *furniture* of the mind. In addition, however, Kingsley refused to concede the commonly held notion that the study of French and German was more practical than Latin and Greek. "The literature of every country of Europe," he claimed, "is founded more or less on classical literature, and derives from this source its most important illustrations."[16] To engage in any sort of literary inquiry, then, required a familiarity with these classical sources. Without mastery of the classical languages any scholar "immediately feels a deficiency in his education, and is convinced that he is destitute of an important part of practical learning."[17] Moreover, as a preparation for the professions, particularly divinity and law, a classical education was unrivaled. As for the modern languages, they simply did not provide sufficient mental exercise. "To acquire the knowledge of any of the modern languages," Kingsley argued, "is chiefly an effort of memory,"[18] and, although they may be "recommended on their own merits,"[19] they certainly do not provide a substitute for the kind of mental gymnastics that Greek and Latin provide. "To establish this truth," Kingsley asserted, "let a page of Voltaire be compared with a page of Tacitus."[20]

A humanistic curriculum justified in mental disciplinarian terms remained practically unchallenged for about half a century. It would be to overemphasize the impact of the Yale Report to attribute this continued success to the arguments of Day and Kingsley in particular. But if these arguments did not actually influence the course of the American curriculum in the next five decades, they accurately reflected the mainstream of thinking as to what constituted a proper education. If humanistic subjects were not immediately practical in the sense that surveying or French might be, they had great potential for indirect utility. The subjects that comprised the humanistic curriculum, with only minor modifications, had the power to strengthen the individual faculties of the mind, and, properly balanced, they created a mental harmony, a mind ready to undertake the work of the world. Nothing could be more practical than that. Even so momentous an event as the emergence of the American common school in mid-nineteenth century offered little immediate threat to the established order of school subjects except, perhaps, insofar as it helped create a population of persons whose children and grandchildren would be prepared to move to the next step on the educational ladder; and, in the long run, mass education on the secondary level profoundly affected the course of the humanistic curriculum. Moreover, the rise of experimental psychology, which coincided with a dramatic increase in the population of secondary schools, served to weaken the psychological foundations of mental discipline, a theory that had served so well as a justification for humanistic subjects.

The Challenge to the Old Order of Subjects

Around 1880, when the high school surpassed the academy as the most populous form of secondary education, a major threat to the humanistic curriculum emerged. It was, of course, not the fact of the new population itself that changed the course of the American curriculum, but that fact as interpreted by a variety of pedagogical reformers and leaders. There had been, after all, an industrial revolution that had profoundly affected the social fabric and a Darwinian revolution that had rent the intellectual world apart. One could hardly cling, many reformers reasoned, to a mode of education tied to aristocratic origins and to a curriculum that only minimally reflected the rise in scholarly status of scientific inquiry. It was not simply that more scientific subjects ought to be added; the curriculum itself had to be determined scientifically rather than by vague speculation. Moreover, the social institutions, such as family and church, that had served so well to socialize the young in a preindustrial society no longer functioned successfully. The school as a social institution, it was felt, had to take a stronger hand in the socialization process. Vice and corruption in the cities, a problem presumably exacerbated by waves of immigrants from Southern and Eastern Europe, had to be controlled.

"We find," said Edward A. Ross, the noted sociologist, "*an almost world-wide drift from religion toward education* as the method of indirect social restraint."[21] The problem as Ross saw it was that education had "become less an instrument of social control than an aid to individual success."[22] It was not that an intellectual education was "without a moral value"; but it was not enough merely to "open a range of new and healthy interests" that would divert the young from vice. "The cry goes up," he proclaimed, "for a secular civic and moral education that shall effectively minister to peace and order."[23] What we find in the last two decades of the nineteenth century is a heightened perception of a profound change in American society, in many cases an apocalyptic vision, and with that perception a demand for a new role for the schools. The role and function of the American school had to be redirected away from simply purveying intellectual culture or the development of the faculties of the mind, and toward direct and conscious social well-being. That new role, many reformers argued, could be accomplished by nothing less than a thorough transformation of the outmoded curriculum.

It would be easy to exaggerate the degree of consensus that was reflected in the 1890s, particularly in secondary schools. The decade of the 1890s, after all, marked the beginning of a massive influx of new students, the secondary school population rising from a mere 6 or 7 percent of the population fourteen to seventeen years old in 1890 to more than 50 percent by 1930. But while the desire to reform the curriculum was virtually universal, there was wide disagreement as to what direction that reform should take. There were those, like Ross, who took their cue from the demands of a modern industrial society and particularly from the feeling that the school should undertake the functions of social control once performed by other, now decaying, social institutions. There were those, like G. Stanley Hall, who drew their inspiration from Rousseau, and who saw in an education according to nature the possibility of a new scientifically determined curriculum that would be in tune with the true interests and needs of the children and adolescents. Even the leading defenders of humanism in this period, Charles W. Eliot, the patrician president of Harvard University, and William Torrey Harris, the powerful Commissioner of Education, were themselves reformers, in essence, seeking modest reforms in the American curriculum that would retain and revivify the humanistic ideal. And, hovering over the battle, there was the figure of John Dewey, critical not only of the old education but of the reformers of the period as well, while at the same time beginning to forge his own proposals for the reconstruction of American schooling. Around the turn of the century, the principal antagonists were humanists like Eliot and Harris and the child-study educators under the leadership of Hall. By the second decade of the twentieth century, social efficiency emerged as the predominant educational ideal, and while humanism showed surprising resilience, its decline was inevitable.

The most important single event in the battle for control of the school curriculum during the 1890s was the National Education Association's Report of the Committee of Ten.[24] The immediate reason for the creation of the Committee was the desire on the part of high school principals for greater uniformity in the curriculum. With different colleges varying widely in their admissions requirements (such as the ability to translate particular works in Latin and Greek), high schools had a virtually impossible job. But beyond this sticky practical problem, there loomed the distinct possibility that the high school would be transformed from a rather elite institution serving a tiny minority of the adolescent population into a mass popular institution. The profound question that the Committee had to deal with, therefore, was whether the curriculum that had held sway in this country, practically since its founding, could continue to serve in the period beyond elementary school.

The Committee was headed by Eliot, whose reputation as an educational reformer had extended beyond his support of the elective system as president of Harvard University to various changes he recommended in elementary and secondary schools. Like Day and Kingsley, Eliot was a mental disciplinarian, but, perhaps because of his training as a scientist, his version of mental discipline took a somewhat unusual turn. Eliot believed that any subject, so long as it were capable of being studied over an extended period (thereby excluding practical subjects), had the power to train the mind. It was possible, therefore, to broaden the curriculum, including even elective subjects, and still preserve the humanist ideal (or one form of it). The full development of the innate human capacities, then called faculties, could be accomplished by intensive study, not of a highly restricted set of subjects, but of a wider range of studies. This broadening of the range of subjects appropriate for the curriculum was more in the tradition of Rabelais than Erasmus. At least in principle, French thus had as much disciplinary value as Latin (although Eliot himself seems to have had some doubt about that claim in practice). The actual recommendations of the Committee of Ten for the high school curriculum can best be interpreted through this set of fundamental assumptions.

The main feature of the Committee's Report when it was published in 1893 was four recommended "programmes," each acceptable both for college admission and for what was then called "life," that is, for those who did not go beyond their high school education. The four courses of study, the Classical, the Latin-Scientific, the Modern Languages, and the English, probably did not go as far as Eliot would have liked in the direction of electivism, but at least they offered students an option as to course of study. By modern standards, each of these courses of study would be considered highly academic. In fact, in the contemporary mythology of the education world, the recommendations of the Committee of Ten are regarded anachronistically as designed to impose college domination on the high school curriculum. Eliot is seen as an archconservative who vainly sought to fend off an appropriate adaptation of the high school curriculum to the new high school population. Actually, however, modest, even significant, changes are apparent in the Report. Considered as a whole, only the Classical program retained Greek as a requirement, and even there, it was reduced from the customary three years to two. (Professors of Greek back at Harvard were outraged.) Even more significant was the fact that in two of the programs, the Modern Languages and the English, there was no Latin requirement at all. Had these two programs been recommended only for the non-college-going population, there probably would have been little controversy, but the Committee unanimously refused to make any distinction between preparation for college and preparation for life. In the mental disciplinarian context, such a distinction was unnecessary because the ultimate purpose of education was the fullest possible development of native capacities, and this was true whether one went on to college or not.

By far the greatest criticism of the Report came from those who saw the need for a much more thoroughgoing reform of the high school curriculum. Led by G. Stanley Hall, one of America's foremost psychologists, the criticism centered on the conviction that the Committee had underestimated the impact of the new high school population. The impact, as seen by critics of the Report, was not so much the implication of sheer numbers, but that the new population was qualitatively different; these new students simply lacked the ability to cope with the programs the Committee recommended. Referring to the new population as a "great army of incapables,"[25] Hall chided the Committee for not recognizing the huge differences in mental capacities of high school students. For Hall, high school programs of study had to be sharply differentiated according to students' mental capacities and therefore indirectly to their future place in society and occupational role. Eliot, while recognizing that differences in ability did exist, did not regard those differences as so significant as to require different curricula for different identifiable groups in the school population. At the heart of Eliot's position was his fundamental optimism with regard to human intellectual capacities. Essentially all human beings were capable of studying and profiting from the subjects now regarded as academic. In this sense, Eliot represented a position that regarded the basic humanist curriculum, expanded and with a few modifications here and there, as appropriate not only for an elite, but for the great mass of people as well.

Whatever may have been the merits or defects of the Committee of Ten Report, it was eventually the position represented by Hall, combining as it did the idea that a curriculum could be scientifically constructed with what might be called a pessimism about human intellectual capacities, which became ascendant in twentieth-century curriculum thinking. A crushing blow to the mental disciplinarian justification for the humanist curriculum was delivered by growing experimental evidence that seemed to contradict some of the fundamental assumptions of faculty psychology. Without specific faculties to be trained, it would hardly be possible to maintain that certain subjects had the special power to train them. As early as 1890, William James reported, as a result of a modest experiment he conducted with his students at Harvard, that the faculty of memory was not improved by continued practice in memorizing.[26] By the turn of the century, Edward L. Thorndike and other psychologists brought experimental evidence to show that abilities developed in one context were not easily transferred to new situations.[27] The implication that professional educators drew from this evidence was that, in the absence of broad faculties to be developed, education had to be directed toward the development of highly specific skills pertinent to very specific situations. These new beliefs about the working of the mind, combined with a new sense of what schools were for, posed a formidable threat to what remained of humanistic studies.

Humanism as the Preservation of the Cultural Heritage

If humanistic subjects did not have the power to develop thinking ability in its several manifestations, what good were they? A new justification had to be found, and the chief spokesman for that new justification was the Commissioner of Education, William Torrey Harris. Harris was undoubtedly the preeminent figure in education during the last quarter of the nineteenth century. The fact that he never produced a magnum opus may lead us to underestimate the significance of his position and the pivotal role he played in the pedagogical world of the time. During his long career, he addressed national meetings of the National Education Association scores of times, and one attempt to compile his bibliography listed 479 publications.[28] The force of his intellect and his incredible energy were undoubtedly vital ingredients in Harris's national stature, but beyond the question of his personal influence, which was considerable, he gave voice to that large constituency of school teachers and administrators who were made uneasy by the threat of massive reform then looming on the horizon. In particular, Harris helped build a plausible platform for that segment of the educational world who resisted the idea of a massive change in the schools of the nation presumably reflective of the great social transformation that had taken place in American society or, for that matter, the intellectual transformation through the rise of science. He was able to strike a tone of moderation in the midst of cries for a revolution in education. Harris, in a sense, was one of the last great spokesmen for a humanistic curriculum that education was to produce from within its midst. Educational leaders in the twentieth century were essentially spokesmen for change of various sorts, while the banner of humanism in educational policy, usually identified with the school's role in the development of the intellect, was carried by academicians and intellectuals drawn from outside the professional education establishment. Although Harris's position began to lose some ground among the leaders who regularly assembled at major educational conferences and who wrote to prestigious pedagogical journals, it is likely that Harris's basic approach to curriculum continued to hold sway in the schools across the nation for years to come.

Born in 1835 when America was still an agrarian country, Harris was keenly aware of the changes that had been wrought in American society, but he did not regard these changes as dictating a drastic reordering of the school's curriculum. Although certain modest adaptations to modern society could be incorporated, the basic function of the school, the development of reason, remained the same. In fact, the restructuring of American society made it even more imperative that the school perform its distinctive function effectively. Harris's interpretation of Hegelian philosophy permitted him to see industrialization with its profound effect on America's social institutions, not in any apocalyptic sense, but as part of the unfolding of the Divine Will. Harris could, at one and the same time, be an advocate of rugged individualism and believe that the individual achieves realization only by subordinating himself to social institutions, institutions that embody the fruits of civilization. It was through these institutions that the wisdom of the race would be transmitted. A consistent advocate of what he liked to call "self-activity," Harris identified that activity with the rational through the exercise of will,[29] and it was his persistent emphasis on rationality in children that put him into direct conflict with the advocates, like Hall, of "education according to nature." The school, according to Harris, must train children to gain control over their natural impulses, not to submit to them. "Rousseau's doctrine of a return to nature," Harris once said, "must seem to me the greatest heresy in educational doctrine."[30]

As early as 1880, Harris was proclaiming the centrality of the curriculum in educational matters. "The question of the course of study," he said, "is the most important the educator can have before him,"[31] and the curriculum, in Harris's mind, should take its cue, not from the vagaries of children's interests nor their spontaneous impulses, but from the great resources of civilization. For Harris, psychological inquiry into child growth and development had its place, but it could never, in itself, direct the course of a proper education. "Self-activity," he said, "is in every newborn soul as a spontaneity—a possibility of unlimited action, good or bad;"[32] and, essentially, it was the function of the curriculum to direct the development of self-activity in the interest of "a knowledge of truth, a love of the beautiful, a habit of doing good. . . ."[33] Considering the maxim of "the self-styled 'New Education' . . . learn to do by doing,"[34] (a maxim he attributed to the prominent German pedagogue, Friederich Adolph Wilhelm Diesterweg), Harris was careful to point out that it was incomplete without some "guiding direction." That direction would be provided by a properly constructed course of study. Each branch of study in the curriculum (or, as he liked to call them, "coordinate groups of study"), he felt, could open the way for an ever more adequate appreciation of the Western social and intellectual tradition. His "five windows of the soul," represented by arithmetic and mathematics, geography, history, grammar, and literature and art, were chosen because to him they represented the best ways of initiating the child into the kind of self-activity that would lead to a command of the resources of that civilization.

Harris claimed that the school should first provide the command of language in reading and writing that goes beyond the "colloquial vocabulary" the child acquires in the home.[35] That increased command of language opened up the wisdom of the race that is contained on the printed page, thus emancipating the child from "the thraldom of dependence on the spoken word,"[36] and once that command were achieved, the child could reach beyond the world of personal experience and oral language, and the first of the "windows," arithmetic, could be opened. Arithmetic permitted entry into the abstract relationships that govern the physical world. Arithmetic, especially exact measurement, represented for Harris a first step in the conquest of nature, and he favored proceeding expeditiously from basic arithmetic to those mathematical operations that were useful in the natural sciences, opposing extensive drill in arithmetic operations as well as "numerical conundrums and other useless mathematical exercises."[37] Geography, the second of the windows, served to relate the inorganic world to the human world. Harris opposed what he called "sailor geography," the memorization of the names of rivers, islands, and cities, in favor of the "dynamics of geography," the interrelationship between natural forces and human beings that led to different forms of commerce and industry in different parts of the world. History focused directly on the unfolding of the will "realized in institutions rather than in mere deeds of the individual."[38] In historical studies, the State and how collectivities made civilization possible should be emphasized. A particular enthusiast for the study of grammar, Harris, waxing poetic, claimed that the window of grammar "lets in a flood of light for the explanation of all problems which human experience can enunciate."[39] For Harris, the logical structure of language was a kind of model for the nature of thinking itself. And finally, literature opened up that window that permitted us to see life as a totality and to appreciate what is essential in human character. That understanding of human experience, according to Harris, could best be instilled through careful study of standard literary works. These works not only led to an understanding of the root of human action, but provided the principal form of aesthetic appreciation available in the curriculum.

These basic components of the curriculum, Harris claimed, were "the five great lines of study that radiate from the center and relate to the five great departments of human learning."[40] Other subjects were not exactly excluded; they were simply subordinate. Industrial drawing, for example, "should have its place in the common school side by side with penmanship."[41] While his position permitted him to support certain changes in the curriculum of the nineteenth century, such as systematic instruction in art, he was probably the leading champion of the continued study of classical literature and never wavered in his support of Greek and Latin, then becoming a lost cause. Harris's defense of the study of classical languages, however, differed in its rationale from that of the typical mental disciplinarian. While Harris seems to have given qualified support to the proposition that mental power could be developed through use, he was skeptical of the mental disciplinarian's belief that mental power developed in one field could be transferred to another. He was more interested in what the subjects had to offer directly than in their alleged value as vehicles for strengthening innate powers. Thus, memorizing dates may have some positive effect on "the health of the nervous system," but that activity derived its most immediate justification "on account of the intrinsic usefulness of the data themselves."[42] Although, almost inevitably, Harris found himself using the vocabulary of formal discipline on occasion, especially in connection with the development of the will, his fundamental justification for retaining Greek and Latin in the curriculum lay in the fact that Greece and Rome were seminal to Western civilization, and no understanding of modern society would be complete without an appreciation of that heritage. For Harris, it was the content of the subjects rather than the form that was crucial in determining their value. Thus, unlike a mental disciplinarian such as Eliot, Harris opposed the substitution of French and German for the classical languages. While Eliot could argue that French, properly taught, could discipline the mind as well as Latin, Harris would hold that a knowledge of French simply was not as valuable as a resource of our culture as was Latin. Unlike Eliot, too, Harris was deeply suspicious of electives, advocating substitutions only within each of his five coordinate groups of study, where content was sufficiently similar. By emphasizing the virtues of the content of what was learned instead of disciplinary value, Harris was reconstructing the justification for a curriculum that preserved the humanist ideal.

The distance that Harris was able to create between his version of a humanist curriculum and the doctrine of mental discipline was particularly important in an era when the psychological underpinning of that doctrine, faculty psychology, was under serious attack by respected psychologists. William James's experiment on the ability to train memory in 1890, crude as it was, was only one in a series of studies that cast doubt on the idea that a mental ability, such as memory, trained in one setting could function successfully in another.[43] The rise of experimental psychology was seriously undermining the rationale that mental discipline had successfully provided during most of the nineteenth century for the continuance of not only Greek and Latin, but of other humanistic subjects in the curriculum. Undoubtedly, part of the appeal of Harris's educational position was that the basic organizational structure of the school required no radical alteration since essentially the same things were to be taught, but for different reasons. Moreover, the central role of the school, the development of the intellect, remained substantially unchanged. What remains of humanistic studies in the twentieth-century American curriculum follows, at least in broad outline, the program that Harris enunciated.

Humanism in the American Curriculum of the Twentieth Century

During the nineteenth century, humanistic subjects in the American school curriculum were defended, basically, on two grounds. The first, as developed by such leaders in higher education as Day,

Kingsley, and in a modified form by Eliot, was that the study of humanistic subjects (with some additions and modifications) had the power to improve the ability to think. As it happened, the ability to think in this context was accomplished primarily by the vigorous exercise of innate faculties of mind. Since the function of the school, throughout most of the nineteenth century, was seen as intellectual development, the vital importance of these traditional subjects was, for the most part, taken for granted. The second major justification, as represented mainly by the work of Harris, was that humanistic subjects conveyed the vital core of the Western cultural heritage. To be educated in the modern world meant to be educated in the finest expressions of that civilization.

In the context of twentieth-century American education, both these justifications were thought to be seriously flawed. First, faculty psychology as a theory of mind had collapsed and with it mental discipline as an educational ideal. The vast majority of educators no longer believed that certain subjects had the power to train the mind. Not only Latin and Greek, but eventually modern foreign languages and even literature were left without that defense for their existence. Secondly, with the advent of mass education, particularly at the secondary level, the conviction grew that the cultural heritage could only be passed on to a relative handful, while for the great majority of youth, education had to concern itself primarily with social and vocational functions. Ross and his influential contemporaries in the educational world saw the primary function of schools as producing law-abiding citizens properly trained for efficient functioning in their destined social roles. A prominent part of that role was occupational, and vocational education had, by the second decade of the twentieth century, already begun to assume a prominent place in the curriculum. Humanistic studies, in short, were increasingly being seen as remote and irrelevant to the children and youth now attending the schools. Additionally, such early twentieth-century events as arrival of the IQ test and the mental measurement movement that followed served to provide persuasive evidence (however spurious) that only a small segment of the school population was capable of the study of such subjects as literature, languages, history, and higher mathematics. Most of the school population had to be trained to perform efficiently in the social roles that their native capacities dictated.

Three unresolved problems faced the defenders of humanism in the twentieth century, none of which they addressed adequately. The first, going back to its origins in the courtly life of Renaissance Europe, was the fact that humanism was associated with a highly restricted elite. The great defenders of humanism in the twentieth century, such as Irving Babbitt, were never able to reconcile their doctrine to the fact of mass public education. In the main, they simply decried it. Second, by restricting the doctrine of humanism to what they took to be distinctly human in origin, such as literature, humanists set up an unwarranted opposition between humanistic studies and the sciences, an unnecessary dualism between the doctrines of humanism and naturalism which Dewey, for example, continually tried to dispel. The real enemy of humanism in the modern era was not science, but a certain pessimism about the human intellect, particularly the idea that only a relative handful were capable of intellectual development. By directing their arguments against such doctrines as naturalism, the principal advocates of humanism simply picked the wrong enemy. Contrary to popular impression, for example, Dewey, one of modern humanism's principal targets, was probably America's leading spokesman in the twentieth century for the development of the intellect as the central function of education, an ideal he pursued in the face of powerful tendencies in a technological society marshalled against it. In an odd way, Dewey can be seen as attempting to rekindle the mental disciplinarian ideal, although his version of what intellectual functioning consisted of was, of course, vastly different from that of his nineteenth-century forebears. Finally, most humanists continued to insist that the study of certain subjects *in themselves* had the power to develop desirable habits of thought. Thorndike's experimental evidence notwithstanding, it is still plausible to assume that the prolonged and intensive study of certain subjects results not simply in the gaining of knowledge of skills (the furniture of the mind), but in enhancing certain ways of thinking (the discipline of the mind). What is implausible is that the study of these subjects in itself has that effect. The key to a modern version of mental discipline as a justification of humanism lies not in identifying allegedly disciplinary subjects and then proceeding dutifully to study them. The key lies in *how* the subjects are studied. History as a record of names, dates, and events is just a lot of shabby and mostly useless furniture; history as giving order and meaning to human experience is thinking in a certain way. In fact, in a modern sense, what makes any field of study humanistic is not its identification with literature or the arts, but its potential for enlarging and deepening human experience.

The decline of the humanities in the modern American school curriculum is, at least in part, a matter of record. As a percentage of public high school students in grades nine through twelve, the study of Latin declined from a high of over 50 percent in 1900 to less than 8 percent in 1949. Greek as a high school subject has been virtually extinguished in this century. Even French, the "modern," whose place Eliot sought to raise to the status of the classical languages, has declined from over 14 percent in 1900 to under 5 percent in 1949.[44] The decline in the study of other subjects traditionally defined as humanistic is more difficult to document. Subjects like literature (English) and history have not so much suffered a decline in enrollments as they have undergone internal transformations. What we mean by English and what we mean by history are no longer quite the same. Additionally, although the sheer number of public schools in the United States is so large as to make it difficult to generalize, it seems clear that such recent educational fashions as career education and "back to basics" have helped move the center of gravity in the educational enterprise from its place in the development of the intellect to immediate utility and mindless drill in the rudiments. One should not be deluded into thinking, however, that education in the United States before the turn of this century represented some kind of golden age. Most of the evidence that exists indicates that what went on in the schools of the nation was, by and large, not only dull and lifeless, but utterly devoid of intellectual stimulation. Mental discipline as a defense of humanism, noble as that ideal may have been, was translated, more often than not, into monotonous drill and inhumane treatment of pupils. It was these defects that the best of the twentieth-century reformers in education tried to correct.

The rescue of humanistic study from its present state of decay in elementary and secondary schools (and perhaps in colleges as well) lies not in a return to an imagined nirvana in the premodern era, nor does it lie simply in a quantitative shift in the balance of humanities and science in the curriculum. It lies primarily in reconstructing all the studies that comprise the curriculum so that their origins in human purposes and human activity are restored and made the focal point of study. The contemporary American curriculum is not antihumanistic because music, art, literature, and foreign languages are given a secondary role to mathematics, physics, chemistry, and industrial arts. It is because the so-called academic subjects (usually characterized curiously as "college-entrance" subjects, as if that were their only function) are set against the practical subjects; and they have become so abstracted from the world that children and adolescents inhabit, that these studies are no longer recognizable as themselves forms of experience. The problem, as Dewey repeatedly emphasized, is one of restoring the subjects of study to their place *in* experience.

The study of the sciences no less than the study of the humanities suffers from the abstraction of these studies from their origins in human interests and human purpose. The mechanical dissection of frogs in a so-called laboratory and the routine combining of chemical elements to make the mixture turn blue is as antiintellectual as the familiar recitation of *amo, amas, amat* or the recounting of the bare plot of a novel. The vague association of these activities with the aura of scholarly activity serves only to mask their fundamentally antiintellectual character. The marks of scholarship imposed from without, as they so often are, quickly degenerate as Dewey said, into a miser's accumulation, and a man prides himself on what he has, and not on the meaning he finds in the affairs of life."[45] The school subjects, whether they are conventionally categorized as humanities or sciences, if they are perceived and presented merely as badges of scholarship, will remain not only antihumanistic but antiintellectual, precisely because they have lost their human meaning.

One of the salient factors in the decline of the humanities in the American school curriculum is the common perception, reflected in the work of detractors and even many defenders, that, while science and practical subjects concern themselves with the serious business of living, the humanities are to be identified with leisure and vaguely frivolous pursuits. That distinction is rooted partly in the common dualism in ancient Greece between labor and leisure. Thus, their association with leisure makes the humanities a luxury only a few can afford and then only after we have taken care of the really important work. The identification of the humanities with a small, cultured, leisure class, which is a legacy of the Renaissance, inevitably will work to their disadvantage if they are ever to function effectively in an era of mass public education. If the office of education is primarily the cultivation of intelligence, then the humanities, no less than the sciences, must be reintegrated into their place in intelligent action. As such, the power of humanistic studies to invest in ordinary experience what Dewey called "a depth and range of meaning . . . which otherwise might be mediocre," lies at the core of their value.[46] The humanities in this sense should not be seen as enjoyable appendages to the real work of education. The humanities, as Dewey said, "are not luxuries of education, but emphatic expressions of that which makes any education worthwhile."[47]

Footnotes

1. John Dewey, "Whither Humanism?" *The Thinker* 2 (1930): 9-12.
2. Emile Durkheim, *The Evolution of Educational Thought: Lectures on the Formation and Development of Secondary Education in France*, trans. Peter Collins (London: Routledge and Kegan Paul, 1977), pp. 177-226.
3. Ibid., p. 187.
4. Quoted in ibid., p. 194.
5. Ibid., p. 197-98.
6. Frederick Rudolph, *Curriculum: A History of the Undergraduate Course of Study Since 1636* (San Francisco: Jossey-Bass, 1977), pp. 65-66.
7. Brooks Mather Kelley, *Yale: A History* (New Haven, Conn.: Yale University Press, 1974), p. 165. Quoted in Rudolph, *Curriculum*, p. 66.
8. "Original Papers in Relation to a Course of Liberal Education," *American Journal of Science and Arts* 15, no. 2 (1829): 297-351.
9. Ibid., p. 299.
10. Ibid., p. 300.
11. Ibid., p. 301-2.
12. Ibid.
13. Ibid., p. 301.
14. Ibid., p. 303.
15. Ibid., p. 324.
16. Ibid., p. 328.
17. Ibid.
18. Ibid., p. 332.
19. Ibid., p. 335.
20. Ibid., p. 332.

21. Edward A. Ross, *Social Control* (New York: Macmillan, 1901), p. 176.

22. Ibid.

23. Ibid., p. 177.

24. National Education Association, *Report of the Committee on Secondary School Studies* (Washington, D.C.: Government Printing Office, 1893).

25. G. Stanley Hall, *Adolescence*, vol. II (New York: D. Appleton and Co., 1904), p. 510.

26. William James, *Principles of Psychology*, vol. I (New York: Henry Holt and Co., 1890), pp. 666-67.

27. Edward Lee Thorndike and R.S. Woodworth, "The Influence of Improvement in One Mental Function upon the Efficiency of Other Functions," *Psychological Review* 8 (May, July, November 1901): 247-61, 384-95, 553-64.

28. *Report of the Commissioner of Education for the Year Ended June 30, 1907*, vol. I (Washington, D.C.: Government Printing Office, 1908), pp. 37-72.

29. William T. Harris, "The Pedagogical Creed of William T. Harris," in *Educational Creeds of the Nineteenth Century*, ed. Ossian H. Lang (New York: E.L. Kellog and Co., 1898), p. 43.

30. Ibid., p. 37.

31. William T. Harris, "Equivalents in a Liberal Course of Study," in *Journal of Addresses and Proceedings* (Washington, D.C.: National Education Association, 1880): 174.

32. William T. Harris, "Psychological Inquiry," in *Journal of Addresses and Proceedings* (Washington, D.C.: National Education Association, 1885): 157.

33. Ibid.

34. Ibid., p. 156.

35. William T. Harris, "What Shall the Public Schools Teach?" *Forum* 4 (1888): 574.

36. Ibid., p. 575.

37. William T. Harris, "Preface" in James A. McLellan and John Dewey, *The Psychology of Number*, International Education Series, vol. 33 (New York: D. Appleton and Co., 1895), p. 5.

38. Harris, "What Shall the Public Schools Teach?" p. 576.

39. Ibid., p. 576.

40. Ibid., p. 579.

41. Ibid.

42. William T. Harris, *Psychologic Foundations of Education*, International Education Series, vol. 37 (New York: D. Appleton and Co., 1898), p. 178.

43. Harold Ordway Rugg, *The Experimental Determination of Mental Discipline in School Studies* (Baltimore: Warwick and York, 1916).

44. John Francis Latimer, *What's Happened to Our High Schools?* (Washington, D.C.: Public Affairs Press, 1958), p. 26.

45. John Dewey, *Democracy and Education* (New York: Free Press, 1916), p. 288.

46. Ibid., p. 238.

47. Ibid.

CHAPTER II

The Vision of the Humanities for the Young

ROBERT COLES

The humanities ought to offer young people in school a means of fitting various pieces of knowledge into a larger view of things—to draw upon a Latin phrase: *sub specie aeternitatis*. The humanities have to do with perspective—the long haul of time; and they have to do also with values, with a sense of what ought be as well as what is. The humanities begin with language—the distinctive attribute of human beings. We are the ones who become self-conscious, through words; who begin to ask questions as well as respond to reflexes; who gaze and wonder, then put into talk what crosses our minds. With language comes distance, a capacity to draw back and render an account of what is and has been taking place: history. Language is the means by which we keep trying for answers, not only to specific, factual matters, but to the mysteries of this universe. The big questions, those asked by Gauguin and written on his famous Tahitian triptych, are the essence of what the humanities try to fathom for us, through poems and stories and plays and essays and factual narratives: where do we come from, and what are we, and where are we going? Such questions have to do with "the meaning of life," a phrase once summoned commonly, but these days all too sadly left unused. The humanities bring us closest to our essential nature, as the ones who speculate: what, if anything, is the meaning of our existence?

Needless to say, a teacher's point of view becomes a student's experience through the mediation of certain texts. Nor did those who wrote, say, the novels or poems many high school students read, spend a lot of time constructing theories of education, or guides to accompany one or another collection of stories. *A Tale of Two Cities*, for example, is just that, a tale given us by a nineteenth-century storyteller. Each student who reads Dickens makes him his or her own companion—brings to Sydney Carton, let us say, a particular kind of sympathy, or indeed, lack thereof. Put differently, the humanities do not begin in a student's reading experience, but in our lives—the moral preparation we bring to school, to our reading time. Still, there *is* the teacher who uses those books as a means of conversation, speculation, edification, exhortation, and occasionally, imprecation. What goes for the reader, of course, goes for the reader who is called a teacher—a lifetime's preparation for Mr. Dickens. But one need not surrender, yet again, to twentieth-century determinism. *Part* of that lifetime, an important part, takes place in the daily activity of a given classroom, where a teacher can hope for the same transcendence Sydney Carton sought, even as that teacher hopes to spring a few students, each year, from the moral as well as intellectual constraints of their lives.

I feel myself, already, a bit too abstract; and I am not sure that the humanities ought be under such a tether. The humanities have to do with the moral and spiritual concreteness of our everyday lives, as a number of American youths have reminded me in no uncertain terms. Here, for example, is a New Orleans high school student, lecturing a doctor on the significance of another doctor's life—the latter a character in *A Tale of Two Cities*:

> They gave us the book to read, and said we had two weeks, and we'd better settle down and read fast, because we had to finish, and if we didn't, they'd find out, because we'd be tested, and they'd use "spot identifications." "They" were the two of them: the regular (older) teacher and the younger one, helping out—and learning, I guess. They kept on saying Dickens was a tough writer, and we should pay close attention, or we'd get lost in the novel, and we'd lose interest, and it'd be a real disaster for us.
>
> When I first picked up the novel, I was really annoyed: so big, so long! I had a lot else to do! What did they mean, by assigning that book for us to read, and in the spring! I was on the baseball team! I had a job! I had a lot of trouble at home: my dad was sick, and I was the one who took over some of his chores, and I was the one who tried to keep my younger brothers and sisters in line, while my mother was out working, or home cooking. Besides, who can go back into the past that far? They wrote different English back then. Even the teacher admitted that it's hard to understand a writer, if you're alive a hundred or more years after he wrote his novel.
>
> I got into *A Tale of Two Cities* fairly fast! I was surprised! I just picked it up, and I got interested. I now realize that the first sentences are famous, and a lot of people who haven't read the book know those lines: "It was the best of

times, it was the worst of times. . . ." But when I first read them, I thought to myself: yes, that's how it is, right now, for me and my family! We're having trouble, but we're fighting this segregation, and we're beginning to win a few battles, so there's trouble, but there's hope, and it more than balances the trouble.

I got involved with that Sydney Carton, and it was he who carried me through the book. If it hadn't been for him, I never would have finished; I would have skimmed, maybe! Also, Dr. Manette interested me: all the suffering he experienced, and yet he managed to stay alive, and when the right moment came, he got better, or mostly better. I kept trying to figure out how he kept his sanity while in prison; and how he recovered his sanity, once his daughter took him away from Paris. He seems to have lost his sanity in-between—while he stayed with the DeFarges. Do you have an explanation? If they'd sent him to a psychiatrist in Paris, after he was released from jail, would it have helped? What good can a psychiatrist do, when a person is being mistreated very badly, and there's no way of stopping his punishment, even if it's cruel and unfair? The psychiatrist would have to *rescue* the person, not *treat* him!

Among other reasons, novelists obviously write to give others a glimpse of a particular vision. Here in the twentieth-century American South, Dickens had found a spiritual kinsman of sorts—a fellow human being whose mind was utterly responsive to *A Tale of Two Cities*, and more, to the moral struggles Dickens had deemed to be so important. In fact, one wonders whether the young man's English teacher was similarly responsive to Dickens. Are novels meant to be studied as if they are bodies of factuality, to be taken apart, limb by limb, and identified? I fear I went through—in college, never mind high school—an experience not unlike that described above: a course titled "Dostoevski and Tolstoy," in which we had endless multiple-choice tests, all meant to prove we had read the books, remembered the names of the characters, principal or minor, and as well, the various deeds they accomplished. Irony is a favorite device of novelists; but life, as we all know, cannot only prompt art but follow it—when, for instance, one reads stories whose purpose is to help the reader (not to mention the writer) go beyond the narrowness and pettiness of everyday life, but ends up once more constrained now, by a narrow and petty didactic method. The transcendence of both Sydney Carton and Dr. Manette in *A Tale of Two Cities* is not necessarily available to many of us, who face no revolution or imprisonment as our fate.

The youth quoted above was, however, not only a critic of a given classroom. He had taken pains to question the very nature of the humanities—their significance to us, their peculiar way of addressing the broadest, yet also deepest aspects of our human experience. Of course, we teachers have a right to demand that our students do, indeed, pay heed—read the books we assign, remember their "contents." But such activity is a prelude to reflection, and not only the kind that has to do with textual criticism. *A Tale of Two Cities*, one young reader dared notice, is a story brimful of mystery. Not so much the conventional kind—cloak and dagger intrigue; but rather, the mystery we all know as we contemplate this life—even elementary school children, one hastens to add. Here, for example, is a white child who lived in New Orleans during the early 1960s, and who (at nine) had never heard of Charles Dickens or Fyodor Dostoevski or Leo Tolstoy:

I see that colored kid walking past the people, and they're all grown up, and they're telling her they're going to kill her, and I wonder why God put her here, to go through such trouble. In our church the minister is always telling us that God was very unpopular with the important people, because He had His own ideas of what was right and wrong, and He didn't agree with the big shots. On television, I heard that colored girl's daddy say he hoped and prayed the white people would think of Jesus, when they saw his daughter trying to get into the school. So, I did think of Jesus! Then, I thought of the colored kid. Then I had this terrible thought, that she'd die, like Jesus did, only we don't have crosses, to nail people on, I don't think.

I asked my mother what she thought would happen, and she said the colored kid is a pawn, and it's the fault of the Supreme Court. I asked my mother about Jesus, and she said Jesus felt sorry for everyone, and that includes all the colored, but you can't live your life like He did, Jesus, because He was God, and we're just people—and besides, He was killed, and He didn't mean for everyone to go get killed, and if we all did, there'd be no one to worship Him! Then, I asked my mother if God had a plan, when He made some people one way, and some people another way. I mean, some people are always having pain, or they're in trouble, and some people are always hurting other people, and the ones who do the hurting say they're Christians, and the ones who get hurt say they're Christians, too, and you get confused when you hear the minister talk, and your momma, and your daddy, and the teachers; and they all *are* confused, I guess, and even Jesus couldn't convince everyone, so they didn't feel confused, and I guess all you can do is be glad if someone gets you to do some "good asking," that's what my grandma says: "always try to be true to the Lord, and always ask yourself questions, the way the Lord did." So, I try!

So do we all—try to figure out this world, its endless puzzles, paradoxes, inconsistencies. The essence of the humanities has to do with moral inquiry, done, of course, with grace, dignity, aesthetic distinction. When I was a boy my mother took me to the Boston Museum of Fine Arts rather often. (She was an artist.) There, she would not only comment on certain pictures she found appealing, even compelling, but also ask me to let my mind wonder and wander both, prompted by the artists, and yes, by her as their interpreter, my teacher. Her favorite in the entire museum was the powerful triptych (1897) of Paul Gauguin, mentioned earlier—done in Tahiti as he struggled with suicidal despair. The canvas evokes the entire span of this life—infancy to old age. The canvas also evokes questions, not the least three supplied directly by the artist—one of those rare occasions when words are to be found in such a "place." Those three questions, rendered in French and mentioned earlier in this essay, were translated for me, again and again, by my mother until (finally!) I knew them in English by heart—and gladly repeat them here: Where do we come from? What are we? Where are we going? I also remember only too well this pointed observation of hers: "We're the ones on this earth who ask those questions!"

A mother's meditative side! A Boston woman's philosophical affinity with the existentialist tradition! A teacher's insistence that Gauguin's genius be saluted intently, seriously, with continuing respect. And yes, a teacher's desire that Gauguin not be confined (by a given pupil) to Tahiti, to the late nineteenth century, even to a particular profession, or branch of the humanities. Even as he was driven by his anguish—by his talent, as well—to ask the hardest questions in the most enduring manner, a teacher was anxious to pay homage not only to him, but to her own humanity, her student's, by embracing the responsibility that goes with attentive regard, with personal appreciation. Put differently, my mother was doing as that New Orleans child (a mere fourth grader!) was wont to do, as teachers of all "levels" aim to do; she was aiming to exert her intelligence, her imagination, in the direction of a scrutiny directed inward and outward both.

This life is full of questions—the general kind Gauguin posed, and the specific kind generated by the circumstances of one or another life.

The humanities are meant to help us *try*, as the child quoted put it, to find useful, decent, appropriate, sensible answers. Not that there ever will be complete, definite, thoroughly clear answers. The humanities are not, at heart, preoccupied with factuality. One turns to George Eliot not for "data" in its modern sense—the unequivocal information we all learn when we take arithmetic, or science courses, or for that matter, spelling. "The task of the novelist," said Flannery O'Connor, "is to deepen mystery;" and if ever there was both an implied definition of what the humanities are about, and a rebuke to a predominant contemporary sensibility, it is contained in that critical observation—one of many shrewd, pointed, often caustic comments that marvelous and all too short-lived, twentieth-century storyteller from Milledgeville, Georgia, gave to the rest of us who continue to make our way toward the year 2000.

Miss O'Connor added that "mystery is a great embarrassment to the modern mind," and with that aside got to the very heart of what ails so much of the teaching done today in the name of the humanities. Rather more of us in the humanities than we care to acknowledge are all too awed not by this world's mysteries, but by those who claim to have banished them rather thoroughly—the confident technicians, the strutting social scientists, the men and women who know how to punch machines, manipulate "materials," and come up with a yes, a no, a true, a false, a solution, definitive and final. Our "embarrassment" bespeaks our loss of self-respect, our shame, our sense of frustration, our feeling of incompetence: others manipulate things, prove themselves "practical," whereas we "merely" watch, listen, muse, acknowledge the strangeness of things. Why, we even cultivate a many-sided, uncertain, perplexed posture with respect to the world's events!

It is, of course, absurd to expect those of us who teach the humanities (in schools, in colleges, wherever) to ignore the powerful thrust of a culture, a historical moment. The issue, surely, is not our "embarrassment" before the power of technology, but what we do with that "embarrassment": ignore it, pretend it is of little import, make it of consuming import, pity ourselves on its account—or use it, wryly, to further our own purposes, as the ones who hope, always, to reflect upon the nature of things when confronted with this life's numerous moments of trial or error. One of the first "humanists,"

Socrates, asked us to regard ourselves with exceeding care, not with a self-centered orgy of reductionist psychology, as too often is the case these days, but with the conviction that honest self-scrutiny can reveal much about *others*. In that tradition, O'Connor's "embarrassment" tells us not only about the predicament of the humanities, but the situation of all this world's people. We are, so many of us, embarrassed by the seemingly endless evidence that we are finite, flawed, all too clearly fumbling—no matter the computers at hand, or the ponderous phrases committed (if I may call upon W. H. Auden's delicious use of that verb) in the name of sociology or psychiatry. ("Do not commit a social science!")

Moreover, embarrassment has many faces, as Dickens or Eliot, Dostoevski or Tolstoy, always knew: arrogance, preciosity, smugness, self-importance, pedantry, narrowness of mind, smallness of vision, coldness of heart. Have I, with that list, suggested a few traps faced by us who want to teach the humanities—the maneuvers we summon in fear and trembling, because we dare not come out and say, with O'Connor's candor, how hard it can be to press upon others, press upon ourselves, the vexing, alarming, saddening exhilarations of our visionary writers and artists? I remember a hero of my youth, whom I was lucky to know, William Carlos Williams, putting the above this way: "On a good day I see enough to say enough to scare myself. If a reader tells me how *pleasing* a line I've written is, or a story, I always wonder whether I've failed. I want 'them' to be pleased—oh sure!—but I want to dig below the surface, and there's lots of pain in digging, or in becoming a digger, by sympathy, yourself."

I suppose I'd better not *recommend* pain in our classrooms—not in an age devoted to countless utopian dreams, repeated romances with prophylaxis of one kind or another. These days, we want not only penetrations to all of nature's secrets, but protection from all of its hazards and hurdles. Not for us the willing assumption of vulnerability—as in the Christ mentioned by the two children I have brought into this essay, or as in our own nation's forebears, when they eagerly chose jeopardy in order to obtain a greater measure of freedom. For so many of us the point is security, certainty—the eradication of all ambiguity. No wonder we veer strongly to multiple-choice tests, to summaries and more summaries—of plots, of positions, of policies. "I haven't time to read *Middlemarch*," a not so stupid or ignorant Harvard undergraduate once let me know, without O'Connor's "embarrassment," and indeed, almost casually rather than worriedly or apologetically. Where did he learn such an "attitude?" Not, I presume, in the course of going through the "oedipal" stage of his "psychological development." Not in a fancy suburban home, or in a ghetto, either. He learned it in a succession of classrooms. The time has come for all of us to stop hiding behind psychology or sociology; to stop throwing our hands up as we contemplate the erosion of literacy in consequence of television, or the "culture of narcissism," or God knows what else.

The black youth quoted above, whom I regarded as his own kind of Dickensian scholar, could have been quickly assigned to some convenient and faddish sociological ashpile—"culturally disadvantaged," say, or "culturally deprived." Instead, a diligent and thoroughly demanding (without "embarrassment!") teacher had grabbed him (literally, sometimes!), collared him (not literally!), pressed upon him a novel. She read it aloud to him and his classmates. She pointed out what its pages meant. She virtually sang it, as well as singing its praises. She indicated her belief in it, and she persuaded a number of her students to give their assent—to her, to Charles Dickens, to O'Connor's "mystery and manners," which is what, in sum, our novelists, all of them, try to set down for us to contemplate. It is my hunch that the particular teacher in question, and her students, too, require neither exhortation nor analysis from the rest of us—what to do, how to do it. They would like, to be sure, our company as delighted, convinced readers—a burden of work they have assumed, and would gladly have us assume. In the absence of our commitment to their kind of journey, they would probably shrug their shoulders, as Sydney Carton sometimes did—not too hopeful about the prospects of all humanity, but willing to stand up for its worth by standing up for themselves as readers, and thereby, unembarrassed dreamers.

Part Two
HUMANITIES AT THE THRESHOLD OF THE DISCIPLINES

CHAPTER III

Cultural Literacy: Time for a New Curriculum

JOHN J. MCDERMOTT

We always live at the time we live and not at some other time, and only by extracting at each present time the full meaning of each present experience are we prepared for doing the same thing in the future. This is the only preparation which in the long run amounts to anything.

JOHN DEWEY

Contemporary Public Education

In our time and in our nation, public precollegiate education is in serious disarray. It is now a nationally observed phenomenon that despite good intentions on the part of teachers and generally intelligent students, even those students who proceed on to colleges and universities seem culturally deprived. They exhibit a staggering ignorance of history and letters, and their symbolic resources for imaginative reconstruction seem bankrupt. It is as if the soul has disappeared, leaving only a more or less satisfactory standardized test as the approach to learning.

The reasons for this state of affairs are complex and obviously not easy of solution. This is not the place to probe the educational politics of the situation, although they are decidedly relevant, as the Conant report attested two decades ago.[1] We are faced with something of an institutional *fait accompli*, in that colleges of education prepare most of our teachers in a decidedly nonhumanistic[2] and nonspeculative framework. It should not come as surprising that these teachers then teach our children in a similar vein. Nothing less than a radical transformation of the curriculum in teacher education programs can resolve that dilemma, a transformation long overdue.

It is now a truism that students with high test scores and class rank are nonetheless unaware of even paradigmatic events in the history of western civilization, to say nothing of their total innocence of the very existence of major cultural traditions other than their own. In a recent effort to assess the knowledge of highly qualified and academically successful juniors and seniors in a major American university, I was startled to learn that thirty of forty students could not identify Socrates, the Roman Empire, the Protestant Reformation, Newton, or Beethoven. In fact, of the thirty simple identifications requested, the average score for the forty students was six correct. Despite the fact that we now live in a truly global culture, requests for information or insight about Oriental, Indian, African, or Islamic cultures, are met with utter bewilderment.

Still more serious, by far, than the existence of this appalling absence of awareness of our historical and cultural past, is the spiritual context of contemporary public education. Although exceptions exist, it is a safe generalization to describe the ambience of "being in school" as an alternation between boredom and violence. The major escapees from these nefarious poles are those children, due to family or occasionally ethnic pressure, who concentrate on "making it" and see one or more careers as the delineation of their human future. These judgments as to the plight of our schools are not novel. In fact, ample literature, both popular and scholarly, details this situation on a regular basis.

Admittedly, the critique of the studied emptiness of middle-class education and the warnings about the baleful future of those children who know only a career as the meaning of education, is comparatively subtle in a nation that is increasingly characterized by the quick, the shallow, and the ersatz. Not so subtle, however, is the diagnosis of the school systems of our great urban centers. In such settings, involving millions of children, historical and cultural illiteracy is not, alas, the primary concern. Rather, we face dramatically high rates of absenteeism and adolescent dropouts. We face strife, social disorder, and plummeting scores in basic verbal and mathematical skills. Administrators, teachers, and community leaders are often called upon for heroic efforts in their attempt to structure a meaningful educational environment. Yet, despite these efforts, increasingly, even liberal and pluralistically oriented parents choose to ferret their children away in one of the urban private schools which now multiply like mushrooms after a constant rain. When added to the postwar flight of the self-announcing gentry to the suburbs, the rise of urban private schools leaves public education in our cities as something of an embattled redoubt, an abandoned but peopled bunker, left behind.

In our country, the United States, historically and morally committed to a democratic polity, it is essential that we continue, generation by generation, to educate all of our children in the best of our warranted wisdom, so that they may take their rightful and necessary place in the ongoing presentation and continuance of our attempt to build a truly human future. The erosion of humanistic sensibility, awareness of the past and basic competency in literacy and science, as often found in contemporary public education, constitutes a major threat to this essential national endeavor. Granted the occasional worthiness and even curricular imagination of private education, we must acknowledge that it is the quality of public school education which holds the key to the spiritual future of this republic. Therefore, we cannot be sanguine, for it is precisely public school education that mirrors the deepest crisis in contemporary America, namely, the economic and social bifurcation between a struggling and cynical lumpenproletariat, confined to poor rural and inner-urban schools and an affluent, morally laissez-faire middle-class, making their way through private or suburban educational institutions. The separation of blacks and Hispanics from whites is, of course, a looming factor in this division, but it is not the decisive source of the division. Looming larger is the gap between the poor and the affluent, for that gap, regrettably and undemocratically, constitutes the major reason for the double standard as to what constitutes acceptable education for an American child. Despite the penchant for crisis management in American society, the crisis in American public school education remains obdurate and discussed only sotto voce. Highways, potholes, prisons, illegal aliens, and interest rates rank far ahead of the debilitation of millions of our children. The politics of this situation seem impervious to resolution, short of revolution, which, in this century, seems to bring only repression under a different rubric.

Transforming Public Education

Given the skepticism about the salutary effect of recent federal programs for the amelioration of problems besetting the public schools and given the economic climate of America in 1983, it is very unlikely that we will witness the appearance of an educational Marshall plan in the near future. Consequently, the finances, the neighborhoods, and the clientele of the public schools will remain basically the same in this decade. The curriculum, however, need not remain the same. And we can move in the direction of a significant shift in the focus of the teaching process. I now offer some suggestions as to the ingredients necessary for a transformation of public education. Parenthetically, I do not have in mind the simplistic resolution, often put forth by university faculty, of adding materials and subject matter in the earlier years. As one who taught Latin and English in secondary school, I can attest that this would only introduce increased confusion to the curricular bedlam now regnant. Adolescent students who now take six, seven, and even eight different subjects a day, in short time snatches, are in no position to have more subject matter added. Although it is generally lamentable that such areas of important intellectual endeavor, such as philosophy, sociology, psychology, anthropology, the history of religion, and the history of science are not staples in a typical secondary school curriculum, I see no possible way in which they could so become, except by ousting equally important concerns or by making the curriculum more of a patchwork quilt than at present. No, the needed change is in a different direction, entirely. We must demythologize the discipline structure of our approach to education.

I believe that humanistic learning is present in every endeavor and that it is dramatically present in the traditional endeavors of precollegiate education. How did it happen that the discipline known as history became responsible for the history of everything, such that other disciplines became ahistorical? If I am teaching physics to secondary school students, is it not germane to the discussion that for more than two thousand years, physics and philosophy were identical? Is it not significant that the ancient philosopher, Democritus, anticipated modern atomic theory? Should not these students be told that the history of science is pockmarked with errors, many of them propagated far beyond the time of exposure, because of political or ideological reasons? Would not the teaching of science be served well if we were to introduce the students to the contrasting conflicts found in the life and work of Galileo, to that of Lysenko? In this way, the teaching of science involves not only history but ethics and biography, as well. A further example from the sciences pertains to biology. In western civilization, biology was founded by Aristotle and the phyla are his creation. Could there be a better model for students to emulate, relative to the power of observation? And would it not be a contribution to these students for them to know that while learning Aristotle's approach to biology, they were also learning his method of philosophy, a method which infused western culture until the late nineteenth century? Similar examples from the sciences can be multiplied indefinitely, and the historical dimension of every discipline should be an integral aspect of its presentation.

We do not quarrel with the fact that it is necessary and salutary that precollegiate education spend time on mathematics, and on reading, writing, and speaking English and at least one other language, all taught very early in the schooling process. And, whenever possible, computer-assisted instruction should be utilized. But for the rest of the curriculum, at the outset for some years, and then periodically thereafter, we should concentrate on biography-autobiography, the science of living things, that is, botany and physiology, sculpture, and theatre. These suggestions are neither final nor definite, although their interdisciplinary width makes them especially attractive. Properly structured and taught, they would be the filter through which all of the "subjects" now extant in the curriculum would be introduced. Before I attempt to justify the significance of these approaches to a new curriculum, I offer the following commentary on the importance of a cultural pedagogy, by which I mean the common source of our personal expectations, sensibilities, and evaluations.

Pedagogy is hapless and empty if it does not face directly the deep and pervasive dialectic between the historical and genetic conditioning of the person on the one hand and the impress of the novelties of the physical and social world on the other hand. This confrontation between our human heritage and the world in which we find ourselves, is the stuff out of which we weave that fragile creature we call our very own self. The key to a successful mapping of this conflictual terrain is the making of relations, that is, the forging of a distinctively personal presence in the doings and undergoings that constitute our experience. The making of relations is a life-long endeavor, but it is especially crucial in the lives of children, as they struggle to achieve self-consciousness in a vast, complex, and initially undefined environment. Helping our children to learn how to make relations is the central and most important task of pedagogy. To the extent that they do not learn to make their own relations, children are doomed to living secondhand lives, creatures of habituation, who merely follow out the already programmed versions of their experience as inherited from parents, older siblings, and self-appointed definers of reality, such as teachers. Ironically, a child who knows how to make relations can convert even authoritarian and repressive treatment into paths of personal liberation, whereas a child who does not make relations converts invitations to free inquiry into derivative and bland repetition. This irony is made vivid for us when we realize that most often the lives of those whom we regard as "great" are characterized by affliction, suffering, and frequent rejection. In the hands of those who can make and remake relations, even negative events become the nutrition for a creative life.

Just what is it for a child to make relations and why do I regard it as crucial to a humanistic pedagogy? First, we must dispel any naiveté about the allegedly virginal character of the emerging self. The profound and complex preconscious conditioning of the self is a truism in our time. Modern sociology, with its roots in the thought of George Herbert Mead, stresses the social origins of the "I," holding that without the "other," there would be no "me." Modern psychology, with its roots in Freud and Jung, stresses the irreducible presence and power of our unconscious. Or conversely, modern psychology, here following B.F. Skinner, holds that we are totally conditioned by the operant impress of external stimuli. The sociology of knowledge, founded by Karl Marx, contends that our consciousness, far from being original, implies "ours," as derivative of "institutions." For Marx, "institutions" referred to church, state, family, and money, whereas recent thought adds gender, race, ethnicity, language, climate, and region as initiating boxes from which we never really escape.

It is now obvious that as we come to self-consciousness in our early years, we are playing out our inherited genetic and social trappings. None of us can ignore the conditioning power of this inheritance. The existence of a pristine self, free of the entangling alliances of one's genetic and social past is a myth. To be born white or black, male or female, Irish or Jewish, is an inherited context as thick as the earth itself. To experience one's postnatal years in the city or on a farm, in the snow or in the jungle is an informing crucible that our consciousness can repress but never totally dismiss. One could multiply these inheritances indefinitely, and a diagnosis of their significance in the lives of children could become a rich source of self-awareness as well as of awareness of others by contrast. In fact, I have in mind that these diagnoses would be the beginning of the child's self-understanding and the beginning of the child's attempt to build a new, distinctively personal world.

My point here is that the only way to obviate the deleterious secondhandedness of our inherited trappings, is to bring them to the fore and diagnose them as to their richness, their narrowness, and the role they play in our assumptions. Under careful and probing guidance, even very young children are capable of fleshing out their distinctive sense of time, space, place, size, color, tone, and ever more subtle ambiences of the world in which they "find" themselves. In this way, the inheritances are transformed from conceptual boxes in which the child is unknowingly encased, to perceptual fields, fit for romping and reconstructing in the light of present experiences. This is precisely what I mean by the making of relations, namely, taking these inherited conditionings and turning them from conceptual rocks into something more diaphanous, crossed and recrossed with variant images, attitudes, and styles. There is nothing arcane in this, for children, despite their inheritances, seek novelty, naturally, unless they are prevented by a pedagogy which attempts to reduce all of their experiences to a common denominator. For example, just recently, a teacher was queried in a newspaper article as to how she would begin her teaching after the children returned from their Hanukkah or Christmas holidays. She replied that if they insisted, they could take a "few minutes" to say what they did during that time, but then it would be "back to the routine." One can hardly dignify this approach as educational, for the classroom is a morgue and the children are cadavers, passive witnesses to an anatomical dissection on behalf of a fixed curriculum.

To the contrary, is not this the time to assist in the conversion of the children's ordinary reportage of these extraordinary events, celebrated for two millennia, into something extraordinary and within their reach? Is not this the time to read them O. Henry's "Gift of the Magi" and appropriate selections from the *Diary of Anne Frank?* Is not this the time to introduce them to Ramadan, the holy period of Islam and then to contrast Judaism, Christianity, and Islam with Buddhism and Hinduism? Is not this the time to assist the children in leaping upon an experience, about to be had and then just after it is undergone, so that they may open it up and reach out to neighboring experiences, analogous, and starkly different? It is necessary for one to have experience if one is to make relations and create a personal world, tied to others yet distinctive. To have experience without making relations, especially of dissimilarity, is to be left with the inert, repetitious and routine.

Like William James, I too believe that experience grows by its edges.[4] By nature, the child comes into the world, on edge, on the qui vive, with a penchant for making relations. Traditional education, however, seems perversely determined to block this run of the imagination, opting rather for a world made up of boxes, separate one from the other, each defined and named, impervious to the rash of potential relations that yield themselves only to the reflection born of experienced perception. Is it not long overdue that contemporary educational practices integrate the accrued wisdom of this century and come to realize that names, categories, schema, and definitions are but functional placeholders in our experiencing the flow of events, linked to each other in a myriad of ways? With the exception of speculative mathematics and formal logic, percepts should reign over concepts. Definitions should never be taken to exhaust the meaning, texture, tone, or implication of that defined. Ambiguity should be restored to its proper place as the proper response in direct proportion to the importance of the experience undergone. Love and loyalty, for example, are exquisitely ambiguous and no amount of quantitative social science methodology can clarify them sufficiently, such that they become fully understood or manipulable.

I have no objection to the proper utilization of quantitative methodology, and I am aware of the necessity of scientific rigor. Similarly, I endorse the importance of high technology and the utilization of the computer in attainment of ever more sophisticated and accurate access to data. No, my concern is quite different. I lament the suffusion of the elementary and secondary school curriculum with disciplines and approaches whose major task is to prepare students for successful functioning in an ostensibly high-technological future, as though such activity was to be the primary activity of a human life. If we are to survive as an originating human culture, we cannot view the reflective awareness of our past, the extensive knowledge of other cultures and other languages, literature, the arts, and speculative science as activities merely desirable and actually peripheral to the more important task of "getting along" in the future. This approach may enable us to survive as a nation, that is, as the saying goes, to hold our own. On the other hand, we shall become spiritually bankrupt.

Four Curricular Modules

As an antidote to the drift away from having the humanities as the centerpiece of public elementary and secondary school education, I offer that we should make use of four curricular modules: autobiography-biography, the science of living things (that is, botany and physiology), sculpture, and theatre. Taking them seriatim, my justification for this contention will now be elaborated.

AUTOBIOGRAPHY-BIOGRAPHY

How are young persons to find a wedge into the tissue of experience in a way that transcends the narrowness of their own ego development? One way, of course, is to be driven by an event, either magnificent or disastrous. Such events are rare in our lives and even they become meaningful only in proportion to our reflective awareness of their significance. A second possibility exists and although it is less intense, it is more available. I refer here to the way in which we can be carried beyond our immediate ken by virtue of participation in the recorded lives of the many startling and creative persons among our collective lineage. Think, for example, how extraordinarily rich is the prose and the historical content of the life and death of Socrates, as written by Plato. Here we introduce the student to a raft of central concerns: classical Greek culture, philosophy, religion, ethics, politics, and finally, the important and profound question of our death, as raised in the discussion as to whether Socrates committed suicide. Equal wisdom is to be gained from the life of Thomas Jefferson, who also introduces us to architecture and to his deep feeling for the land, on behalf of an agrarian ethic. The meaning of courage and indomitability in the face of adversity, is brought to our consciousness by the study of the lives of Queen Elizabeth or Joan of Arc. Virtually every human characteristic and every cultural and intellectual movement is represented by one or more biographies and autobiographies. Through this medium, we have access to the achievements and the plight of every race, region, ethnic group, religion, and cultural persuasion. And we need not confine our materials to happy endings, for we have much more to learn from the slave narratives, the survivors of the holocaust, or of Gulag, or of Hiroshima. I do not see the study of biography and autobiography as a replacement for systematic study. Rather I view it as propaedeutic and an accompaniment. The plaintive cry, why do I have to study physics, is not well met by the stock reply that someday you will use it. Far better to study the life of Newton and Heisenberg and develop a hunger for the activities of physics.

The biographies of the famous, the great, and the notorious are an obvious way to have students begin to understand the multiplicity of cultures and life-experiences, which then cast light on their own lives. Equally important are the reported lives of those persons who are comparatively unsung or known only for their prowess in a limited area or for a single accomplishment. Their stories do not have a fabled backdrop but the human quotient may be even closer to the experiences of the students. Of recent vintage, is the telling of the lives of the totally unknown, as pieced together from diaries and letters found posthumously. In 1963 and 1967, my wife and I traveled with our five children across America, some 40,000 miles in and out of every continental state. One of the most moving sets of experiences resulted from our indefatigable effort to stop at hundreds of local museums throughout the country. In those modest buildings, on those modest streets, we found the letters and diaries of the founders—men, women, and children. Beautifully written both in prose and in penmanship, belying the fact that their formal education, mostly in the nineteenth century, was limited in scope and time, these documents evoked a sense of the past, of human misery and triumph equal to the legendary figures we celebrate. It is of importance to note that the beauty of the style and the depth of feeling in these documents is accompanied by a simplicity of access. They can be read by children without difficulty. I think of the letters of the people of the whaling community of Sag Harbor and Cold Spring Harbor on Long Island. I think of the letters of the settlers in Texas and Minnesota and Colorado. For every Lewis and Clark, for every Daniel Boone, there are hundreds of people like you and me who wrote of their experience in a moving and telling way.

In addition to the students bathing in the reflective waters of the experience of others, ordinary as well as extraordinary, the pedagogical task is to urge them to keep their own diaries and to save their letters. The keeping of a diary at a young age is often met with an embarrassed incredulity. The responsive refrain is often in the plaintive vein of "who, me?" or "who would care?" Perhaps no one would care. Perhaps someone would care. Perhaps many would care. The significance of the diary does not depend on these future possibilities. Rather, the writing of a diary, contexted by the reading of others' lives, provides the student with a private landscape for self-diagnosis and for the integration of the past with the present. The diary will provide the glare of self-examination. The prose will improve and the life of the student will be privately exposed to the twin canons of evaluation: the niggardliness of the everyday and the occasional breakthrough or conquest. The personal importance of the student's diary will not achieve the significance of the spotlight cast upon the *Meditations* of Marcus Aurelius, but the rhythm of a life living will be notably similar.

THE SCIENCE OF LIVING THINGS

Despite our many differences, one from the other, creature from creature, we share a rich and incontrovertible common bequest, that of being a live creature. The plants, the animals, and human beings are living things. (Some say the stars are as well, but we shall leave that discussion for another time.) With the exception of those few who believe in pan-psychism, an intriguing, although as yet unverified hypothesis, most people accept the distinction between the organic and the inorganic as fundamental to any understanding of reality. The science of living things would introduce the student to the life and death cycles of plants, vegetation, insects, animals, and human beings.

Ideally, this should involve both laboratory and field work. The task here is to introduce the student not only to the names and functions of organisms, but to stress, as well, the dramatic sharing and conflict that is a permanent characteristic of living. It is easy to replicate the life and death cycle of vegetation, plants, insects, and small animals in a classroom setting. Objections to the existence of these living things in the classroom are fey and bureaucratically self-serving. The death of a geranium or a hamster, especially one giving birth, provides an unending and, ironically, fertile source for the exploration of the most important event in our lives, our own death.

Moving to the human organism, considerable time should be given to the liver and the brain, organs which are masterpieces of perturbation, consummation, and messaging. The rhythm of setback and recovery as well as the function of watchdog are salient characteristics of these organs. The liver, for example, nicely and appropriately named in English, has as its obligation the managing of more than five hundred activities, each essential not only to human well-being, but to life itself.[5] I am reminded of the ancient text from the Hebrew scriptures, the Book of Ezekiel, 21:21, "For the King of Babylon stood at the parting of the way, at the head of the two ways, to use divination: he made *his* arrows bright, he consulted with images, he looked in the liver." And from the Greek doctrine of the four humors, through the medieval period and into Shakespeare's *Julius Caesar*, the amount and kind of liver bile was thought to determine whether a person was choleric, sanguine, bucolic, or melancholic. Modern medical science has abandoned these anthropomorphic versions of the liver, yet the urgency and centrality of its function still hold. A biochemical marvel, the human liver is a sorter, a dispatcher, a condemner, a welcomer, and the arbiter of what stays in our body and under what conditions and what leaves our body, namely, the barest detritus of the nutrition cycle. In short, the human liver is a supreme maker of relations, our biological brain. Its malfunction is our serious illness. Its death is our death. For the children, the obvious fallout of this study of the liver, as well as of the brain, and of the kidneys, each a maker of relations, is an awareness of the simultaneous power and fragility of the human body, a dialectic which is repeated in our religious, ethical, social, psychological, and imaginative transaction with the world.

SCULPTURE

What the liver is to the inner world of our bodies, the hands are to the outer world in which we live out our lives. Different from fish and from snakes, we are prehensile creatures. With our hands, we touch, we grab, we hold, we push, and we pull. More subtly, we caress, we knead, we feel, and with our hands, we make sounds and things and signs. Our hands are the major way in which we penetrate the world, seeking to learn its texture and occasionally seeking to remake the world in our image, be it a representation, fantasy, or an original construct. It is with our hands that we touch and care for the most intimate and private parts of our bodies, and as adults, care for the bodies of those we love. Our hands enable the violin and the piano to yield their enchanting sounds. Our hands enable us to write and type the messagings of our person. Our hands go still only in our sleep or at our death. It is well-known that the most human and "living" aspect of a human cadaver is the hand; the fingers are crooked over the palms, seemingly clinging to life when all else has failed.

In this vast variety of activities of the hand, the most distinctive and powerful version is to be found when we sculpt. In this activity, we render the external world in our own image. No matter the material, we can fashion it into shapes and contours which bespeak the press of our desire to build a world that is singular and original. Pedagogically, the intention is to have the student create his or her own imaginative image of the world, experiencing deeply the extension of human intimacy, the hands, into the obduracy of materials. Accompanying this creative and managing activity would be research into the textual makeup and history of the materials utilized. Each student would provide analysis of the materials subject to their sculpturing, and upon sharing this information with each other, the result would be a common apprisal of the history and texture of cloth, paper, clay, plastics, and the wide varieties of woods and metals. Shared, too, would be the range of skills necessary to an effective managing of these materials, such as carpentry, welding, the use of a kiln, and an array of decorative abilities. Salutary, as well, would be the collapsing of the pernicious distinctions between the fine arts, the practical arts, and the industrial arts. Sculpture is remarkable precisely for its capacity to integrate every conceivable human way that we have to effect a change in the nature of material before us, in effect, to make something undreamt of in nature.

In addition to the mastery of technique and the understanding of the potentialities and limitations in the nature of materials, the making of sculpture offers to students an excellent opportunity to forge a relationship between themselves and the world through a personal and imaginative medium. On the basis of my experience with this approach to learning, I have no doubt that the results will range from the obvious to the surreal and from the beautiful to the grotesque, thus bequeathing a mirror image of the dazzling, albeit too often hidden, plurality which is potential to human creative activity. In time, these sculptures will be in every classroom, in homes, and perhaps even in public places. In this way, the community will relive its own fantasies, histories, and personal perspectives through the hands of its children.

THEATRE

The last of our suggested curricular modules is that of theatre. Of all the ways to educate, theatre is the most demanding and complex, both in preparation and execution. The rewards in learning and experience, however, more than justify the effort. Basically, we can either select our source of theatre as pedagogy from plays already written and performed, or we can have the writing of the play as part of the activity.[6] Each source has its advantages. The former provides the students with a play that has been evaluated and represents approved wisdom, style, and dramatic effect. All of the details necessary to staging are provided, so that the students can concentrate on effecting a successful production. I would suggest several attempts at utilizing already written and produced plays, before trying to write an original script. No doubt, starting from scratch will not produce the equivalent quality of plays already extant. Still, the advantages here are considerable. Learning to write dialogue, developing a plot, generating believable characters, and setting out the specifications for stage directions are all extraordinarily valuable in teaching students how to write and how to "set up" a human world. It would be especially valuable if the development of the script could be done in concert, thereby introducing the students to an ongoing and shared community of inquiry, by which they, as generational peers, would evolve their view of their world, its values and pitfalls.

Whichever of the above two methods are followed, plays as extant or original, the pedagogical rewards are considerable. First, theatre is contextual; it is set somewhere. The setting may be ancient Greece as in the *Agamemnon* of Aeschylus or in England during the late medieval age of the history plays of Shakespeare. Or, the setting could be more modest, say Willy Loman's unbecoming home in New York and a small hotel room in Boston, as found in Arthur Miller's *The Death of a Salesman.* Additional sites abound: airplanes, farms, ghettoes, ships, war sites, mountains, and the totally imaginative, such as the fantasy constructs of alien planets. No matter the site, the pedagogical upshot is that the students must enter a world other than their own. Costume, jargon, climate, and an endless set of cultural assumptions will differ from theirs. By virtue of participating in a theatrical presentation of this other world, they will be forced, by contrast, to sharpen their experience of their own world, while obviating the subtle danger of habituation and repetition.

A second positive result of the pedagogy of theatre results from the preparation of the play. Ideally, all of the ingredients necessary to the production should be wrought by the students. Lighting, costumes, scenery, and other appurtenances also should be the responsibility of the students. As with sculpture, this responsibility will bring together the fine arts and the applied arts. As an example of this merging of disciplines and technical skill, take the problem of costumes. They should not be obtained ready-made but rather should be made by the students. What, then, is a toga? Of what material was it made? How did it fit? Were they all identical? What of those worn by a male, female, slave, free person, citizen, or a child? And did the dress differ by the time of the day, or of the year, or of the season, or by ceremonial occasion? Equally tantalizing is the nature and history of footwear, undergarments, and personal weaponry. This historical research is only the first step, for when the knowledge of "what" was worn and "when" and "why" is attained, the students must then attend to "how" it was made and then make it themselves.

One could go further and have the students make the technology, however primitive, which made the clothing and utensils of other, earlier cultures. Not only would this provide a deep and lasting insight to the ingenuity and steadfastness of the children's forebears, it would also cast a light of appreciation and even marvel on the achievements of contemporary technology. Two anecdotes will illustrate this judgment. At the end of the nineteenth century, John and Alice Dewey founded a laboratory school for children. One of the exercises was to bring in a bushel of raw cotton plants and have the children pick the cotton and prepare it for processing. After a day of this, they barely had enough cotton for a pair of socks and their untutored hands were sore and abrased. The children were then introduced to Eli Whitney and the invention of the cotton gin. The second anecdote comes first-hand. When our son, Brian, the fourth of our five children, was in the fourth grade, his public school teacher devoted a major part of the year to having the class build a replica of the Mercury capsule, launched just a year earlier. The children read articles on aerodynamics, the mysteries of space, and were taught the elementary physics of this astonishing phenomenon. They did all of the carpentry and other material preparation. The capsule grew, imposing, dazzling, and mysterious, although accessible to its creators. It stood in the center of the classroom and each day took on portentous stature as it neared completion. For our son, now a secondary school teacher of the industrial arts and a master carpenter, the experience in the fourth grade was incomparably the richest of his eighteen years of schooling. Depressingly, although not surprisingly, this story has a bitter ending. Despite the protests of irate parents, our fourth-grade teacher was fired at the end of that memorable year. It seems that he did not complete the fourth-grade syllabus.

A third reason for introducing the pedagogy of theatre as a central module in our curriculum is the reenforcement of effort and experience by virtue of doing the play for an audience, either student peers or perhaps parents and relatives. The best of these dramatic productions could even be shared with the community at large. As a medium, theatre surpasses the symphonic concert and even cinema, in its ability to draw the audience out of its consciousness and into a different and often novel setting. The legendary excitement of the "opening" is deserved, for the footlights are just that, lights which illuminate the walking of an audience into the lives of others, rhetorically and scenically embracing. Song and dance are infinitely more alive and captivating when they are aspects of theatre, thus the power of opera and ballet. The most ordinary of plots and most banal of prose turn into excitement in the context of music and song, as when the libretto of *La Boheme* is rendered operatically by Puccini. The simplest of tales rise from their obviousness when Tchaikovsky offers us the ballets, *Swan Lake* and *The Sleeping Beauty.* Even the dramatic starkness of *Our Town* by Thornton Wilder draws the audience into its ken and then back again to their own consciousness for a nostalgic rumination of their childhood. To create theatre is not only to create a human world. More, it is to create so that others, the audience, can participate, can share, and can enter into the process. No medium, no art form, no human activity, can make relations in so many ways, so expansively, so extensively, so multiple in style and theory and artifact, so subtle, so explosive, so clear, so ambiguous, so deft, so explicit, and so rich in implication as can be found in the doing, making, and offering of theatre. If I am correct in this assessment, then our children must have the opportunity to develop these theatrical skills, attitudes, abilities, failures, and successes from their preschool years through their adult life.

I do not have an idêe fixe on these four modules for a revised precollegiate curriculum. Other possibilities come to mind, archaeology, pathology, dance, and comparative anthropology, to cite some of many. Frankly, they, and others, seem absorbable and able to be taught within the imaginative pedagogical approach to autobiography and biography, the science of living things, sculpture, and theatre. Actually, adjustments to these curricular suggestions and even replacements are not destructive to the above discussion, so long as the main contention is honored, that is, the irreducible task of pedagogy. By this task, I mean the helping of others to make relations, such that the deepest recesses of personal privacy transact with human others, with an external world, and with the images gleaned from a storied and even repressed past. In this way, we build our world. It is a world borrowed, stolen, hidden from others, shared, lamented, celebrated, and occasionally the result of personal triumph.

Surely in a nation ostensibly committed to excellence and to equality, we cannot afford to deprive our children of access to the wisdom of the past and to the stirring and value-laden modalities and media of the arts and the humanities. They have every right to be taught how to write, listen, read, and speak with a deep understanding of our full cultural heritage. The computer is a parrot and will be only as meaningful as the quality of our input. If we render generation after generation culturally deaf and dumb, the rising spires of high technology will be but a contemporary parallel to the Tower of Babel.

Footnotes

1. James B. Conant, *The Education of American Teachers* (New York: McGraw-Hill, 1963). Although published twenty years ago, this "Report" retains its significance. The situation is now worse and the reforms suggested have not been implemented. Of the twenty-six recommendations, the most telling is that fledgling teachers be certified after having successfully majored and graduated in a field or discipline in the arts, sciences, and social sciences and having completed successful student teaching. This procedure enables some prospective teachers to bypass the College of Education curriculum and offers a new source of competent teachers in our schools. Learning how to teach, after all, is significant in direct proportion to whether one knows something worth teaching others. For a recent statement on this issue, see David Stewart, "Schools of Teacher Education Should Be Eliminated," *English Journal* 71 (December 1982): 8, 10, 12.

2. Unfortunately, it is necessary to clarify the term humanistic. In my use, it has no relation to the contemporary conflict between the "moral majority" and its alleged opponent "secular humanism." To the contrary, humanistic education appeals to the entire history of human activity, including religion and religious experience, as reflectively undergone and aesthetically articulated. Equally germane to this effort is the thought of Cicero, of St. Teresa, and of the revelation scriptures, and Goethe's *Faust.*

3. The reeducation of teachers so that the humanities become the matrix on and through which education takes place is precisely the ongoing legacy of the work of the National Humanities Faculty. It is extraordinary to witness the impact of a visiting N.H.F. member when he or she provides insight as to how to galvanize and enliven an existing curriculum.

4. Cf. "A World of Pure Experience," in *The Writings of William James*, ed. John J. McDermott (Chicago: University of Chicago Press, 1977), pp. 212-13. "Experience itself, taken at large, can grow by its edges. That one moment of it proliferates into the next by transitions which, whether conjunctive or disjunctive, continue the experiential tissue, can not, I contend, be denied. Life is in the transitions as much as in the terms connected; often, indeed, it seems to be there more emphatically, as if our spurts and sallies forward were the real firing line of the battle, were like the thin line of flame advancing across the dry autumnal field which the farmer proceeds to burn. In this line we live prospectively as well as retrospectively."

5. See Carroll M. Leevy, *Evaluation of Liver Function in Clinical Practice* (Indianapolis: Lilly Research Laboratories, 1965).

6. Another alternative is to have the students rewrite an extant play in their own words, or, again, to put an extant biography or short story into dramatic form. The latter was done some years ago at Huntington High School in New York. The students rewrote and dramatized Vonnegut's "Harrison Bergeron" with electrifying success, even as gauged by a sophisticated community audience. Believe me, it can be done!

CHAPTER IV

The Place of Languages in the Precollegiate Humanities Curriculum

GERMAINE BRÈE

What is it that learners are expected to speak, read and write? The language they are learning. What do we mean by this?

H. G. WIDDOWSON

Situation of the Topic

Language, its nature and functions, its capacity to produce and communicate meaning at a variety of levels—conceptual, poetic, mythic, religious, quotidian—has become one of the more active and controversial areas of research in the Western world. It lies at the intersection of such disciplines as anthropology, linguistics, psycholinguistics and psychoanalysis, sociolinguistics, philosophy, and the many contemporary schools of literary criticism both theoretical and applied. There are divergencies between theoreticians as to how language is acquired, how it functions, how it relates to modes of behavior and belief, collective and individual. There is no disagreement as to its major role in the development of human affairs, nor as to the many questions still to be answered in this relatively new area.

"Despite the substantial volume of theory, little is actually known about the language acquisition process," wrote Postovsky in 1970.[1] Although we know more today, the situation has not greatly changed: "language and language-learning are such," warns Widdowson, an eminent British linguist and—in the best sense of the word—pedagogue, "that it would be irresponsible to be anything but tentative. But it would be still more irresponsible to avoid investigation and to pretend that there are no problems."[2] It is in part this uncomfortable position that has kept language teaching in a state of imbalance. It has taken some years of experience to see that only to a certain degree can theoreticians of language offer precise answers to problems of classroom methodology. Insofar as they have done so, we cannot, as language teachers, ignore them. But we cannot overlook the warning signals they are sending out, and which our experience corroborates. We cannot single-mindedly deduce method from theory and impose it on our pupils.

The very mass of the material on the topic of language makes it difficult to keep up with more than a fraction of the whole; but if we do not get at least the gist of it, we may be as lost, professionally, as the baseball player who has stumbled into a soccer game and persists in playing according to the rules of baseball.

A different kind of bewilderment may overtake us as the reams of literature dealing with the educational role of the humanities pour from our presses. This literature is sometimes sensible and heartfelt, sometimes smug and hardly convincing. It only sporadically looks into the interrelationships of language and the humanistic disciplines. When it does, the word "language" usually refers to the English language, and the context is usually that of higher education. In a recent investigation of the state of our high schools, the editor noted the invisibility of the teachers.[3] High school teachers have not been invisible in the language sector, but they seem to prefer to remain within their specific area—the teaching of French, Russian, Spanish, et al., and the discussion of the practical applications of methodology in the successive stages of language learning.

I must confess to personal perplexities. I have never attended an American secondary school. Long ago, between the ages of nine and fifteen, I attended an English public school (in the English sense); then for a couple of years, two French schools; all three, I think, were excellent and all three were strictly in the liberal arts tradition. In the United States, where I have taught almost uninterruptedly since 1936, I have had all too few contacts with our schools. I have sometimes been invited to speak to classes, generally on Albert Camus. I have never encountered an apathetic class.[4] My one claim to some competence in regard to my topic is that I was born in a bilingual family and the vagaries of my career reinforced my bilingualism. I can truthfully say that I have always been language-conscious. Nonetheless, for all practical purposes, I have lost the Latin I studied for six years in school, and the German required for my French degree. Schools can do just so much in this area. Unused, language slips its moorings in our mind. But I do not consider that the time I spent in language study was wasted.

With these thoughts in mind, I can approach my topic only with caution. I have, I hope, gauged its complexities. I know that the place of language study and of the humanities in our educational system seems to be shrinking in proportion to the rhetoric lavished upon them. Statistics tell us that 75 percent of our young people now graduate from high school, and that 50 percent of them are headed for further schooling in colleges, universities, or vocational schools. Of those 75 percent "only 15 percent now study a foreign language" and "only one out of twenty public school students studies French, German, or Russian beyond the second year." Since only 8 percent of American colleges and universities now require a foreign language for admission, high school students, who are in the narrower sense "precollegiate," have little incentive to so.[5] In this essay I shall attempt not to repeat the excellent analyses of the *Report of the President's Commission on Foreign Language and International Studies.* I should hope it has been thoroughly discussed. I shall not enumerate the often carping criticisms so profusely bestowed upon language teachers, and high schools in general, by people like myself who have rarely set foot in a classroom. One of the roadblocks in my path has been the manifest uncertainty and lack of consensus among these people as to the goals of high school education.

Aware of the difficult conditions under which some of our schools operate,[6] I shall nonetheless assume that today the ultimate goal of a high school curriculum is to open the minds of all young Americans—and I mean *all*—to the perils, joys, opportunities, and responsibilities of living as conscious human beings in the world of the here and now.

The conviction may seem naive, given the overtly utilitarian tendency of much educational rhetoric. Though I situate myself within the liberal arts tradition, I do not share the belief that a "return" to the past is viable. The position I have taken, vague though it may be, is the only one that allows me to approach my topic with some degree of consistency.

We cannot, I think, attribute a "place" to language study in "a" humanities curriculum, unless we have some idea of the general goals the schools set for themselves. What can language study contribute to those goals that other disciplines do not? Given our sense of what efficacious language study requires of school, teacher and learner, what is feasible in the often far from ideal conditions in which classes must function? When we promote the cause of language in our schools are we merely defending our professional interests or the larger educational needs of our students?

I think we are only now becoming aware of the role of language in all the facets of our lives—collective, public, and private. I think that this growing interest is significant at this moment in our history. As a society, we are not particularly moved by the question of our deficiencies in foreign language study. But we are deeply concerned with the question of literacy. The use of a language is related to the awareness of its many potentialities, and its multilayered character. It is thus closely linked to the sense of the vast dimensions of culture explored by the humanities. Language study and an interest in the humanities, as we tend to see it now, wax and wane together. Lately the pairing of the two has moved from a peripheral status to become central.[7] The "humanities-language" connection proposed here for scrutiny suggests a shift in our educational perspectives. Without some background, some understanding of that connection, even such well thought out recommendations for language study as those presented by the President's Commission might prove useless, like so many others formulated in the past.

Anticipating my theme, I chose as a guidepost a quotation from Widdowson. He scrutinizes those shibboleths of pedagogical theory that formulate the goals of the language learner in terms of the famous four skills (to understand, speak, read, write). "But what," he queries, "is it that learners are expected to understand, speak, read, and write?" And he answers: "The language they are learning. What do we mean by this?"[8] Yes, indeed, what *do* we mean?

With no claim to exhaustiveness, and only insofar as they bear on my topic, I shall take a brief look at a few facts that may furnish some solid ground to my discussion. We tend, in these matters, to be bright on theory and dim on specifics. Our thinking is swung by statistics and abstractions. We are horrified by the statistics in the Commission's Report. But we might look at it differently. There are 47 million high school students; if even one out of twenty studies language beyond the second year, it still makes a sizeable group of two and a quarter million. Why blot them out? We may be helping to generate the situation we are deploring. A study of the *successful* high school language students would be enlightening. Which ones go on? Why? What schools are they attending? What happens to them later? There are too many variables to be considered when dealing in such broad categories to be able to build entirely upon them.

Changing Contexts

THE SCHOOLS

In its Summer and Fall issues in 1981, *Daedalus*, the journal of the American Academy of Arts and Sciences, ran a set of essays on America's schools. The Fall issue described three different models of "exemplary schools." One is an inner-city vocational high school with an "overwhelmingly black majority" and a very small contingent of academically oriented pupils. The second is a comprehensive public school in an affluent suburb, whose pupils are multiracial and multilingual in origin. It combines a standard curriculum—English, mathematics, foreign language, social studies, fine arts, and physical education—with a large number of other offerings, some 165 courses in all, responding to a diversity of needs and interests. The third is an expensive boarding school "for the privileged few," overwhelmingly white, "preppies" en route to Ivy League schools. There may be other exemplary models, but certainly the differences between these three models are marked. Their educational goals, thence the place of language study in each of them, are not the same. These schools qualify an otherwise grim picture. "The evidences of disarray in the American educational system are too numerous, too obvious, to escape detection," notes the general editor, Stephen Graubard, not unexpectedly, in his preface to the Summer issue (p. v). Distressing to some contributors, that "disarray" is challenging to others who see it as a transitional stage in the implementation of a desirable educational goal. As one contributor puts it, "it is the result of the first genuine experiment in universal schooling." But what of the implications of the three models? They warn us not to take for granted that there is such a thing as a curriculum in the humanities. We should then think in terms of more than one model. This runs counter to the ideal of an egalitarian education offering equal opportunities to all.

I shall, for a moment, introduce an apparent digression. In his survey of the essays, Graubard makes an interesting observation:

> It is noteworthy that none of the authors deemed it necessary to locate those purely American educational developments in a more global context, that no one thought it imperative to see what others—not so different from ourselves—were also doing during this period. . . . No one, for example, asks how any of Europe's democracies, influenced by their own social-democratic and liberal traditions, and no less preoccupied with the extension of educational opportunity, sought to incorporate the children of less privileged families. . . . Nor, for that matter, does there seem to be conspicuous interest in how multinational and multiracial societies have handled the education of their "minorities." The rhetoric in this volume is markedly American.[9]

And he wonders "if there is any loss in such total absorption in the American perspective." The answer would seem to be "yes." For all the countries of Western Europe are experiencing the same disarray; a break or "rupture" in the community of the culture, manifest in a breakdown in the previously accepted patterns of "literate" language, as defined in terms of a national high culture. The break is seen as more than a generational gap. That "literate" language was in fact the language of the "privileged few," which established a frontier or line of demarcation between the classes. Through that "rupture," new layers of young people are making themselves heard, using forms of expression that cross the linguistic boundaries of the past. The media provide their hidden grammar and overt semantics and furnish an effective, if inchoate, bond between them, an inarticulate culture transmitted horizontally instead of vertically from past to present. It might be one of the strongest bonds between our three culturally segregated high school groups. In the frame of a pervasive cultural mutation, traditional patterns of speech may carry no credence in our classrooms. Nor will any number of humanities courses bridge the cultural gap between teacher and learner unless the teacher can find the area where the two languages mesh. This does not mean the teacher should use questionable patterns of language. "We must find other modes of insertion which can give these groups rooted in the web of collective life their capacity to innovate and to invent," writes Jean

Duvignaud, a French sociologist, speaking of the rift in cultural continuity. Otherwise what we call our culture "will become a nostalgic image of the past," in fact an intellectual ghetto, the happy hunting ground of an elite; while on the periphery a mainstream culture is developing with little sense of the long-term implications the humanities curriculum could bring.

Let me now examine a couple of terms I have been using. The first is "American" used as an adjective: "American schools." The scantiest acquaintance with language patterns shows that to designate our geographic location it is more elegant to use the term "American" as an adjective than "United States." "United States schools" is awkward to pronounce because of the clash of the "s's," an oral phenomenon. So, adventitiously, we have been led to equate the continent of America with our own more restricted part of it. Insidiously, the rest of the continent becomes "not-American," the home of "non-Americans" of various brands. This linguistic phenomenon may ipso facto create a spurious sense of superiority, a sense that Cubans, Canadians, Peruvians, et al. do not qualify as Americans, while it convinces them of our inherent arrogance. It may be one factor in an unconscious ethnocentricity.

Of different origin, historically and culturally determined, is a semiunconscious belief that the "American" speaks English. It has produced that wonderfully effective whipping boy, the "monolingual American."[10] The monolingual American speaks only English and sees the world through monocultural eyes. As high school teachers know, the reality is different. They confront multilingual classes every day. But what language do they speak? "The phenomenon of a 'mixed language' or 'emigranto,' as it is sometimes called, is all too common among us," notes a teacher of German.[11] The "monolingual American" under attack is in fact an abstract figure. It emerges from a past phase of American culture when masses of immigrants were to be integrated into a cultural mold through the assimilation of a common language. Many Americans are speakers of "emigranto," a language very loosely connected with weakened cultural traditions, not at all with the tradition associated with the English language. They are concerned with the immediacy of their own experience. Like French or German, English has to be learned. It is and is not a "foreign" language.

Of whatever variety, these "mixed languages" do not prepare the high school students to "see through American eyes." They are and they are not "American." These students might perhaps eventually, Graham observed, more easily see beyond the ethnocentricity of the anglophobe. Commenting on the Report of the President's Commission, a distinguished scholar and language teacher wrote:

> I think it might be appropriate to include some thought about the quality of the modern teacher's life nowadays, about the felt reality of working with so many students who lack even a veneer of piety to an idea of culture. The sense of despair we often feel in confronting the students is worth mentioning; their nearly exclusive orientation to the here and now presents us with a formidable obstacle in motivating foreign language teaching.[12]

Yet, she notes, if one can "break through, " the students are open and generous. The metaphor of the wall, implicit in the expression "break through," is instructive. Teachers and students actually do not use the same language, or at least do not relate to it in the same way. Again we should not overgeneralize. But the question arises, should we then abandon the teaching of foreign languages in the schools and direct our energies to the teaching of English? We have tried bilingual schools for the "Hispanics" and in a very few cases for the French-speaking immigrants of Canadian origin. When doing so, are we increasing the confusions of "in-between," "mixed" languages? For some the answer is "yes." If we concentrate on English alone, are we adding to the "monolingual" population so roundly denounced in the Commission's Report?

In this section I have deliberately stressed the paradoxes in our educational positions—the coexistence of contradictory patterns. In essence, a homogeneous vocabulary attempts to cover over a heterogeneous reality; a strong stress on "global" vision accompanies an equally strong "absorption" in the American scene; a view of the matrix of American culture as founded on the English versions of the "canons" of Western culture accompanies the urgent call for a multicultural America. At the same time, schools are being called upon to assure "literacy" in English. And above all, perhaps, I have noted the discrepancy between our egalitarian educational goals and the obvious class distinctions mirrored in the diversity of our schools. I have further suggested that though we speak of "global perspectives" we may remain culture-bound; that, in contrast, our pupils may *have* global perspectives, vague though they be, but they are language-bound, since they tend to a greater or lesser degree to be "illiterate" in regard to the conventional exigencies of syntax and to the coherence of the national language. "Literacy becomes the first priority for high schools to require for its graduates," writes Graham.[13] She makes the point that the definition of "literacy," in its basic sense designating the ability to read and write, has greatly changed. It used to be limited to the ability to sign one's name. This is a far cry from what we mean by the word in a humanities context: the capacity to relate to a high culture, to relate to it pertinently and with ease. Our present world, Graham notes, requires of everyone a high degree of literacy in the first sense. We require of our people at large the ability, daily, to read and apply more and more intricate instructions accurately. In our academic setting, "literacy" in the cultural sense seems, in contrast, to be in crisis. In its two senses, the word needs to be redefined. High schools may have a chance now to narrow the gap between the two meanings. The "disarray" in the schools can in part be attributed to the uneasy relation to the language of teachers and pupils, caught between the two meanings.

Can high schools deal simultaneously with the problem of literacy as defined by Graham and the "global" literacy advocated by many, which includes some acquaintance with a foreign language and a critical evaluation of the unconscious ethnocentricity of our culture? How can language study help to make the impact of a humanities curriculum more effective, language study in general and foreign language study more particularly?

"TO LEARN A LANGUAGE"—WHAT DO WE MEAN?

By this we mean many things. One thing, however, we do *not* mean: that a language can ever be "known" in the way one can know the names of the Roman emperors or the dates of the two world wars. We also know under what conditions students in our schools might acquire the minimal proficiency that would allow them to develop further their ability in this area. Research and experimentation have outstripped the physical cadre and scheduling habits of most of our schools. The "why" of language classes cannot be answered at present in terms of its "usefulness." Three years of language study limited to three or four fifty-minute periods a week, plus an hour or so of drill in a laboratory, broken by vacations, in classes that group thirty or more students, cannot prepare those students to "understand, speak, read, and write" a foreign language with any degree of proficiency. This will be the case until such time as at least some of the recommendations of the President's Commission are implemented; or until such time as more of the affluent private and public schools are willing to give language study a high priority. I shall briefly consider the various answers we have given to the question "to learn a language, what do we mean by this?" in regard to precollegiate education.

In the 1930s, when I started to teach at Bryn Mawr College, freshmen entered with four or five years of foreign language study, often including Latin. They came from elite private schools. They were prepared, if they wished to "major," for a four-year study of the major literary works in the area of their chosen language; they spent the junior year abroad. The program of study was geared to the traditional concept of a liberal arts education patterned on the offering of the English department. The schools these students came from stressed grammar, reading, and translation, but combined these skills with the use of the "direct method." The result was reasonably good; those who wanted to teach could, if they chose, increase their proficiency by building on a fairly secure base. The break came with the great variety of teaching postures regarding the use of a foreign language in graduate schools and schools of education.

I shall not recapitulate the erosion of that pattern, as the high school population increased massively. The belles-lettriste approach to the study of languages came under attack, often violent. The "tool" approach to language learning now predominated. The 1950s had inherited a model from wartime experiments for the quick acquisition of "functional" patterns of language. Linguistics and sociolinguistics of that period furnished theorizations that seemed pertinent—essentially the notion of language as "learned behavior," acquired through the mechanical interiorization of the code that governs the organization of words so that they "make sense." The explosion of technology offered the ideal methodological equipment to implement the new situation—large classes—and the aims proposed. Materials were prepared for use in "laboratories." The audio-lingual method was in full sway.

To learn a language was to appropriate the "codes" or conventions that assure its cohesiveness as a formal system which "makes sense" to the users. It was acquired in stages by memorization, based on repetition, in sequentially arranged "drills." It was a "learned behavior," the processes of which, in the absence of a natural context could, to a certain degree, be duplicated in a laboratory. Seated in closed booths the learners listened, repeated, answered according to given scripts. They were passive. The method was oppressive, contrary to the human impulses that provide the impetus to produce language. The results were disappointing.

Reappraisals followed, based on more complex theories of how language works. Essentially, language now appeared as an *instrument* (rather than a tool) of communication. The musical metaphor likened the manifest language to a score that one deciphers in reference to a double register; in other words, a notation and the vast edifice of music to which it refers. A language then is "played" by each and all in relation to more than one context: the grammatical rules of "usage" assure its communicability; the subjective selection gives it its significance in a specific context and its generally unconscious relation to the cultural context that the language conveys, what Widdowson calls its "use."[14]

"Meanings," Widdowson notes, "do not exist ready-made in the language itself. They are worked out. We are given linguistic clues and on the basis of these clues we make sense of the sentence." The laboratory method was concerned only with the linguistic code. It communicated nothing to the learner and so did not give him the desire to say anything himself. As Postovsky noted: "Language in any meaningful sense cannot develop without thought, because it is for the very purpose of the transfer of thought that language develops."[15] To learn a language, then, is to learn to translate it into the "inner language" of thought and to communicate that thought outwardly and appropriately within a context. In that sense, it is defined as a form of self-knowledge and an instrument of communication.

Granted that language is a "tool" that allows the user to obtain factual information, let me consider briefly two versions of the most trivial dialogue: (a) "Have you had lunch yet?" "No, have you?" (b) "Djeet yet?" "No dju?" (Did you eat yet? No, did you?)[16] They transmit the same approximate information perfectly conveyed. But the language itself suggests an infinitely wider area of reference which

I need not "decode." We can all do it. And it is not proven that the first speakers would understand the second. "Communication," then, requires a broad, shared area of reference.

We now reach a third answer to the question: "what does it mean to learn a language?" It means that the learners get a sense of how the language *works* and, conversely, how they can "work" it. This is the area that properly belongs in a humanities high school curriculum. The liberating effect of language study is inherent in the remark that "meanings do not exist ready-made in language." This realization makes critical analysis possible. But beyond that, it leads to the creative delight all people share in the spontaneous play of language: the puns, the imaginary creations, the language games; the unexpected meanings and quid pro quos created by the hazards of homophones or the transfers of a word from one register to another. Language presents itself through a wide range of organized "discourses" which can all be analyzed or "deconstructed," as the saying goes, to reveal the covert messages it transmits. But we also take delight in seeing it "explode" the familiar forms. We do not always communicate what we think we are communicating. One small anecdote can illustrate this. A little girl had taken great delight in the old folk story of the "mother goat and the seven little kids." But the storyteller's complacency dissolved into laughter when she heard her niece proclaim ecstatically that she had been told the lovely story of the "mother ghost and the seven little children." The confusion engendered a simple form of aesthetic pleasure.

Language is a tool, yes. A complex, subtle, and powerful tool. But what is the use of a tool if the user does not know how it works? From the earliest stages of language study, the learner should become alert to how language works. The study of a foreign language has a place in the humanities curriculum in the schools because it is free of a heavy burden of association, and "value" judgments. It can open, for learners, new perspectives on how they may relate to language; how one can let forms of language drive one into deadends; or how one can use language for one's pleasure, or situate oneself as an individual within a group. What came through quite clearly in the first phase of the experiments with laboratory techniques is that a learner can, temporarily, acquire the "skills" required to speak, hear, even put together separate sentences without being able to "say" something, "listen," and "understand." The analysis of the relation of language to "discourse" can most fully be carried out in the study of "literary" texts.

Foreign language, because it does not involve one's own self-image so immediately, may be an asset in the development of that "inner speech" so necessary to humanistic understanding. It may also help the student to see how language patterns become stereotypes, whether individual or collective, that, more particularly in times of rapid change, must be reexamined. In my brief review of the various approaches to language learning, I have condemned none. All are grounded in reason; there are rigorous linguistic conventions to be learned. Without the knowledge of these conventions, words juxtaposed do not make sentences. In oral exchange, where facial expression and gesture support them, they may communicate at least an intent, in regard to a context which has to be understood. The basis of effective language "use" is most exactly to "use" the many registers of the language. Methods are subordinated to that end, not the other way around. The main intellectual incentive must come from the students' sense that the "codes" are necessary to achieve their goal as "users" of the language. What has been called the Dartmouth-Rassias method of teaching,[17] a highly successful method, uses all the approaches we have outlined, from drill to active participation in the classroom. High school students are in a crucial stage of development, more crucial perhaps for the less privileged. The process of becoming linguistically awake, however, may be slow and difficult to "measure." We are deluding ourselves and our pupils if we assume that, even in the best conditions, they will emerge from foreign language study in high school in possession of a second language. Unless they continue to study, they will forget the language they studied, through no fault of the school. What they might not forget is their own new relation to language, almost a sine qua non of literacy.

Options

My argument for a central place of language study in a high school curriculum, in all high school curricula, may not be persuasive. The convergence of the problems encountered by teachers of English and teachers of a foreign language may help support it. But it must also be positively accepted by the teachers in the humanities curriculum if it is considered seriously; and further, it must be given more than lip service by the principals, superintendents, and school boards. At a time when new funding may not be available, what may be required is a reallocation of funds.

This raises the problem of how to implement such a study; how to find the time and means to bring about the integration of language study and the humanities within the framework of the schools in this period of penury.

Should the schools limit language study to English? This solution would seem to me perverse in the face of the Commission's 1979 Report. Clearly, however, where no foreign language studies are offered, it would still be valuable to apply some of the insights we have gained to the study of English. Personally, I deplore what I call the admonitory use of statistics. Why stress that some six thousand high schools do not offer courses in foreign language study instead of stressing that well over twenty thousand do? Some reference to their *quality* would be pertinent. We should play to our *strengths.* Perhaps then some schools of different kinds could see whether collaborative programs could be developed which integrate language study, English and one or more second languages, within a humanities curriculum.

All the work that has recently appeared dealing with language learning and pedagogy stresses the need for the personal and vigorous involvement of the teacher. Like the learner, the teacher must *want* to speak, or else the class goes dead. Furthermore, the *physical* response and participation of the learners must be stimulated, although perhaps not to the extent that the Rassias model inspires. No teachers can be content to teach according to established routines, nor can they be uncertain as to what they are doing. But they must be fully supported.

It is clear that the rigidity of the scheduling in high schools and, in some, the disciplinary problems, are insuperable obstacles to the freer structuring of language classes. Furthermore, they make the "immersion" techniques impossible. There are, besides, schools that habitually use procedures detrimental to the requirements of the classes where, in the middle of the class period, the interoffice communication system comes on with five or ten minutes of announcements in English, disrupting the class and destroying its concentration. A large number of pupils in the class is also detrimental to successful language teaching.

We know that language learning requires continuity. It is utterly frustrating to teachers and students when no continuum of study is assured even from junior high to senior high, to say nothing of the continuum from kindergarten to twelfth grade. Some of these disadvantages could be mitigated, but it does mean that the place of foreign language study is better assured in the good private schools, where the task of integration into a humanities program would be easier.

It seems unlikely that any one model of language study would fit all the schools. If there is a humanities "program" rather than a set of courses, the students registered in the program could be asked, for instance, to impersonate the characters introduced, or to describe them, with whatever range of language they have acquired. There are other strategies. I should say in passing that, as suggested by Shaugnessy, the language teacher needs inexhaustible patience and judgment in showing learners when, because of faulty grammar, a sentence means nothing or means perhaps the opposite of what was intended.[18] If there is to be some coordination between the language classes and the humanities program, each school, I think, would have to find its own format.

Even should nothing further ensue, I am inclined to think that if the schools, and the language teachers therein, renewed their understanding of the humanistic values of *language study* as empowering the *teaching of languages*, schools, teachers, and learners would be the better for it. It might contribute its mite to the ultimate needs for all of us today to give a full "human" dimension to our consciousness, and carefully to examine the implications of what we say, profess, and write. In other words, it would help create an intellectual climate favorable to the "literacy"—in the broad sense of the word—required of us as we move into the twenty-first century.

FOOTNOTES

1. Valerian A. Postovsky, "Effects of Delay in Oral Practice at the Beginning of Second Language Learning" (Doct. diss., University of California, Berkeley, 1970), p. 2.

2. H. G. Widdowson, *Teaching Language of Communication* (London: Oxford University Press, 1979), p. ix.

3. Stephen R. Graubard, "Preface," in "America's Schools: Portraits and Perspectives," *Daedalus* 110 (Fall 1981): xvi.

4. I do not mean to be facetious. High school students respond to Camus. I have from time to time also received interesting letters from them. I found both the classes and the letter writers alert and well-informed.

5. *Strength through Wisdom: A Critique of U.S. Capability*, Report of the President's Commission on Foreign Language and International Studies (Washington, D.C.: U.S. Government Printing Office, 1979), p. 7.

6. The difficulties in the inner-city schools, the book burnings in rural areas, and the wide variables in the background of the student body have all been abundantly discussed.

7. It has been discussed in workshops funded by the National Endowment for the Humanities and in Modern Language Association commissions and colloquia, stimulated by grants from private foundations. The programs of the National Humanities Faculty have been quite naturally concerned principally with the humanities part of it. One of the more significant recent publications in this context is the May 1981 issue of the *Bulletin* of the Association of Departments of Foreign Languages (ADFL).

8. Widdowson, *Teaching Language of Communication*, p. ix.

9. Stephen R. Graubard, "Preface," in "America's Schools: Public and Private," *Daedalus* 110 (Summer 1981): xxii. See also two reports of the Quebec Royal Commission on Education: *Parent Report* (Quebec: Royal Commission on Education, 1968) and *Team Report* (Quebec: Royal Commission on Education, 1981).

10. Here again, the vast generalization obscures the facts. In a half-century of teaching in the United States, I have met many bilingual, sometimes trilingual Americans, among them a number of high school teachers. School superintendents might well call upon their expertise when considering such questions as the one I am here tentatively exploring.

11. Herbert Lederer, "The 'Native Speaker' Issue: Problem or Pretext," *ADFL Bulletin* 12 (May 1981): 1-4. In one of her last articles, Margaret Mead concluded from her work with immigrants that for those mired in "in-between" languages the best solution is to make a fresh start on a third.

12. Madelyn Gutwirth, "Responses from Members," in *Profession 81*, ed. Richard I. Brod and Dexter Fisher (New York: Modern Language Association, 1981), p. 8.

13. Patricia Albjerg Graham, "Literacy: A Goal for Secondary Schools," *Daedalus* 110 (Summer 1981): 119-34.

14. Widdowson distinguishes "usage" from "use." "Usage" concerns the capacity to organize sentences correctly according to grammatical conventions; "use" is the capacity to select the appropriate combinations within specific contexts. See Widdowson, *Teaching Language of Communication*, p. 50.

15. Postovsky, "Effects of Delay in Oral Practice at the Beginning of Second Language Learning," p. 31.

16. This double dialogue, I understand, is in current circulation in New York as a joke on "Brooklynese."

17. John Rassias developed the model in the late 1960s. It has been spectacularly successful. It could only be applied completely in the affluent secondary schools. It requires of the teacher a personal involvement, great energy, and imagination, to say nothing of a good command of the theory and practice of language learning. It is "an immersion model whereby students spend ten hours per week in the foreign language classroom and two and one-half hours in the language laboratory." Besides the Master Teachers, it requires small classes and the assistance of trained apprentice teachers. It is, admittedly, an expensive undertaking; but its spirit and some of its features could inspire

fresh developments in high school classes. For further information, see Charles Stansfield and Jeanne Hornor, "The Dartmouth-Rassias Model for Teaching Foreign Languages," *ADFL Bulletin* 12 (May 1981): 23-27. The success of the FLES (Foreign Language Program in the Elementary Schools) was probably due to the uninhibited participation in song, dance, and mime of the children. The willingness to use the media in an attempt to cope with the new layers of student population was highly commendable in the "audio-lingual" period and is not to be jettisoned but is not used with the same near exclusivity.

18. See Mina Shaugnessy, *Errors and Expectations* (New York: Oxford University Press, 1977).

CHAPTER V

The Teaching of History in American Schools

ABRAHAM ASCHER

According to the historian Henry Johnson, in 1933 a distinguished philosopher declared that "any philosophy of education more than five years old was antiquated."[1] The philosopher's comment, made in all seriousness, can be taken as a rationale for one of the most distinctive features of the American school in this century—rapid change. Over the past six decades or so professional educators in the United States have formulated a dizzying array of theories about how to educate our youngsters, and their influence on school curricula has been very marked. But of all the areas of study none has been revised more frequently or drastically than history. In many schools, in fact, the very word "history" is hardly encountered; insofar as the subject is taught it tends to be subsumed under "social studies."

In recent years this situation has given rise to a considerable amount of concern among educators and parents who believe that the decline in the rigorous study of traditional history has contributed to a slippage in the quality of education of American youngsters. The most startling evidence of such a slippage came to light in 1975, when it was revealed that during the preceding decade there had been a steady erosion of scores on the Scholastic Aptitude Test. Both the average scores as well as the proportion of students performing with distinction declined. In 1972, for example, 5.3 percent of all high school seniors taking the verbal test scored over 650; in 1980 only 2.9 percent did that well.[2] There are other indications to suggest that our youngsters are not being as well educated as they should be. A study by the National Assessment of Educational Progress, published in 1977, showed that 47 percent of our seventeen-year-olds did not know that each state elects two United States senators. A survey of college freshmen administered in 1976 by the Educational Testing Service in Princeton for the *New York Times* discovered that American youngsters had a very superficial knowledge of their own country's past. Two-thirds of the 1,856 high school graduates who were tested had little understanding of the origins of religious toleration or the nature of Reconstruction. Over 70 percent did not know which powers Congress derives from the Constitution. Social science coordinators or chairmen of history departments claimed that students going on to college should have been able to answer at least thirty of the forty-two questions. But fewer than 9 percent scored that well.[3]

The causes of this widespread ignorance are in dispute, but there can be no doubt that for some time now the traditional history courses in our schools have been under attack and that the trend has been toward their elimination as requirements for all students. In 1977, Richard E. Gross reported that "many pupils do not get U.S. History either in grades seven or eight or in the senior high school."[4] In several states students are permitted to substitute courses in such fields as anthropology, law education, and ethnic studies for American History. The decline in the study of World History has been even more dramatic. To cite but one statistic, in the years from 1962 to 1973 the total enrollment in our public schools, grades seven through twelve, rose from 11,700,000 to 18,500,000 but the number of students taking courses in World History rose by only 70,000.

Equally noteworthy is the fact that the social studies courses that students do take have been watered down. Some schools incorporate into them sex education, drug education, and even driver education. An examination of a few recent yearbooks of the National Council for the Social Studies suggests how far-reaching the movement away from the teaching of history has been during the past decade. The volume for 1971 was entitled *Values Education* and carried articles such as "Objectives of Value Analysis," "Teaching Strategies for Value Analysis," and "Resolving Value Conflicts." The yearbook for 1972, *Teaching about Life in the City*, published articles on "The Unfinished Identity of Metropolitan Man," "Exploring Urban Cultural Variations through Anthropology," and "Reflections on Urban Life." In 1974 the Council put out a volume entitled *Teaching American History: The Quest for Relevancy*, in which the emphasis was on current issues such as "What is Liberation? A Closer Look at the Women's Equal Rights

Movement," "Developing Empathizing Skills," "Inquiring about the Development of a Myth: The Melting Pot," and "Appalachian Coal Miners: A Simulation." The 1975 yearbook featured discussions of "Should Traditional Sex Modes and Values be Changed?" "Should the Study of Death Be a Necessary Preparation for Living?" "Should the Nation-State Give Way to Some Form of World Organization?" In the 1977 yearbook the focus was on "Developing Decision-Making Skills"; the volume contained articles on "Small Group Decision-Making for Social Action" and "Developing Decision-Making Skills in Elementary Schools."

Publications of this kind, distributed under the imprimatur of the most prestigious organization of social studies teachers, were bound to influence the content of classroom instruction, particularly since so many of our teachers have themselves been exposed to very little serious study of history. In several states, among them New York, Indiana, Iowa, Oklahoma, and Oregon, "virtually no training in history is demanded" as a qualification for a teaching position in social studies at the secondary school level. In about one-third of our states, prospective teachers of history are expected to have taken four to six three-hour history courses in college. Fewer than one-sixth of the states require at least seven three-credit courses in history.[5] It is not surprising that teachers inadequately trained in history are lured into teaching contemporary issues, an area in which opinions often count for as much as knowledge.

The decline in the study of history has been a gradual development caused by a variety of factors. Early in the twentieth century our schools, strongly influenced by two reports of the American Historical Association, made the study of history a central feature of the curriculum. In 1899 the Committee of Seven proposed that all high school students take a year of ancient and medieval history (up to 800 A.D.), a year of medieval and modern European history (from 800 A.D.), one year of English history, and a year of American history and civil government. Ten years later a Committee of Eight recommended that in grades seven and eight youngsters should also be exposed to a year of American history taught chronologically. The college professors who dominated both committees believed that rigorous study of history trains youth for citizenship in a democracy by inculcating in them sound habits of thinking and sound values. It forces youngsters to learn to arrange facts logically, to understand the relationship between cause and effect, and to appreciate the inevitability of change. According to the Committee of Seven, students taking history would come to realize that "virtue must be militant if it is to be triumphant."[6]

But history did not retain its exalted place in the curriculum for very long. Far-reaching demographic changes in the United States and the emergence of new academic disciplines led to major revision of the educational system. A few statistics will suffice to indicate the dimensions of the change that occurred in four decades. In 1900, 518,251 youngsters, about 10 percent of the population aged fourteen to seventeen, attended secondary school; by 1920 the number had jumped to 2,200,389; by 1940, to 6,601,444; and a decade later 82 percent of our eligible youth were in high schools. One consequence of the great increase in the secondary school population was the transformation of the American public high school from an institution that was essentially college preparatory to a comprehensive school that stressed technical and vocational studies. To be sure, attendance at college also rose sharply during the first half of the twentieth century, but most students were not expected to enroll in programs traditionally required by our most demanding colleges. Moreover, during that era such social sciences as anthropology and sociology became part of the college curriculum, and a growing number of educators became convinced that these disciplines were more suitable than history for young people who had to make their way in a modern industrial society.

School administrators and teachers responded quickly to these developments. For our purposes, the critical date was 1916, when a commission created by the National Education Association to examine secondary education published its report on the teaching of history. Significantly, whereas the Committee of Seven had consisted of six professors of history and one private school headmaster, the new committee was composed of two professors of history, one college teacher of home economics, one of rural sociology, and eighteen secondary school teachers, administrators, and employees of government education departments. Clearly, in the formulation of educational policy a decisive shift had taken place within a few years from specialists in the traditional disciplines to those who were considered experts in "school administration, instruction, and supervision."[7]

The Commission of 1916 proposed that instead of the existing requirements in history, students in junior high school should be given a choice of courses. In grade seven, for example, students would be able to replace the course in American history with a term of geography and a term of European history or with a year of European history in which geography was fully integrated. Instead of taking ancient history in the ninth grade, students would be allowed to choose from a variety of courses in "vocational and economic civics." In grades ten, eleven, and twelve, students would enroll in a sequence of courses on Europe since 1700, American History, and Problems of Democracy.[8]

The real significance of the Commission's report lay not so much in the courses it recommended as in its underlying rationale. As Arthur S. Bolster, a historian of American education, has pointed out, the Commission did not advocate a change in ends, only in means, because the stated goal of secondary school education was still to be "an appreciation of the nature and laws of social life . . . a sense of responsibility of the individual as a member of social groups . . . the intelligence and will to participate effectively in the promotion of social well-being. More specifically, social studies in the American high school have as their conscious and constant purpose the cultivation of good citizenship."[9] What was new, according to Bolster, was the contention that these aims of education could not be realized if traditional history remained a focal point of the curriculum.

The Commission's argument deserves to be quoted at length:

> From the standpoint of the purpose of secondary education it is far less important that adolescent youth should acquire a comprehensive knowledge of any or all of the social sciences than it is that he should be given experience and practice in the observation of social phenomena as he encounters them; that he should be brought to understand that every social problem is many-sided and complex; and that he should acquire the habit of forming social judgments only on the basis of dispassionate consideration of all the facts available. This this committee believes can best be accomplished by dealing with actual situations as they occur and by drafting into service the materials of all the social sciences as occasion demands for a thorough understanding of the situation in question.[10]

It may be true that the Commission of 1916 proposed only a change in means, but its recommendations nevertheless amounted to a radically new educational policy. In elevating concern with contemporary problems to a central place in the curriculum, the Commission repudiated the notion that the goal of education was to impart to youngsters the skills and knowledge hitherto considered to be a prerequisite for the handling of these problems. Or, as one historian has put it, the Commission "assumed that the present problems of adult society were the present problems of the pupil."[11] Such an approach was bound to undermine the study of traditional history. To be sure, students were to be trained to "understand," not "solve," contemporary problems, and chronology was not to be abandoned completely in the new courses. Nevertheless, history as a discipline loses its integrity if the overriding purpose for its study is no longer to explore past societies in their own terms and to examine their evolution but rather to shed light in an immediate and direct way on issues of current interest.

It has been estimated that by 1948 at least a majority of our secondary schools and even more of our elementary schools had changed the curriculum in conformity with the recommendations of the Commission of 1916. In junior high schools, courses in social studies (to use the term coined by the Commission) became especially widespread. Many senior high schools adopted the Problems of Democracy course in lieu of history, but even in those schools where history was still taught, teachers stressed questions of contemporary interest. In addition, elective courses in social science, economics, and occasionally in psychology were introduced.

In the 1950s and 1960s the principles underlying the Report of 1916 came under attack. The reformers of this era, inspired by the theories of Jerome Bruner and generously financed by the National Science Foundation, the U. S. Office of Education, and private foundations, argued that what students needed to learn was not the content of any discipline but rather the structure and methodologies of the social sciences. Under the "new social studies" curriculum youngsters were to develop "inquiry-oriented skills." They would locate a problem, seek out all the relevant information, and reach a tentative conclusion, the validity of which they would test by analyzing additional data. "Once this procedure became second nature through repeated practice," we are told, "students were less likely to be fooled or misled by vague statements, myths, or stereotypes in textbooks or those advanced by some politicians, journalists, salesmen, teachers, neighbors, or friends, and, equally important, by the students themselves. Neil Postman and Charles Weingartner have termed such training the development of an ultrasensitive 'crap-detector.' "[12]

The proponents of the new social studies were only in the early stages of preparing their innovative teaching materials when they came under criticism from advocates of the "new" new social studies. The rallying cry of this group of reformers, who emerged in the late 1960s, was relevancy. They did not reject the notion that students need to master methodologies rather than facts, but they insisted that in addition there must be "renewed emphasis on affective-type goals which build upon cognitive objectives." Historical events and social issues were to be examined for the specific purpose of impelling "students to question, express interest, experience empathy, or seek to analyze objectively and clarify their own values or those held by others, past and present." The advocates of the "new" new social studies consider it especially important to inspire their students with empathy. How that goal was to be attained can be seen in Allan O. Kownslar's description of the use in the classroom of R. Garry Shirt's *Star Power*, a simulation that has allegedly been effective at the elementary, secondary, and college levels of education:

> Through the distribution of wealth in the form of plastic chips it is a game which builds a mobile three-tiered society. Students playing the game have chances to move from one level of society to another by amassing wealth as the result of trading chips with one another. Once a given society has been established, that group with the most wealth receives the right to determine the rules for the remainder of the game. This "wealthy" group usually makes rules which the other groups of students feel are unfair, dictatorial, or racist. What usually results is protest or revolt against the rules as well as the rulemakers. Once this occurs, or is about to occur, the point is made and the teacher must end the simulation.

The author of these lines assures us that students who have played the game are in the proper frame of mind to examine thoughtfully other rebellions, such as the "Civil Rights movement of the 1960s, the Civil War of 1861, or the American Revolution of 1776."[13] The trouble with such an approach to the study of the evolution of societies is that it is thoroughly ahistorical and is therefore likely to produce terribly simplistic analyses of past events. Moreover, under this teaching strategy insufficient attention is paid to the reading of texts and documents, and one of the most serious indictments of our schools is that many students are not learning to read and write the English language properly. In the spring of 1982, for example, it was announced that 47.7 per cent of New York City's ninth graders read below grade level. Under the circumstances, it seems wasteful to devote class time in high school to games, however stimulating they may be.

But it is not enough for educators who believe in the restoration of traditional history to the curriculum to deplore the present state of affairs in the public schools. They must also refute the arguments against the study of history and make a convincing case for its inclusion in the school curriculum. During the past few decades professional historians have not paid much attention to this question, probably because they have felt overly secure about the importance of history and have emphasized specialized research at the expense of teaching. Indeed, in 1968 the American Historical Association officially severed its ties to the National Council for the Social Studies, clear evidence of the gulf that has emerged between colleges and the schools in the field of history. The professional historians' indifference has certainly made it easy for the proponents of social studies to gain for their field a strong place in the curriculum.

Although many of the social studies courses may be shallow, not all the arguments against traditional history are frivolous. For example, Bolster subjected the teaching of history to a critique that calls for a serious response, all the more so because his views are widely shared by proponents of social studies. Bolster pointed out that historians have rested the case for their discipline on three claims: that it promotes the exploration of "social issues in the perspective of time"; that it encourages "critical judgment" and therefore helps train students for responsible citizenship in a democratic society; that the study of our cultural heritage will deepen the student's understanding of and commitment to democratic values. Bolster contends that even if these arguments were convincing, there still exists the problem of how to incorporate history into the curriculum, for the discipline is so vast that difficult decisions must be made about what to teach. Clearly, students cannot be expected to know everything about past societies.

But Bolster also doubts that the study of history will sharpen students' analytical abilities. It will not "teach the critical judgment of the historian any more than the memorizing of Euclidian proofs, no matter how carefully laid out, teaches youngsters to think like geometricians." Only if students write their own history will they become acquainted with the skills of the historian. Nor does Bolster believe that history as it is generally studied can contribute to the solution of contemporary issues. To be sure, our problems are rooted in the past, but a knowledge of that past is of little help, for history is as much an art as a science. Because it has no "predictability value," it is "useless as a guide to appropriate action on contemporary problems."[14]

This argument can be convincing only to those people who still believe in the feasibility of applying the methodology of the natural sciences to the study of human affairs. It has often been tried, but it has never been productive and is not likely to be in the future. There can be no laws of human conduct for the simple reason that man is not a robot who reacts to processes beyond his control. He is a cultural creature of infinite complexity whose reactions to any particular set of circumstances cannot be foretold with scientific certitude. Thus, no historian can predict under what conditions war between nations will break out. If he is bold enough to formulate a hypothesis about the origins of war, he obviously cannot test his theory by artificially creating the preconditions for military conflict.

In any case, the historian is not unique in his inability to predict the future course of events. The sociologists, psychologists, anthropologists, and economists have been no more successful in their attempts to do so, and yet it is their disciplines that are replacing history in our schools' curricula.

The truth is that the humanities, social sciences, and history are worth studying in large measure precisely because their methodologies are different from those of the natural sciences. There are many vital decisions that human beings in our society must make without being certain of the consequences. They often make moral judgments on a wide range of issues, they vote for candidates for office, they decide on their careers, and they are likely to make large purchases. In all these matters they are influenced by their experiences, informed opinion, assessment of evidence—in short, by wisdom. The application of wisdom does not, of course, guarantee that the right decision will be reached, but would any argue that it would be better for human beings to abjure wisdom?

There is, then, a good practical reason for offering history in our schools: it is a discipline that provides students with data and perspective for judgments on contemporary issues. Is it sensible, for example, to favor one set of proposals against another for the improvement of race relations in this country without an awareness of the sources of racial conflict? Would it be wise to advocate the abolition of the electoral college for the selection of the President of the United States without understanding why that system of selection was established by the Founding Fathers and how it has functioned for over two hundred years? Merely to raise these questions is to answer them. Courses in which students and teachers dwell excessively on contemporary issues simply will not devote adequate time and effort to examining the historical background necessary for an understanding of those issues.

Now this is not to suggest that the concepts and insights of the social sciences should be ignored. But it does mean that history possesses certain virtues that are absent from the other disciplines devoted to the study of man and society. History deals with the development of human societies chronologically, and thus makes us aware, on the one hand, of the inevitability of change and, on the other, of the gradualness of change. For youngsters who are often dismayed by the imperfections of our society, this in itself is a useful lesson to learn. Moreover, unlike the social sciences and humanities, which tend to focus on one major aspect of a culture, history seeks to shed light on an entire culture and the interrelationships between its various aspects.

But it would be a mistake to rest the case for history merely on utilitarian arguments. It is a subject that can be enormously exciting. It can be exhilarating to read about the achievements and failures, the great discoveries and follies, of man. For whatever reason, human beings have always been interested in their "roots," in the developments—political, military, economic, and cultural—that have shaped the world in which they live. With the steady increase in leisure time, adults at least have the possibility of reading more than they have in the past. It seems altogether appropriate for our schools to train youth to read history thoughtfully and critically. We consider it proper for schools to teach literature and music, neither of which is "practical" in the narrow sense of the word. Why not history?

There is one further argument of the opponents of traditional history that deserves scrutiny, and that is that those who teach history in our schools do a very poor job of it. They rattle off facts from their notes, raise no stimulating questions, rarely offer courses that go beyond the 1930s; in short, teachers fail to engage the interest of students "who are expected to be passive listeners only, passive notetakers, or passive memorizers."[15] This is a serious indictment and most probably accurate, but it hardly justifies the removal of the discipline from the curriculum. It is doubtful whether teachers of other subjects are, as an aggregate, much more stimulating, but no one would suggest that mathematics or biology should cease to be taught in high school. Still, like other instructors, teachers of history have an obligation to stimulate their students intellectually, to demonstrate that the study of history can be absorbing.

The first requirement for effective teaching of history (as of any subject) is a sound grasp of the discipline. If traditional history is to be returned to the classroom, state education departments will have to establish rigorous prerequisites for those wishing to teach history. Nine or ten undergraduate courses in history would seem to be a minimum. But equally important, greater efforts should be made to provide teachers with opportunities for intellectual renewal, or in-service training of a serious and challenging kind. Several programs for such renewal already exist. For example, the National Humanities Faculty makes it possible for a limited number of schools to send teachers to summer seminars, to invite scholars to discuss special problems in the curriculum, and to obtain guidance from a college professor with expertise in both scholarship and pedagogy. The National Endowment for the Humanities is about to launch a series of summer seminars for teachers in various disciplines in the humanities. In the fall of 1983, the Graduate School of the City University of New York plans to institute a long-range association with the city's school system. Established scholars will offer seminars for teachers and will regularly visit classrooms to become better acquainted with the problems encountered in precollegiate education. Such links between colleges and schools throughout the country could benefit both higher education and precollegiate education, for they would break down the artificial distinctions between them and restore the professoriat's interest and involvement in improving instruction in our schools, in history and in other subjects.

We already have some evidence that institutions of higher education can cooperate successfully with public schools. Yale University has conducted a program of intellectual enrichment for New Haven schools for the past four years, and recently the National Endowment for the Humanities acknowledged the achievement of the Yale-New Haven Teachers Institute by awarding it a grant of $368,000. One teacher declared that "people in New Haven have always had some access to Yale, but there was nothing like this in which professors and teachers worked closely together in ways that can have an impact on the public-school students." Another teacher said that "the attitude of teachers has changed, and Yale is no longer seen as an ivory tower separated from New Haven." As Richard Ekman, Director of the Division of Education Programs at the National Endowment for the Humanities, has pointed out, the link between Yale and local schools is especially noteworthy because the university does not have a school of education. The intention is not "to teach teachers to teach, but to immerse them in the humanities—such as philosophy, history, and foreign languages—so that they will be better equipped to teach their students."[16]

I put so much stress on the teachers' intellectual renewal because I am convinced that this is a necessary first step in any endeavor to improve instruction. Most teachers carry so heavy a burden in discharging their obligations at their schools that they have little opportunity for academic pursuits. They have neither the time nor the incentive to read extensively in their fields or to discuss issues of intellectual substance with their peers or with scholars. If teachers themselves are intellectually alive they are more likely to be able to stimulate their students. And it seems to me—I base this on my experience as an occasional speaker to high school students—that the interest of youngsters can be aroused if they are challenged to think analytically about historical events and trends, if they are made aware of the complexity of the historical process, and if they come to be persuaded that as adults they will often have to cope with difficult problems, the dimensions of which cannot be grasped without a knowledge of history.

Classroom discussions and frequent writing assignments should concentrate not only on how a course of events evolved but on why it evolved as it did. Youngsters are capable of understanding that to a considerable degree the historical process is determined by human beings who are constantly faced with the need to choose between alternative actions or policies. Thus, in discussing the origins of the American Civil War the surest way to bore students is to list four or five causes and then take up one by one the various sources of conflict between the North and South. A much more provocative and interesting way to proceed is to begin by asking the class what were President Lincoln's options in 1861 in response to the southern states' decision to secede from the Union. Why did he act as he did? Would any other course have been sensible, plausible? Skillfully handled, such a discussion would quickly require a consideration of a large body of historical data and would make students aware of the interconnection between events. But teachers are not likely to conduct a history class in this manner unless they are well versed in the subject and students have been required to read a fair amount of history. Teachers might be surprised to discover how many students, challenged to think analytically and treated as young adults, would rise to the occasion.

The selection of appropriate reading material is, of course, critical. Many of our textbooks in history are indeed dull and condescending to youngsters because they simplify historical accounts to the point of utter lifelessness. But interesting textbooks as well as more specialized works of history are available for use in precollegiate courses.[17] There is no reason why more gifted students should not be assigned historical fiction or some primary sources, such as major speeches by statesmen or important governmental documents. An ideal assignment for the lesson on the Civil War would be Lincoln's inaugural address in March 1861, in which he analyzed the question of secession in masterly fashion.

Some educators object to the rigorous study of history in elementary and secondary schools on the ground that our youth are not capable of it. We know, however, that in other countries, most notably Japan and France, youngsters do cope successfully with serious intellectual challenges. "All French adolescents," Ravitch tells us, "not just the select few, receive an education by the age of fifteen or sixteen that is the equivalent of what an American student covers by the end of the sophomore year in college."[18] It is not believable that our adolescents are any less gifted than their French counterparts. To be sure, the restoration of traditional history to our curriculum as a requirement for all students would signify the beginning of a drastic revision of our educational system, but the time may be right for such an ambitious enterprise.

This call for a return to traditional history is not meant to suggest that our schools should now resurrect the curriculum of 1900. New fields such as social history and the history of the non-Western world need to be incorporated into the offerings. Because of the vast increase in our knowledge of the past, it is no longer feasible to expect all students to take courses in ancient, medieval, modern European as well as American history.

In *Making History Come Alive*, Howard and Mendenhall argue for an "irreducible minimum" of history for our youth. An exploration of the past should begin in elementary school, but the courses in history should become increasingly sophisticated and rigorous in high school. During the last four years in school every youngster should be required to take a topical course in U.S. history and a "survey of European history, followed by a survey of U.S. history." The authors also *recommend* a "history of a non-Western country or region" for every student.[19] This seems to be an eminently reasonable proposal, though some school districts may find it advisable to diverge somewhat from this sequence.

It may also be advisable to devise different approaches for different groups of youngsters. "The challenge that has not been met," to quote Ravitch again, "is to present the same subject matter through a variety of teaching techniques and to make it immediate and valuable to all. This may be an impossible dream, but it is a dream worth pursuing."[20] The critical point is that all young people ought to be exposed to the study of the evolution of several different civilizations. The purpose is not to turn them into historians, but to give them a glimpse of what it means to "think historically."

The debate over the place of history in the curriculum of our schools is really part of the larger debate over the function of education in our society. Simply put, the question is whether the primary concern of teachers ought to be to train the intellect of youngsters, or to mold their character.[21] "The original view," according to Hofstadter,

> which remained in the ascendant until 1910 and continued to have much influence for at least another decade, might be dubbed old-fashioned or intellectually serious, depending upon one's sympathy for it. The high school, it was believed by those who held this view, should above all discipline and develop the minds of its pupils through the study of academic subject matter . . . the pupil, whatever the precise content of his curriculum, should pursue every subject that he studied long enough to gain some serious mastery of its content.[22]

But it was also assumed that the students' experience in the school would have beneficial influence on their character. Teachers would set good examples in the classroom and the reading of great works of literature and history would inspire students with respect for virtue, personal achievement, and democratic institutions.

The fate of traditional history in our schools' curriculum exemplifies the successful challenge to this general view of education. True, the educators who initially criticized the teaching of history intended only to make the study of the present rather than the past the focal point of precollegiate instruction in the social studies. But the change in emphasis was significant, for "the child was now conceived not as a mind to be developed but as a citizen to be trained by the schools."[23] Ever since the 1920s this view of education has inspired several movements of curriculum reform, each successive one moving further and further from the ideals and practices that predominated at the turn of the century. By the 1970s many opponents of traditional history argued that in social studies the principal goal must be to train youngsters to "empathize" and to devise solutions to social and political problems. The reformers of the 1970s received a respectful hearing and for a few years they exerted a considerable amount of influence on the curriculum of our schools. But their position has recently been subjected to widespread criticism. For one thing, many people seem dubious about the wisdom of having pupils solve problems before they have mastered the intellectual skills necessary to understand them. By the same token, the steady decline in the quality of education has prompted some professional educators and an increasing number of citizens to demand the restoration of the cultivation of minds of youngsters as the primary objective of teachers. If this conception of education were to achieve ascendancy, traditional history would inevitably come to occupy once again a central place in the curriculum of our schools.

FOOTNOTES

1. Henry Johnson, *Teaching of History in Elementary and Secondary Schools*, rev. ed. (New York: Macmillan, 1940), p. 74.

2. Diane Ravitch, "The Schools We Deserve," *New Republic* 184 (April 18, 1981): 24.

3. *New York Times*, 2 May 1976, pp. 1, 65.

4. Richard E. Gross, "The Status of the Social Studies in the Public Schools of the United States: Facts and Impressions of a National Survey," *Social Studies* 41 (March 1977): 196-97.

5. Richard S. Kirkendall, "The Status of History in the Schools," *Journal of American History* 62 (September 1975): 558-59.

6. Quoted in Arthur S. Bolster, Jr., "History, Historians, and the Secondary School Curriculum," in *Democracy, Pluralism, and the Social Studies*, ed. James P. Shaver and Harold Berlak (Boston: Houghton Mifflin, 1968), p. 214.

7. Ibid., p. 216. The statistics on enrollments in high school are on p. 215.

8. Ibid., pp. 216-17.

9. Quoted ibid., p. 217.

10. Quoted ibid.

11. Johnson, *Teaching of History in Elementary and Secondary Schools*, p. 65.

12. Allan O. Kownslar, "Is History Relevant?" in *Teaching American History: The Quest for Relevancy*, ed. Allan O. Kownslar, Forty-fourth Yearbook of the National Council for the Social Studies (Washington, D.C.: National Council for the Social Studies, 1974), p. 5.

13. Ibid., pp. 7-8.

14. Bolster, "History, Historians, and the Secondary School Curriculum," pp. 225-29.

15. Allan O. Kownslar, "The Status of History: Some Views and Suggestions," *Social Studies* 40 (October 1976): 448.

16. *New York Times* 26 September 1982, p. 51.

17. A useful list of history books appropriate for youngsters may be found in Appendices B, C, and D in a recently published volume by James Howard and Thomas Mendenhall entitled *Making History Come Alive: The Place of History in the Schools* (Washington, D.C.: Council for Basic Education, 1982).

18. Ravitch, "The Schools We Deserve," p. 27.

19. Howard and Mendenhall, *Making History Come Alive*, pp. 49-63.

20. Ravitch, "The Schools We Deserve," p. 27.

21. Frances FitzGerald touches on this theme in her *America Revisited: History Schoolbooks in the Twentieth Century* (New York: Little, Brown and Co., 1979), pp. 170, 208, 214.

22. Richard Hofstadter, *Anti-intellectualism in American Life* (New York: Knopf, 1970), p. 329.

23. Ibid., p. 335.

CHAPTER VI

Values, Ethnicity, Social Science Research, and Educational Policy

JAMES A. BANKS

Since the ethnic revitalization movements of the 1970s, educational reformers and researchers with diverse and often conflicting philosophical commitments and beliefs have set forth proposals designed to improve the schooling of ethnic minority youths and to promote educational equity. The basic values, assumptions, and inquiry modes of these diverse groups of reformers and researchers have rarely been critically analyzed in the social science and educational literature.

The inquiry modes, conceptual frameworks, and basic assumptions of educational reformers and researchers—such as the geneticists and sociobiologists, the integrationists, the cultural deprivation theorists, and the culturally different theorists—emanate from implicit value commitments and ideological positions. The humanities are vitally concerned with human values and with the analysis of assumptions and concepts that express fundamental beliefs. This chapter discusses how values, fundamental beliefs, and ideology influence social science research and public policy, and it examines the implicit values of several major theories related to the education of ethnic minority groups.

The Humanities Teacher and Social Science Knowledge

Two of a teacher's most important roles are the selection of knowledge for instruction and the design of pedagogy to teach that knowledge. Each of these tasks is important and difficult. The selection of knowledge in the form of concepts, generalizations, and theories is difficult because much of the knowledge from which teachers must select consists of factual statements that are not clearly related to major concepts, generalizations, and theories.

The selection of knowledge for instruction is especially difficult in the social sciences and humanities because knowledge in these disciplines is often undergirded by implicit values, latent assumptions, and ideology. This is especially true of knowledge about ethnic groups, because race and ethnicity are emotion-laden topics in American society. Knowledge about pedagogy is also undergirded by implicit values and assumptions.

When teachers select knowledge for instruction and to guide pedagogy, they are making important value choices. Consequently, it is important for teachers to be knowledgeable about the values and assumptions which underlie the knowledge they use so that they are fully aware of their own value choices. Teachers can make value choices only when they are fully aware of value alternatives and their possible consequences. A major goal of this chapter is to help educators become more aware of the nature of social knowledge and the assumptions and values that underlie knowledge about the education of ethnic groups in the United States.

Social Science Knowledge and Values

Kuhn uses "paradigm" to describe the "entire constellation of beliefs, values, techniques, and so on shared by members of a given [scientific] community."[1] The laws, principles, explanations, and theories of a discipline are also part of its paradigm. Kuhn argues that during the history of a science, new paradigms arise to replace older ones. He calls this phenomenon a "scientific revolution." Kuhn refers primarily to natural science disciplines and draws most of his examples from the natural sciences. It is not clear whether or not social science has developed true paradigms because of the paucity of universal laws, principles, and theories in social science, and because social science is still characterized by many competing systems of explanations. Writes Kuhn, "It remains an open question what parts of social science have yet acquired such paradigms at all. History suggests that the road to a firm research consensus is extraordinarily arduous."[2]

Social science has also been able to develop few grand theories that are universally accepted in the social science community. According to Merton, social science has been able to develop only partial theories or theories of the middle range. Merton believes that it is premature for social scientists to develop grand theories because "not enough preparatory work has been done."[3] He argues that the grand theories in social science, such as the Freudian theory and the Marxist theory, have a number of major limitations. According to Merton, social scientists who use grand theories to guide their research often manipulate their data and findings to fit into preexisting conceptual and theoretical frameworks. This leads to conclusions that are faulty and misleading.

The diverse and conflicting theories and schools of thought that characterize social science raise the question as to why there are perhaps no true paradigms, little universal acceptance of grand theories, and many countertheories and counterexplanations in social science disciplines. The complexity of human behavior, the relatively short history of social science, the nature of social science research, and the influence of values on social science research explain, to a large extent, why social science theory is often diverse, conflicting, and controversial.

Human behavior is much more complex than animal behavior and other scientific phenomena. Consequently, it is easier for natural scientists than for social scientists to develop consensus and paradigms. However, Merton believes that we greatly overestimate the status of grand theory in the natural sciences and underestimate the difficulties natural scientists experience in building grand theories. He writes, "Sociologists sometimes misread the actual states of theory in the physical sciences. The error is ironic, for physicists agree that they have not achieved an all-encompassing system of theory, and most see little prospect of it in the near future."[4] The social sciences are also newer than the natural sciences; consequently, they have had less opportunity to develop theories, consensus, and paradigms. Social science had its birth in philosophy, which has historically been as concerned with normative as with scientific questions and explanations.

In its ideal and purest form, science searches for explanations and theories without influence from human values and human subjectivity. Peirce writes about the method of science, "To satisfy our doubts, . . . therefore, it is necessary that a method should be found by which our beliefs may be determined by nothing human, but by some external permanency—by something upon which our thinking has no effect. . . . The method must be such that the ultimate conclusion of every man shall be the same. Such is the method of science."[5] Peirce describes the ideal rather than the reality of science. Science, in the real world, is influenced by the values and the social contexts in which scientists live and work.

The subfield of sociology known as the sociology of knowledge is concerned primarily with studying the ways that the social context influences the construction of knowledge.[6] Karl Mannheim was one of the first influential social scientists to describe the ways in which society influences the work of social scientists. Mannheim believed that thinking was not an activity free of group influence, and that it had to be both understood and interpreted within the context of society. He argued that thinking was influenced by both the historical time and the social structure and that thought was perspectivistic.

Mannheim used the concepts *ideology* and *utopia* to describe perspectives that emerge from political conflict. *Ideology* describes the tendency of ruling groups to become so "intensively interest-bound to a situation that they are simply no longer able to see certain facts which would undermine their sense of domination."[7] *Utopian* describes oppressed groups that are "so strongly interested in the destruction and transformation of a given condition of society that they unwittingly see only those elements in the situation which tend to negate it."[8] Mannheim describes how perspective influences concepts:

> Even in the formulation of concepts, the angle of vision is guided by the observer's interests. Thought, namely, is directed in accordance with what a particular social group expects. Thus, out of the possible data of experience, every concept combines within itself only that which, in the light of the investigators' interests, it is essential to grasp and incorporate.[9]

Perspective and values influence the questions scientists ask, their theoretical frameworks, paradigms, research methods, explanations, and conclusions. These factors probably influence research more in the social than in the natural sciences because humans are usually more emotionally involved when studying questions related to themselves than when studying questions about atoms and amoebas.

Ethnicity and race are highly emotion-laden issues in a society as stratified by class and race as the United States. Perspective and values are more likely to influence strongly research related to emotion-laden issues than research on issues and problems that evoke few emotions.

Because race and ethnicity are issues highly charged with emotion in the United States, research related to these issues is likely to be more emotion-charged and value-laden than research on a less emotion-evoking topic, such as the housing patterns and population distribution of males between the ages of twenty-five and thirty who live in New York City.

Social scientists often reach divergent conclusions when studying issues such as the effects of school desegregation on students' attitudes and academic achievement, the extent to which genetic variables influence the academic achievement of black and white students, and the effects of bilingual instruction on the academic achievement of Hispanic students.[10] The generalizations that social scientists have reached on these problems are related to the perspectives, values, assumptions, and attitudes they bring to the research process. The conclusions that social scientists have reached regarding these issues, and the public policies they have recommended, are so divergent and conflicting that only initial perspectives and values can explain them.

Ethnic Subsocieties and Social Science Research

I have argued that social scientists, because of the cultures and/or subcultures in which they are socialized, inculcate specific values, perspectives, ideologies, and beliefs that often influence their research questions, assumptions, methods, and explanations. In a complex, pluralistic society such as the United States, which is not only characterized by a mainstream culture shared by all ethnic groups but also by ethnic subsocieties, the work of social scientists is often influenced by both the mainstream society and the ethnic subsocieties in which they are socialized.

Many nonblack social scientists conducted studies of blacks prior to the civil rights movement of the 1960s—studies that were strongly attacked by black social scientists in the 1970s. Much of this controversy focused on historical interpretations of topics such as slavery and the Civil War, sociological interpretations of the black family, and descriptions and interpretations of black English and black culture.[11] Traditional research assumptions, methods, and conclusions of nonblack social scientists often differed sharply from those of the new black social scientists during this period. Traditional interpretations often portrayed black slaves as happy and contented, paying little attention to the complexity and totality of their lives and to their struggle to remain human while experiencing tremendous adversity. Many traditional interpretations of the black family described it as a disorganized institution that negatively influenced the socialization of black children. Prior to the 1960s, black English was often regarded by social scientists as a bastardization of standard American English rather than as a legitimate language with its own phonology and lexicon.

During the 1960s and 1970s, many black scholars challenged traditional interpretations of black slavery, the black family, and of black English that had been made by nonblack social scientists and had become institutionalized in the social science literature and in the curricula of the schools and universities. They also developed studies that suggested the complexity of black slavery, the strengths of the black family, and the nature and function of black English.[12] Several scholars also described the importance of black English in the historic and contemporary lives of Afro-Americans.

Although the research and interpretations of slavery, the black family, and of black English were fairly clearly divided along ideological lines (that is, whether the researchers were assimilationists or pluralists), they were not consistently distinguishable by the race of researchers. A few black social scientists endorsed traditional interpretations of the black family and of black English, while nonblack social science academics, such as Eugene D. Genovese, Herbert G. Gutman, and Joan Baratz, presented and supported nontraditional interpretations of slavery, the black family, and black English, respectively.[13]

The relationship between race of researchers and their interpretations indicates the complex ways that social contexts influence social science data and explanations. It is much easier to describe the behavior of groups of social scientists—such as the new black group in the 1960s and the traditional nonblack group—than it is to predict or describe the behavior of individual social scientists or subgroups at any particular time in history. Marx, another student of the sociology of knowledge, recognized this phenomenon when he pointed out "that particular individuals might not always think in terms of their class interests, that they are not always influenced in their attitude by the class to which they belong."[14] However, he suggested that "categories of people, as distinct from individuals, are so influenced."[15] The influence of class interests on scholars, as described by Marx, seems similar to the influence of ethnic and racial interests. Individual members of specific ethnic or racial groups frequently promote the overarching values of the nation-state, such as equality and justice, rather than their own immediate ethnic interests. The nontraditional, nonblack social scientists, such as Genovese, Baratz, and Gutman, supported public policies in their research in the 1960s and 1970s that were highly consistent with the interests of low-status ethnic groups and with American ideals of justice and equality.

Social Science Research and Public Policy

The influence of the social context on the work of social scientists creates complex problems in a field such as multiethnic education, which is not only interdisciplinary (and consequently inherits debates and controversies from a number of disciplines), but is also a policy discipline with a particular set of goals. Therefore, values not only influence the research in the field, but policy makers influence which research studies get support and public attention, and consequently influence the nature of the research process itself. Research with different values, assumptions, and outcomes is given visibility and high rewards in different times, depending on the ideologies of the individuals and groups that have the most political and economic influence.

During the 1950s and 1960s, a civil rights movement emerged which highlighted the social, economic, and political discrimination that blacks were experiencing in American life, and called for a redress of these injustices. Social science research that supported equity for blacks became highly visible and was influential in shaping public policy.

The most noted example of the influence of social science research on public policy during this period is the citation in the historic Supreme Court decision in *Brown v. Board of Education* (1954) of research documenting the negative psychological effects that racism has on black children. The Court ruled that segregated educational facilities are "inherently unequal" because of the psychological harm they cause black children and youths. Chief Justice Warren, for the

Court, wrote, "To separate them [black children] from others of similar age and qualifications solely because of their race generates a feeling of inferiority as to their status in the community that may affect their hearts and minds in a way unlikely ever to be undone."[16] The now famous footnote 11, which contains the social science citations, includes works by Clark, Witmer and Kotinsky, Deutscher and Chein, Frazier, and Myrdal.

A range of studies published between 1960 and 1980 supported more liberal policies toward black and other ethnic minority groups. These studies emphasized the importance of school desegregation for student achievement and positive racial attitudes, the ways in which teacher attitudes and expectations influence student achievement and behavior, the positive aspects of black family life, and the functional characteristics of ethnic minority languages, such as black English and Spanish.[17] The findings of this series of studies suggested that institutions such as schools had a major responsibility to help improve the education of ethnic minority and poor youths, and that the quality of schools was a significant factor in determining whether or not minority group students achieved well in school. These studies also suggested a substantial role for the federal government in the education of poor and ethnic youths. One of their basic implications was that the federal government had a major responsibility to help all youths experience equal educational opportunities. These studies implied that the federal government not only had a responsibility to help poor and minority youths to achieve, but that schools could be reformed in ways that would enable them to achieve this goal.

Many of these studies, which presented new perspectives on ethnic life and culture, were conducted by the black intelligentsia. They included Smitherman's research on black language, Williams's work on black intelligence, and Billingsley's study of the black family.[18] Many studies in this genre, however, were conducted by nonblack social scientists, such as Pettigrew, Leacock, and Valentine.[19]

The Limitation of School Theorists

It would be misleading to suggest or imply that only studies that supported liberal policies and a substantial role for the federal government in the education of ethnic groups were published during the time of the civil rights movement of the 1960s and 1970s. Several important and influential studies appeared which suggested either that the school was limited in its ability to increase equality for poor youths because of the nature of class stratification in American society, or because of the genetic characteristics of ethnic minority students.

Jensen's controversial study of black-white intelligence appeared in the prestigious *Harvard Educational Review* in 1969, during the height of the movement to secure more rights for blacks and other ethnic groups.[20] His study indicated that the genetic characteristics of blacks was the most important reason that compensatory educational programs, designed to increase the IQ of black youths, had not been more successful. The publication of Jensen's study at a time when a liberal ideology was being widely voiced in the nation suggests the complex relationship between science, values, research, and public policy in a democratic, pluralistic nation such as the United States.

In a pluralistic society in which freedom of speech, academic freedom, and the quest for truth—no matter where it leads—are important and publicly affirmed values, there can and does emerge research that contradicts other overarching societal values such as justice, human dignity, and equal educational opportunity. Thus, the publication of Jensen's research was justified on the grounds that Jensen was involved in a scholarly quest for truth about the relationship between race and intelligence. In this instance, the quest for truth was a higher value for the editors of the *Harvard Educational Review* than the possible role that Jensen's study might play in denying black children equal educational opportunities. The editors believed that their primary responsibility, after publishing the Jensen study, was to allow other scholars opportunities to respond to it. They devoted an entire issue of the journal to the Jensen study, which was unprecedented in the recent history of the journal. In their introduction to the Jensen study, the editors wrote: "Because of the controversial nature of Dr. Jensen's article, the Spring Issue of the *Review* will include a discussion of the article by five psychologists."[21]

In the same issue in which he published an article by Shockley, Stanley M. Elam, editor of the *Phi Delta Kappan*, included an article by Gage that refuted Shockley's hypothesis. Elam wrote: "We hope that *Kappan* readers of all persuasions will view the Shockley-Gage encounter as what we have tried to make it: an examination of the questions fundamental to enlightened educational policy. . . . Even in a period of great racial tension, the investigation must proceed."[22]

The editors of the *Atlantic Monthly* published a highly controversial article by Richard J. Herrnstein in September 1971.[23] Herrnstein, a Harvard psychology professor, argued that "social classes reflect genetic differences."[24] Herrnstein's hypothesis differed from Jensen's and Shockley's because he suggested that social class rather than race was related to heredity. Because nonwhite ethnic groups are disproportionately represented in the lower classes, however, many of his readers called his hypothesis racist. As a result of publishing his unorthodox views, Herrnstein was publicly ridiculed, physically harassed, unable to deliver a public lecture at the University of Iowa, and forced to cancel a lecture at Princeton. It is possible that Herrnstein's views were more vigorously attacked than Jensen's and Shockley's because he argued that social class rather than race was related to heredity. Thus, his views can be used to justify antiegalitarian public policies for whites as well as for blacks.

Pluralistic democratic societies and institutions are often faced with decisions that involve conflicts in deeply held values, such as equality and academic freedom. They have to weigh and balance values that, as ideals, are equally important. These kinds of decisions create moral dilemmas that are difficult and complex. Whether the editors of the *Harvard Educational Review* and the *Phi Delta Kappan* would have made the same decisions if Jensen and Shockley had hypothesized that whites rather than blacks were genetically inferior is an important question that can only be speculated about and never answered. It is clear, however, judging from the reactions of black scholars to the publication of these articles, that few black academics would have chosen to publish the articles by Jensen and Shockley. Most black scholars view the research by Jensen and Shockley as threats to their survival as dignified human beings and to equal educational opportunity for black children and youths.

Jensen's research is based on what many eminent geneticists consider faulty assumptions and logic. It has antiegalitarian policy implications and was antithetical to the frequently articulated liberal ideology of the late 1960s. Consequently, his work triggered an acid debate and a storm of controversy. Shockley, who set forth views similar to those of Jensen but who enjoyed less academic respect in the educational research community, was frequently not taken seriously by academics. However, he made a number of highly publicized and controversial appearances on television and on college campuses.

Jensen, Shockley, and Herrnstein, of course, were not the only academics who published research during this period suggesting that the school could do little to increase the academic achievement of ethnic and poor youths. Other theorists, who were liberal to radical in their perspectives, argued that the school was limited in what it could do to help ethnic and poor students attain equality because the school was not a very important variable in determining academic achievement levels and adult income. Social class, family background, and luck were more important factors in determining adult income and the life chances of students. These theorists stressed the limited effects of schools on the adult life of all students.

Christopher Jencks became one of the most widely known and frequently quoted "ineffectiveness of school" theorists.[25] He argued that the most effective way to bring about equality for poor people is to equalize incomes directly rather than to rely on the schools to bring about equality in the adult life of students. He suggested that the schooling route was far too indirect and would most likely end in failure.

Jencks's critics were often harsh in condemning both his research methods and the policy implications of his research. They argued that his recommendations would be used to justify a retreat from liberal policies and inaction by the federal government and by school officials. They also believed that Jencks's radical solution to the problem of inequality—the direct equalization of incomes—would be ignored by policy makers because it was neither politically realistic nor feasible.[26] Kenneth B. Clark, one of Jencks's harshest critics, wrote:

> The Jencks report cannot successfully obscure its arrogant demeaning of contemporary social science. . . . White policy makers generally do not find this type of historical and empirical distortion difficult to accept when the victims of educational neglect are nonwhite. These social science rationalizations for the benign neglect or malignant rejection of nonwhite human beings in America both reflect and reinforce the pervasive racism of America.
>
> Social scientists, who by their glib, fatuous willingness to compromise the fundamental humanity of dark-skinned children and who by doing so provide

public officials with rationalizations for policies of malignant neglect, are not only accessories to the perpetuation of injustices; they become indistinguishable from the active agents of injustice.[27]

The Neoconservatives

During the late 1970s and early 1980s, a neoconservative movement emerged in the social science community. It seriously questions whether the national legislation of the 1960s and 1970s and the war on poverty had any appreciable effect on reducing poverty and increasing educational equality for minority and poor youths.[28] Irving Kristol, Daniel Bell, Norman Podhoretz, and Daniel Moynihan are some of the leading neoconservatives. The neoconservatives also question the extent to which the Supreme Court is involved in determining social and educational policies. In general, they believe that the Court is making decisions that sharply conflict with public sentiment and the public interest. The neoconservatives are especially disillusioned with the role of the Supreme Court in legally mandated public school desegregation cases. Many of them believe that the Supreme Court is too adamant in pushing for racially balanced schools and that it ignores other approaches that might be used to increase the achievement of minority group students.

Coleman has been widely quoted by the neoconservatives since he published a highly publicized and controversial study which suggests that whites usually flee from cities when their schools become desegregated by court order.[29] Coleman's "white flight" thesis was harshly criticized by the integrationists.[30] Neoconservatives doubt the beneficial effects of legally mandated school desegregation on student achievement and student racial attitudes. They also question educational programs such as bilingual education, compensatory education, and current attempts to infuse more ethnic content into the school curriculum.

Values and Theories in Multiethnic Education

Multiethnic education, like the social science disciplines from which it draws heavily, does not have a paradigm in the sense that Kuhn uses that term. However, theoretical schools of thought in multiethnic education can be identified, such as the geneticists and sociobiologists, the cultural deprivation theorists, the integrationists, and the cultural difference theorists. It is important to examine each of these theories to identify their major goals and implicit values, and to determine the extent to which they are consistent with the values and ideals expressed in the American Creed.

Equality and justice are key components of the American Creed. A frequently expressed goal of American public education is to educate all children to the limits of their potential, regardless of their social class, ethnic, racial, or religious affiliations. Historically, we have viewed the school as an institution to help all children attain the skills, attitudes, abilities, and knowledge needed to become effective and productive citizens of the commonwealth.

THE GENETICISTS AND SOCIOBIOLOGISTS

Geneticists such as Jensen, Shockley, and Herrnstein believe that heredity places severe limits on what the school can do to increase the academic ability and achievement of ethnic minority and poor students. Jensen argues that about 80 per cent of the variance in IQ is the result of heredity and that only 20 per cent is caused by the environment. He consequently concludes that social class and racial variations in intelligence must be explained primarily by genetic rather than environmental differences. Geneticists such as Jensen believe that compensatory educational programs that are designed to increase IQ are misdirected since an "enriched educational program cannot push the child above [his or her] potential."[31]

Sociobiologists also emphasize the role of genes in human behavior. They believe that some human behavior is an outgrowth of the human genetic makeup and that some elements of human culture are products of evolution.[32] Sociobiologists approach the study of culture in the same way that they approach the study of biological phenomena. Culture is viewed as an extension of the genes and the result of superior adaptive value. Behavior such as incest inhibition, bond formation, sexual practice, warfare, male dominance, and racial and ethnic sentiments are social behavioral characteristics.[33] Sociobiologists believe that these characteristics are a probable consequence of evolution. As such, they are seen as integral parts of human nature.

Genetic and sociobiological theories can be used to justify antiegalitarian policies and educational practices. Consequently, public policies that emanate from these theories often conflict with American Creed values such as justice and equality. If a child's intellectual capacity is severely limited by heredity, then the school is limited in what it can do to bring about educational equality. The perpetuation of the status quo and the support of an educational elite are public policies that can be defended with genetic and sociobiological theories.

THE CULTURAL DEPRIVATION THEORISTS

Cultural deprivation was one of the first theories that emerged in the 1960s concerned with the education of lower-class students. Cultural deprivation theorists assume that lower-class youths do not achieve well in school because of the dysfunctional social and cultural characteristics of their families and communities.[34] They believe that characteristics such as poverty, disorganized families, and fatherless homes cause children from poor communities to experience "cultural deprivation," and "irreversible cognitive deficits."

The cultural deprivation theorists, unlike the geneticists and the sociobiologists, are strong environmentalists who believe that the school not only has a responsibility to help poor and minority students to learn but that it has the ability to achieve this goal. These theorists assume that the learning problems of lower-class youths result primarily from the cultures in which they are socialized. They will achieve academically if the school is able to compensate for their deprived cultural environment and alienate them from it. Cultural deprivation theorists see the major problem as the culture of the students rather than the culture of the school.

Cultural deprivation theorists assume that a major goal of the school is to provide "culturally deprived" children with cultural and other experiences that will compensate for their cognitive and intellectual deficits. These theorists believe that lower-class children can learn the basic skills taught by the schools, but that these skills must be taught using intensive behaviorist teaching techniques.[35]

The goals of cultural deprivation theorists are highly consistent with the historic goals of American education. They believe that the school should help poor students learn and that it is capable of achieving this goal. However, by trying to alienate poor youths from their cultures, by blaming their cultures for their academic failures rather than the school, and by evaluating their cultures negatively, they violate what Ramirez and Castañeda call "cultural democracy."[36] In a pluralistic democratic society, children have a right to an education that respects and values their family and community cultures, as long as their cultural characteristics do not conflict with the overarching goals of the schools or the nation.

THE INTEGRATIONISTS

The integrationists are strongly committed to a society in which children from diverse racial and ethnic groups will freely interact, have positive racial attitudes, and will voluntarily associate with members of other racial and ethnic groups.[37] The integrationists believe that ethnic groups such as blacks and Mexican Americans can best attain an equal educational opportunity by attending integrated schools. They cite research by Coleman[38] and the reanalysis of the Coleman data by the U.S. Commission on Civil Rights[39] when they argue that the social class and racial composition of the school are the most important correlates of academic achievement for black and other minority students. Integrationists believe that the best way to increase the achievement of black and other ethnic minority groups is to place them in racially integrated middle-class schools.

Integrationists are strongly committed to equal educational opportunities for minority group youths and to other American Creed values. Their commitment to racially desegregated schools often becomes passionate, especially when they try to defend their plans that are attacked by harsh critics of legally mandated desegregated schools. Few issues have polarized American communities in recent years more than the issue of legally mandated desegregated schools.[40] In some communities, plans for desegregated schools have received mixed or hostile reactions from various ethnic groups including blacks, Anglos, and Mexican Americans.

Individuals and groups frequently oppose legally mandated desegregated schools for diverse and complex reasons, including fears of racial groups, a strong commitment to the concept of the neighborhood school, a belief that the burden for desegregating schools falls primarily on minority students and parents, and fears that the quality of education in the schools will drop when they become racially integrated.

The research on the effects of desegregated schooling on academic achievement and racial attitudes is conflicting and frequently reflects the perspectives that researchers bring to the research process.[41] While supporters of school desegregation are strongly committed to equal educational opportunity for all students, they sometimes support policies that do not consistently support cultural democracy for minority group students.

THE CULTURAL DIFFERENCE THEORISTS

Cultural pluralists, biculturalists, and multicultural theorists are distinguishable but can be categorized as one group because of the research assumptions and values they share. Unlike the cultural deprivation theorists, they reject the idea that ethnic minority youths have cultural deficits. They believe that ethnic groups such as blacks, Mexican Americans, and Indians, have strong, rich, and diverse cultures.[42] These cultures, argue the cultural difference theorists, consist of languages, values, behavioral styles, and perspectives that can enrich the lives of other Americans. Ethnic minority youths, contend these theorists, fail to achieve in school not because they have deprived cultures but because their cultures are *different* from the school culture.

Cultural difference theorists believe that the school, rather than the cultures of the minority students, is primarily responsible for the relatively low academic achievement of ethnic minority students. The school must change in ways that will allow it to respect and reflect the cultures of minority youths and at the same time use teaching strategies that are consistent with their cultural characteristics. These kinds of teaching strategies will help ethnic youths to achieve at higher levels. The schools, argue these theorists, frequently fail to help ethnic minority students to achieve because schools often ignore or try to alienate them from their cultures, and rarely use teaching strategies that are consistent with their life-styles. Cultural difference theorists frequently cite research that shows how the cultures of the school and of ethnic minority youths differ in values, norms, and behavior.[43]

Cultural difference theorists are strongly committed to helping ethnic minority youths experience educational equity and to protecting their rights to cultural democracy. Cultural democracy guarantees them the right to keep ties with their ethnic families and communities and the right to maintain their dialects and languages, while at the same time developing competency in standard American English. Ramirez and Castañeda write:

> Cultural democracy, as we define it, states that an individual can be bicultural and still be loyal to American ideals. Cultural democracy is a philosophical precept which recognizes that the way a person communicates, relates to others, seeks support and recognition from his environment (incentive motivation), and thinks and learns (cognition) is a product of the value system of his home and community. Furthermore, educational environments or policies that do not recognize the individual's right, as guaranteed by the Civil Rights Act of 1964, to remain identified with the culture and language of his cultural group are culturally undemocratic.[44]

Cultural difference theorists maintain that every nation needs an overarching set of values and goals to which all members of the nation-state are committed and that there is a need for a national identity shared by all ethnic and racial groups. Members of all ethnic and racial groups should also have the skills and attitudes needed to participate effectively in the political, economic, and social institutions of the nation-state, and should be given the opportunity to participate in these institutions.

However, the cultural difference theory also recognizes the need for Americans to maintain attachments to their ethnic communities.[45] For many, especially those who are members of visible ethnic groups, their attachments to their ethnic families and communities are strong and important. It provides them with a sense of group identification, a sense of peoplehood, and psychological support. When members of these ethnic groups are provided the opportunities and skills to participate in the shared American culture and in their ethnic cultures and communities, they can make their maximum contributions to the civic culture because both their personal and civic needs are being satisfied and are given the richest opportunities to grow and blossom.

Knowledge, Equality, and Humanities Educators

I have described how research related to multiethnic education supports a basic principle of the sociology of knowledge, that is, knowledge reflects the social context and times in which scientists live and work. The influence of society on knowledge and thought causes knowledge to be perspectivistic, according to Mannheim. While accepting Mannheim's basic premise, I described how the relationship between the social context and the production of knowledge and thought in a pluralistic democratic nation such as the United States is complex rather than linear.

The United States consists of a mainstream society as well as ethnic subsocieties. Each of these social contexts influences the production of thought and knowledge. Important publicly affirmed values in our nation include equality and justice, yet research is often published that is used to support inequality and other values that contradict American Creed values. This happens because intellectual freedom is a publicly affirmed American value, and inequality is an important structural characteristic of the United States which public decision makers often wish to defend with legitimate social science research.

Because pluralism and intellectual freedom are important American values, research which both supports and refutes public policies that promote equality usually coexist in the United States in each historical period. However, research that is most consistent with the dominant ideologies of the individuals and groups in power is given the most visibility, financial support, encouragement, and prestige. Scientists who do research that counters the dominant economic, social, and political order are often relegated to obscurity, and usually have little influence on public policy.

Educators, like social scientists, have perspectives on knowledge about ethnic groups that reflect the social contexts in which they live and work. Educators bring their perspectives, values, and assumptions about ethnic groups to the schools. They are reflected in their instructional objectives, teaching strategies, and classroom behavior. Most educators are not keenly aware of their attitudes toward ethnic groups and the perspectives they convey to their students.

Educators communicate their perspectives, values, and attitudes toward ethnic groups to students primarily through unwitting actions and words. Consequently, it is important for humanities educators not only to examine the knowledge that underlies their curriculum and methods, but also their own values and perspectives to determine the extent to which they promote equity and justice for all students.

FOOTNOTES

1. Thomas S. Kuhn, *The Structure of Scientific Revolutions,* 2d ed., enl. (Chicago: University of Chicago Press, 1970), p. 175.

2. Ibid., p. 15.

3. Robert K. Merton, *Social Theory and Social Structure*, enl. (New York: Free Press, 1968), p. 45.

4. Ibid., pp. 47-48.

5. Justus Buchler, ed., *Philosophical Writings of Peirce* (New York: Dover, 1955), p. 18.

6. Peter L. Berger and Thomas Luckmann, *The Social Construction of Reality: A Treatise in the Sociology of Knowledge* (Garden City, N.Y.: Doubleday, 1966).

7. Karl Mannheim, *Ideology and Utopia: An Introduction to the Sociology of Knowledge* (New York: Harcourt Brace Jovanovich, 1949), p. 36.

8. Ibid.

9. Ibid., p. 245.

10. See especially: *School Desegregation: The Continuing Challenge* (Cambridge, Mass.: *Harvard Educational Review*, Reprint Series no. 11, 1976); *Environment, Heredity, and Intelligence* (Cambridge, Mass.: *Harvard Educational Review*, Reprint Series no. 2, 1969); and Noel Epstein, *Language, Ethnicity, and the Schools: Policy Alternatives for Bilingual-Bicultural Education* (Washington, D.C.: Institute for Educational Leadership, George Washington University, 1977).

11. For examples of these studies see: Ulrich B. Phillips, *American Negro Slavery* (New York: D. Appleton and Co., 1918); Daniel P. Moynihan, *The Negro Family: The Case for National Action* (Washington, D.C.: U.S. Department of Labor, Office of Planning and Research, 1965); and Carl Bereiter and Siegfried Engelmann, *Teaching Disadvantaged Children in the Preschool* (Englewood Cliffs, N.J.: Prentice-Hall, 1966).

12. John W. Blassingame, *The Slave Community: Plantation Life in the Ante-Bellum South* (New York: Oxford University Press, 1972); Andrew Billingsley, *Black Families in White America* (Englewood Cliffs, N.J.: Prentice-Hall, 1968); Geneva Smitherman, *Talkin and Testifyin: The Language of Black America* (Boston: Houghton Mifflin, 1977).

13. Eugene D. Genovese, *Roll, Jordan, Roll: The World the Slaves Made* (New York: Pantheon Books, 1974); Herbert G. Gutman, *The Black Family in Slavery and Freedom, 1750-1925* (New York: Vintage Books, 1970); Joan C. Baratz, "Teaching Reading in an Urban Negro School System," in *Language and Poverty: Perspectives on a Theme*, ed. Frederick Williams (Chicago: Markham Publishing Co., 1970), pp. 11-24.

14. Lewis A. Coser, *Masters of Sociological Thought*, 2d ed. (New York: Harcourt Brace Jovanovich, 1977), p. 54.

15. Ibid.

16. *Brown v. Board of Education of Topeka*, in *The Annals of America*, vol. 17 (Chicago: Encyclopedia Britannica, 1968), p. 257.

17. Examples of this research include U.S. Commission on Civil Rights, *Racial Isolation in the Public Schools* (Washington, D.C.: U.S. Government Printing Office, 1967); Ray C. Rist, *The Invisible Children* (Cambridge, Mass.: Harvard University Press, 1978); James P. Comer, *School Power: Implications of an Intervention Project* (New York: Free Press, 1980); Billingsley, *Black Families in White America*; and Smitherman, *Talkin and Testifyin.*

18. Smitherman, *Talkin and Testifyin*; Robert L. Williams, "Abuses and Misuses in Testing Black Children," *Counseling Psychologist* 2, no. 3 (1971): 62-73; Billingsley, *Black Families in White America.*

19. Thomas F. Pettigrew, *A Profile of the Negro American* (Princeton, N.J.: D. Van Nostrand Co., 1964): Eleanor Burke Leacock, *Teaching and Learning in City Schools* (New York: Basic Books, 1969); and Charles A. Valentine, *Culture and Poverty: Critique and Counter-Proposals* (Chicago: University of Chicago Press, 1968).

20. Arthur R. Jensen, "How Much Can We Boost IQ and Scholastic Achievement?" *Harvard Educational Review* 39 (Winter 1969): 1-123.

21. Ibid., p. 2.

22. Stanley M. Elam, editor's introduction to William Shockley, "Dysgenics, Geneticity, Raceology: A Challenge to the Intellectual Responsibility of Educators," *Phi Delta Kappan* 53 (January 1972): 297.

23. Richard J. Herrnstein, "I.Q.," *Atlantic Monthly* 228 (September 1971): 43-64.

24. Richard J. Herrnstein, *I.Q. in the Meritocracy* (Boston: Little, Brown and Co., 1971), p. 14.

25. Christopher Jencks et al., *Inequality: A Reassessment of the Effect of Family and Schooling in America* (New York: Basic Books, 1972). See also, *Perspectives on Inequality* (Cambridge, Mass.: *Harvard Educational Review*, Reprint Series no. 8, 1973).

26. See especially, Alice M. Rivlin, "Forensic Social Science," *Harvard Educational Review* 43 (February 1973): 61-75.

27. Kenneth B. Clark, "Social Policy, Power, and Social Science Research," *Harvard Educational Review* 43 (February 1973): 118-19.

28. See, for example, David L. Kirp, "School Desegregation and the Limits of Legalism," *Public Interest* 47 (Spring 1977): 101-28; and Peter Steinfels, *The Neoconservatives: The Men Who Are Changing America's Politics* (New York: Simon and Schuster, 1979).

29. James S. Coleman, Sarah D. Kelly, and John A. Moore, "Recent Trends in School Integration" (Paper delivered at the Annual Meeting of the American Educational Research Association, Washington, D.C., April 1975).

30. Thomas F. Pettigrew and Robert L. Green, "School Desegregation in Large Cities: A Critique of the Coleman 'White Flight' Thesis," *Harvard Educational Review* 46 (February 1976): 1-53.

31. Jensen, "How Much Can We Boost IQ and Scholastic Achievement," p. 2.

32. Arthur L. Caplan, ed., *The Sociobiology Debate: Readings on the Ethic and Scientific Issues Concerning Sociobiology* (New York: Harper and Row, 1978); Michael Ruse, *Sociobiology: Sense or Nonsense?* (Boston: D. Reidel Publishing Co., 1979).

33. Edward O. Wilson, *Human Nature* (Cambridge, Mass.: Harvard University Press, 1978); Pierre L. van den Berghe, *The Ethnic Phenomenon* (New York: Elsevier, 1981).

34. See Frank Riessman, *The Culturally Deprived Child* (New York: Harper, 1962), and Bereiter and Englemann, *Teaching Disadvantaged Children in the Preschool*, for examples of this theory.

35. Bereiter and Engelmann, *Teaching Disadvantaged Children in the Preschool.*

36. Manuel Ramirez III and Alfredo Castañeda, *Cultural Democracy, Bicognitive Development, and Education* (New York: Academic Press, 1974).

37. See Pettigrew and Green, "School Desegregation in Large Cities."

38. James S. Coleman et al., *Equality of Educational Opportunity* (Washington, D.C.: U.S. Government Printing Office, 1966).

39. U.S. Commission on Civil Rights, *Racial Isolation in the Public Schools.*

40. See Diane Ravitch, "The 'White Flight' Controversy," *Public Interest* 51 (Spring 1978): 135-49.

41. See Coleman et al., "Recent Trends in School Integration" and Pettigrew and Green, "School Desegregation in Large Cities."

42. Stephen S. Baratz and Joan C. Baratz, "Early Childhood Intervention: The Social Science Base of Institutional Racism," *Harvard Educational Review* 40 (Winter 1970): 29-50.

43. See Geneva Gay, "Interactions in Culturally Pluralistic Classrooms," in *Education in the 80s: Multiethnic Education*, ed. James A. Banks (Washington, D.C.: National Education Assocation, 1981), pp. 42-53, and Barbara J. Shade, "Afro-American Cognitive Style: A Variable in School Success," *Review of Educational Research* 52 (Summer 1982): 219-44.

44. Ramirez and Castañeda, *Cultural Democracy, Bicognitive Development, and Education*, p. 23.

45. James A. Banks, *Multiethnic Education: Theory and Practice* (Boston: Allyn and Bacon, 1981).

CHAPTER VII

Can the Humanities Be Taught in American Public Schools?

ELLIOT W. EISNER

The Context of Humanities Education

The saliency of the humanities in American schools is extremely low. The reasons are not particularly difficult to discern. In the first place, American schools embrace, whether they know it or not, a positivistic attitude toward education. This attitude looks with suspicion on forms of understanding that rely upon judgment, intuition, metaphor, and other nonquantitative and hence "imprecise" forms of disclosure. The humanities as typified by literature, history, and ethics are hard pressed to employ the kind of criteria that a positivist view of knowledge requires. In education we tend to get nervous about making decisions that depend upon judgments, preferring to rely upon those procedures that lead to "certain" answers. Ambiguity has never been a load that Americans have liked to carry. We have little tolerance for it in political leaders, but even less in education.

Second, American schools, especially at present, are preoccupied with the achievement of prespecified outcomes. This is not a new phenomenon but it has been exacerbated in recent years by the accountability movement in education. What this means for curriculum and for classroom practice is that the character of the journey is less important than arriving at the destination on time. Measured payoff in relation to conventionally defined competencies is the current theme song among educators; hence talk about so evanescent, ineffable, and difficult to measure outcomes as those achieved through humanistic studies receives less than an enthusiastic welcome. When one believes one has an angry or anxious public barking down one's neck, measured outcomes on noncontroversial skills appear much more sensible.

Third, American educators are influenced by a practical public which often finds it difficult to understand why so impractical a body of studies as the humanities should be given serious attention in the public schools. Given the high rate of unemployment, the widespread concern about basic skills, and the pressure to get rid of the frills, studies that seem to lead to few vocational outcomes and which, in any case, one cannot confidently evaluate are not given high priority.

Fourth, and related to the foregoing, is the educator's concern with time. In American culture, time is treated as a commodity. It is something we buy and sell. Given the pressure upon teachers to get students to perform up to standard, time cannot be squandered on what is not truly of importance. While time for physics, chemistry, biology, and calculus is seldom questioned, the same cannot be said for humanistic studies.

Fifth, most Americans still harbor the illusion that schooling is or should be a value-free enterprise. The humanities are riddled with values. They deal with issues that are controversial; they expose students to ideas and that might encourage them to become critical of the values that their families and community embrace. Hence, a course that deals with values, such as *Man: A Course of Study*, is first proscribed in Arizona and later has its funding cut by the Congress of the United States. What the public seems to want is a form of schooling that is designed to teach children to think, but not to become critical of the status quo. The humanities, dealing as they do with values rather than facts (in the eyes of the public at least), are troublesome in this regard.

Finally, the humanities as a general field has no effective professional constituency. Teachers of each of the fields or disciplines that typically constitute the humanities owe their allegiance to their own disciplines; hence, seldom are their common aims and the means appropriate for achieving them considered. In fact, given tight budgets and reduced time, the members of this humanistic family of fields often compete with each other for the few scraps that are left after the really important subjects are assigned time and resources.

The point of the foregoing narrative is not to depress the reader but to avoid engendering the illusion that because a yearbook of the

National Society for the Study of Education is devoted to the humanities in American schools, the humanities occupy a place having curricular significance in the schools or that light is soon to be found at the end of the tunnel. I do not believe that this is the case, and unless your eyesight is keener than mine, I see no light yet. In fact, I believe that the pressures I have described have led to a deterioration of the quality of schooling—and I do not mean a deterioration of test scores. On the contrary, pressure to increase test scores *could* contribute to a further decline in the quality of education *if* higher test scores are secured at the cost of neglecting the very mental skills and curriculum content that the humanities require. A public anxious about test scores and a body of school administrators concerned about their jobs do not augur well for programs that give flight to the spirit. We are still very much on a "back-to-basics" kick in American education.

Humanities Education

So much for context. What is it that the humanities provide in education?

To raise this question implies that we desire but frequently do not have a positive conception of the humanities. For example, the National Endowment for the Humanities lists the following as constituting the humanities: history, ethics, law, philosophy, linguistics, archeology, literature. . . .[1] It does not include the arts in its list. Nor does it provide a discussion of the criteria used to select those particular fields and not others. One might say we have in the National Endowment for the Humanities an ostensive definition. Yet our mind yearns for something more. We want to know what essential properties, if any, constitute fields such as these and we want to know why the arts are excluded. We want more than a list of fields; we want a principle that sheds light upon them and that helps us rationalize the distinctions we make.

But because we are educators, we want not only to know what counts as a humanistic study; we want also to know about the distinctive educational import of humanistic studies. Indeed, if such studies have no distinctive educational import, identifying the essential properties of the humanities is of little use. It would be both arrogant and foolish for me to write about the humanities as though no one had given any thought to the subject prior to my writing. The variety of conceptions of the humanities are as diverse as the disciplines and fields of study that are said to constitute them. Yet, the various conceptions that have been advanced do share certain common qualities. First, there is a shared agreement that humanistic studies shed light on what it means to be a human being. While the natural sciences focus on the operations of the natural world, the humanities have something important to say about the cultural world so that through the study of the humanities one learns about man. Even more important, the student of the humanities learns something significant about himself. For example, Shakespeare's *Othello* has much to say about jealousy as experienced by its central character, but it says much more than that; it tells us about jealousy in general and it helps the competent reader understand through feeling what jealousy means in his or her own life. Somehow *Othello* becomes a vehicle, to be sure to be enjoyed in its own right, but also to help us reflect on our feelings of jealousy and on the frailties that all humans share.

The second function of the humanities that most conceptions of them describe is the contribution humanistic learning makes to our powers of critical appraisal. In some ways this is a necessary offshoot of the nature of humanistic content. We have not devised a way to determine within small errors of measurement the intellectual or aesthetic value of humanistic scholarship or of works of art. There is no scale, no yardstick, no measure that can be applied to such works to determine the value of what we encounter. Such judgments as the humanities require attention and sensitivity to nuance; they require appreciation for context; they require the ability to deliberate and judge. These processes are utterly fallible; they are swayed by argument, moved by rhetoric, and altered as time changes. It is precisely these features that make human judgment acute. Where an infallible yardstick exists, judgment is unnecessary. Participation in the questions that humanists ask requires one to sharpen one's critical sense. Upon this too there is consensus.

Attempting to encapsulate the defining features of the humanities, the Commission on the Humanities writes:

> The essence of the humanities is a spirit or an attitude toward humanity. They show how the individual is autonomous and at the same time bound, in the ligatures of language and history, to humankind across time and throughout the world. The humanities are an important measure of the values and aspirations of any society. Intensity and breadth in the perception of life and

power and richness in works of the imagination betoken a people alive as moral and aesthetic beings, citizens in the fullest sense. They base their education on sustaining principles of personal enrichment and civic responsibility. They are sensitive to beauty and aware of their cultural heritage. They can approach questions of value, no matter how complex, with intelligence and goodwill. They can use their scientific and technical achievements responsibly because they see the connections among science, technology, and humanity.[2]

Such an accolade might be faulted for what it fails to omit. Yet, its general thrust is consistent with the views of those who have attempted to provide a conception of the humanities. For some readers conceptions such as the foregoing may seem imprecise, too global, leaving too much to matters of taste and judgment. Yet would it not be peculiar to provide a definition or conception of a field whose very characteristics controverted the properties that it was designed to define? Definitions of the humanities are "imprecise" precisely because they are in keeping with what humanists do. They are definitions that invite deliberation, argument, counterpoint. It seems unreasonable to seek precise definitions in a field in which the drawing of precise lines is an anathema.[3]

I concur with the spirit of the Commission's efforts to say what the humanities are. Humanists regard knowledge as fallible, believe that no single method has a monopoly upon inquiry, believe that the fundamental human questions are ineluctably enduring and that over the course of human history some extraordinary human beings have made some remarkable efforts to answer those questions. Humanists place premium on the human's ability to be critically rational, that is, to reason deeply and sensitively about important human matters. And they believe that a dialectical engagement with the works of the humanities helps man not only to view the world in useful, illuminating ways, but also helps man learn something about himself.

How is it that one learns about oneself through the humanities? Consider first an example from music, and then one from literature. In the fifth movement of his Ninth Symphony, Beethoven slowly begins to build a pattern of rhythms that gain increasing momentum. This rhythmic sequence appears to crescendo when it is made to retreat to a more modulated dynamic range and then made to crescendo again. Moving toward still another crescendo, Beethoven suddenly introduces an unexpected cacophony that is immediately followed by a baritone voice singing the lines from Schiller's "Ode to Joy." The poem becomes the lyrics of a moving melodic theme that builds to a perfect finale within a huge symphonic score. By the time one reaches the coda, the dynamics, the rhythm, and the melodic line of this movement bring the listener rising to his feet. Feelings are experienced that one could not know prior to hearing the symphony. The musical forms that Beethoven creates reveal to the competent listener a new source of personal discovery. It is by virtue of the music that one aspect of the self and its capacity to respond is known.

In Arthur Miller's play, *The Death of a Salesman*, Willy Loman, a middle-aged, ne'er-do-well salesman, creates a world of self-deception through which he avoids the reality of a declining career and of recognizing that his two sons are not what he wants them so desperately to be. It is only when he is confronted by the loss of his job, which was the hub of his life, and by pleas from his son, Bif, to see Bif as he really is, that reality breaks through.

Miller's play is a powerful vehicle that sheds light on the human tendency to bypass reality and to substitute for it a fantasy or a dreamlife that is often unproductive and unsatisfying. While few of us are as immersed in a private, illusory world as is Willy Loman, all of us share aspects of his life. Through Miller's work we are able to discover those aspects. We come to recognize some of our own weakness and come to share an affinity with Willy Loman. By distilling a human weakness and giving it a vivid presence, Miller affords us a means for discovering what we might not otherwise see in ourselves.

These contributions to self-discovery are, of course, indirect. The humanities do not aim at psychotherapy. Furthermore, to recognize oneself in the content that the humanities provide requires one to be able to read their messages; great humanistic works require great audiences. Yet the fact that such contributions are indirect does not diminish their significance. The humanities are both a lamp and a mirror. While neither a lamp nor a mirror guarantees insight, they do help make sight possible.

If we use as one defining characteristic of the humanities the capacity of a work to help us understand the nature of human nature, it seems to me that there is no field or discipline that could not be treated in a way that is humanistic in character. Physics and chemistry are normally not taught or thought of as being a part of the humanities, yet one could easily imagine how physics and chemistry, when put into historical context and treated as examples of intellectual history, could become humanistic studies. What do Kepler's epicycles tell us about Kepler and the times in which he lived?[4] What does the race of Watson and Crick with Pauling tell us about the role of human motivation and competition in scientific inquiry?[5] What moral obligations, if any, does a scientist have with respect to the uses of the ideas he or she creates? Such questions broaden the context of scientific understanding and give it a cast that is thoroughly humanistic in flavor. My point here is that even disciplines that appear to be outside the arena of the humanities can be placed within them if the focus and the approach to learning is humanistic in character.

The Arts and the Humanities

What about the arts? What claim, if any, can they make to being a part of the humanistic tradition rather than distinct from the humanities? There are, of course, traditional separations that have been made between the arts and the humanities. For example, the Commission on the Humanities writes:

> Whether defined by questions, methods, or fields, the humanities employ a particular medium and turn of mind. The medium is language. Discourse sets in motion and supports reflection and judgment. The humanities have close ties not only with speech but especially with writing and the thought processes writing makes possible. Study in the humanistic disciplines is not limited to texts—oral cultures have reflected deeply on human experience and have achieved great wisdom—but it cannot proceed without creating and using texts.[6]

From a political perspective as well, the humanities have been separated from the arts. Congress saw fit to create two endowments: the National Endowment for the Arts and the National Endowment for the Humanities. On our own university campuses we often distinguish between the arts faculty and the humanities faculty, or the arts *and* humanities faculty and the science faculty. Tradition seems to lead politics, and the distinction, rarely defined, is built into our language and our way of doing business.

I have no trouble with such distinctions as long as one does not take them too seriously. If the distinction between humanistic and artistic work is simply a carry-over from an ancient legacy, and if such legacies make people comfortable, okay. But if the distinction implies a difference in social or intellectual status or in our conception of the source of the work—for example, intelligence as contrasted with talent—then the distinction is mischievous, or worse, misleading, and should be abandoned.[7]

The use of language, which appears to be crucial to the Commission, must be treated just as qualitatively or artistically in writing poetry and literature as a composer must treat sound, or a painter space and form. As for the idea that a humanistic work conveys ideas while the arts convey feeling, that distinction simply will not hold water. Works of visual art have as much to say about man and his world as any writer can convey or any historian can describe. The paintings of Francis Bacon and Georgio De Chirico, the sculpture of Marcel Ducamp, the drawings of Daumier, the music of Stravinsky, Wagner, Mahler, and Schoenberg are riddled with ideas about man, music, and the world. Hence, from a substantive point of view I can find no sound basis for distinguishing between the arts and the humanities when one focuses upon either their aims or their achievements. Both the works we call the humanities and those we call the arts are artifacts, man-made constructions, the off-spring of the human imagination, and they reveal aspects of the world in ways that are *sui generis* to their form. The works created within each of these historically inherited categories are achievements of the mind, produced by people of genius and are there to enhance the lives of those who can "read" them.

The Mission of Schools and Colleges for Teaching Humanities

It is precisely in the realm of helping students learn to read the arts and the humanities that the school has one of its most important but most neglected missions. I have already alluded to some of the factors that have militated against the teaching of the arts and the humanities in the schools. If one were really skeptical, one might seriously question whether the arts and the humanities can be taught in the majority of schools in the nation. Such skepticism has been expressed by those social theorists who see the school as an institution designed—intentionally or not—to sustain the inequities that currently exist in our society.[8] They claim that schools merely echo the messages of the larger social order and are used to prepare people who will be willing workers within an economic system that places little value on what is most precious about human beings—their capacity to use their rationality and to exercise free will. They claim that schools militate against the development of such competencies by enveloping students in an organizational structure that allows primarily for one-way communication, from the top down, and that makes horizontal communication difficult. Furthermore, the schools are said to emphasize a sociology of knowledge or a knowledge hierarchy that places a premium on being able to follow prescribed rules in order to arrive at known ends. In sum, these and other features of schooling produce what one writer calls a type of structural violence.[9] Such violence, he claims, is not direct, it is indirect; it pervades the culture of schooling silently, and therefore is even more insidious than if it were blatant, since in silence the aggressor is even more difficult to identify.

When one adds to such analyses the fact that most college graduates choosing teaching as a career come from the bottom quarter of the college graduating class, the prospects for teaching subjects in a manner consistent with the humane becomes even more problematic.[10] Unlike teaching simple arithmetic, punctuation, spelling, and the rules of grammar, the arts and the humanities demand attention to nuance; they place a premium on deliberation; they ask students not only to cope with ambiguity and uncertainty, but to enjoy them. Can teachers who are likely to be among the least able intellectually and who work in an environment in which the arts and humanities are regarded as marginal, create the kind of classrooms and provide the kind of curriculum that will truly be in harmony with the spirit of the arts and humanities? Put another way, can teachers who themselves have little understanding of what the humanities are and do, help the young learn to appreciate them?

From my point of view the likelihood of achieving such goals is dim—*unless* there is a turnaround in what universities emphasize and a change in the public's view of the mission of the school.

I indicated above that those currently entering the teaching profession are among the least intellectually able of their cohorts. According to the best data available these are the facts. But I would be only marginally more sanguine about the humanities in the schools if it were those in the first rather than in the fourth quartile who were entering the teaching profession. This is due to the fact that regardless of the intellectual level of prospective teachers, university programs, like programs in elementary and secondary schools, are not characterized by a deep commitment to the spirit of the arts and humanities. Most colleges and universities are essentially extensions of secondary education; they have a wider curriculum, to be sure, but they provide the same climate of expectations for students. As a result, note-taking and "cramming" by students sitting in large lectures has unfortunately become characteristic. In research-oriented universities the premium paid to good teaching is small, and in land-grant universities that have no clear research orientation, the size of classes, except in the most exotic of specializations, makes the kind of deliberation and critical analysis characteristic of humanistic inquiry all but impossible to achieve. When accompanied by a preoccupation among students with grade-getting and careerism, it matters less than it would otherwise who elects to go into education as a career. In addition, the impact of misguided but well-intentioned missives from prestigious private universities to American secondary schools is difficult to underestimate. Most such prestigious institutions are unhappy with the quality of their entering freshmen; they complain about their lack of adequate preparation and decry what has come to be called "grade inflation." Yet the solutions that they prescribe—tougher standards, harder courses, more homework—are almost always prescribed without a shred of philosophical context or empirical justification. The quick-fix, get-tough policy they prescribe is so denuded of theory that those same academics would raise the roof if similar nostrums were prescribed by others for the improvement of teaching in their own fields. The recommendations for educational improvement that have appeared have, on the whole, been contrary to the spirit that I believe resides at the heart of humanistic learning. Indeed, if one were to cast blame for some of the weaknesses of American primary and secondary schools, I would want to lay some of that blame on the doorstep of the university.

New Dimensions of Schooling for Humanistic Learning

Yet I am not willing to give up the aspiration to create schools whose programs and whose climate are humane in spirit. Education is, after all, an optimistic enterprise. What would it take to create schools in which humanistic learning could flourish? The answer to that question leads us to the major dimensions of schooling that would need to be changed if such an aim were to be achieved. These dimensions include (a) the character of the curriculum, (b) the structure or organization of school, (c) the competencies of the teacher, and (d) the conduct of evaluation programs. It is on these dimensions that I will focus in the remainder of this chapter. In focusing upon these dimensions of schooling I do not claim that they exhaust all of the dimensions that could be considered. Nevertheless, the ones I have identified, to my way of thinking, are the most important. One other caveat. Although I have distinguished among these dimensions for analytic purposes, in fact, these dimensions are intertwined: what is taught, at base, cannot be separated from how something is taught; the curriculum and the organizational structure of the school shape each other.

THE CHARACTER OF THE CURRICULUM

As far as the curriculum is concerned, I have already indicated that any subject, if treated as an aspect of man's intellectual history and taught in a spirit of deliberation, would be a humanistic study. The sciences, which are most often contrasted with the arts and the humanities, could be taught in a way that illuminates man's struggle to understand nature; they could be taught as a human quest characterized by all of the foibles that humans possess—self-doubt, jealousy, ambition, weakness; they could be taught for their moral implications. The sciences could be taught with special attention to the public status of their processes and claims, to the social burdens of some of their conclusions, and they could be taught with an eye to the responsibilities of the public to the scientist and to the social conditions that make scientific inquiry possible. The point here is that even those areas of the curriculum that appear most remote from the humanities could be studied for their humanistic potential.

Yet, notwithstanding this potential, insofar as the humanities shed light on what is most human about man, there are studies that take that subject matter as their major focus. Perhaps nowhere is this more vivid than in literature, drama, and poetry. The world of literature is replete with material that helps the competent reader to participate empathetically in the lives of others, and through such participation to know what cannot be known directly. Literature does this not only through the topics or themes writers choose to attend to, but because of the way in which its characters are revealed, the atmosphere that is created, the plot that is made to unfold, the way in which a theme is embedded within the story. These devices make literature and drama powerful modes of psychological transportation. The book, as vehicle, can be an escape from "reality" or a means of access to it; it can lead one away from significant human issues or it can present them vividly to our consciousness. What we regard as great books written by great writers emphasize the significant, not the trivial. They help us see more clearly the world in which we live. They do not lead us away from that world. Even *Alice in Wonderland* is referenced to human-kind.

STRUCTURE AND ORGANIZATION

If students are to have access to such works, at least two conditions must be present. First, students must be sufficiently skilled in reading to find such works meaningful. Second, opportunities for reading and discussing such works must be available. As far as the former is concerned, reading skills are not wholly independent of subject matter. If students are to develop the skills needed to read literature, they need opportunities to read literature. The idea that students can develop such skills on nonliterary material and then apply them to literature or poetry underestimates the extent to which different written forms make different intellectual demands upon students. The acquisition of reading skills and the content to be read are not independent activities. With respect to the school curriculum, this implies that a program of study be defined in which a significant array of humanistic literature, including poetry, be available as an ongoing part of the school day, that such material be selected so as to be compatible with the existing reading competencies of students, and that such material serve as the basis for discussion.

The importance of discussion in helping students—even young students—penetrate the surface of what they have read should not be underestimated. Reading need not be a solitary activity. Common reading and the encouragement of diverse but relevant interpretations and implications of what has been read are of paramount importance for eliciting the full educational value of reading and for illuminating what is significant but subtle in the work. Discussion has become a dying art in our culture, despite the fact that when it goes well it is a stunning example of the capacities of the mind. Novels, poetry, works of visual art and music, these can be sources of such celebration. What school programs need are the time, space, and support for such activities to occur.

The importance of time in learning has been most recently highlighted by researchers studying what has come to be called "time on task."[11] Put simply, the more students are actually engaged in tasks that have academic importance, the greater the likelihood they will learn what is being taught. Put conversely, if students are not given an opportunity to learn something, it is not likely that they will learn it. Such research conclusions appear to belabor the obvious; nevertheless, these conclusions are educationally important: if students are to reap the benefits of what the humanities have to provide, the curriculum of the schools should provide them with time and access to humanistic content. Given such a conclusion, it behooves school administrators to get some sense of the quality and quantity of the opportunities for learning that students are afforded. One ought not to assume that English I or that "reading" from 9:15 to 10:30 A.M. implies that material from the humanities will be read or that it will be discussed in the manner alluded to above.

The skills needed to discuss the important ideas found within books, music, and the visual arts and the ability to analyze such works can be developed by teachers who themselves know how to lead such discussions and to critique relevant humanistic work. Yet, on the whole such skills are rare for reasons related to the ones I described earlier. These reasons relate to our antipathy toward discussion and critical analysis in schools; it simply is not a salient feature of what children or teachers do there. The primacy of achievement over inquiry is not new. Thelen wrote about it over two decades ago.[12] Unfortunately, things have not changed. As long as one is centered upon reaching fixed goals in a systematic way, the quality of the journey and the uncertain destination that genuine inquiry often creates are bound to suffer.

But school climate and the general expectations affecting the teacher—expectations of students, administrators, and parents—are not the only reasons why the kind of critical discussion on topics that pervade humanistic subject matter, or subject matters that are humanistically treated, is not characteristic of school classrooms. Teachers themselves are seldom taught how to lead discussions, how to dissect and help students analyze issues, how to penetrate the surface features of argument and to locate the author's starting point. It might seem remarkable, but few teacher training programs provide courses, or even significant sections of courses, on the conduct of class discussions. The difference between open and closed questions, the uses of probes, the application of skills needed to draw out students, or to elicit alternative views on the same issue are virtually absent in the repertoire of skills prospective teachers are asked to develop. The reasons for such neglect are obvious: such skills are not considered important because such processes are not considered important within the classroom. Indeed, in the past two decades the apotheosis of pedagogical virtue has been and still is something called individualized instruction. The educational ideal is a single track for each student who works in his own lockstep fashion by himself until he reaches an objective set by someone else. These locksteps are often color-coded so that the child can see the progress he has made and can compare his progress to others. The ideas that students can actually face each other and discuss what they had read, seen, or heard simply has no saliency in contemporary images of good educational practice. "Individualize" has come to mean "alone."

I hope it is clear from the foregoing how intimately related are the curricular and the pedagogical: what one teaches cannot be easily separated from how one teaches. This lesson was first taught to us by artists; form *is* content.

But before we leave the curricular and the pedagogical, I believe it is important for the reader not to come away with the conclusion that the content of the humanities is simply the classical disciplines or the great humanistic works. I believe that the contemporary world that students inhabit provides an enormously rich source of material for humanistic inquiry. I speak here of television, the mass-printed media, the architecture of shopping centers and local communities, the advertising that surrounds virtually all Americans. These sources, sources that have been called the vernacular arts, provide much in the way of issues, ideas, and themes that can be related directly to the kind of life human beings lead, to the forces and factors that influence their lives, and to the values that these sources reflect, engender, and reward. There is much to be learned from the very material that artists and writers have used as substance for their own work. There is no good educational reason why the study of contemporary life should not be used to develop the kind of skills and insights that one seeks in humanistic learning.

THE COMPETENCY OF THE TEACHER

The features of schooling needing attention if the humanities are to thrive include the competencies the teacher brings to teaching. As I have already indicated, the curricular and pedagogical are not easily separated. How one teaches colors what one teaches; indeed, the messages that students secure from teachers often have more to do with how teachers go about their tasks than what precisely it is that they are teaching. Consider for a moment the fact that teachers who care deeply about their subject matter and who express that caring to students are likely to generate a level of interest in that subject than can be secured in few other ways. The teacher who is genuinely excited by the ideas he or she treats in class, who does not feign enthusiasm, tells students indirectly that there is something here in this field that is worth knowing.

The difficulty, of course, that one encounters with teacher enthusiasm and commitment as valuable pedagogical traits is that these traits are extremely difficult to engender in teacher training programs. This does not diminish their significance; it simply diminishes the possibility of developing them in programs that prepare teachers.

The type of skills—rather than traits—that can be developed that are relevant to humanistic learning in schools focuses upon the ability of teachers to analyze materials that are read, seen, or heard with respect to themes and issues that are significant but subtle. The skills of interpretation, the ability to employ metaphor in the explication of text and image, the skills needed to elucidate relationships between particular humanistic works and, say, the historical context in which the work was created, are skills that should be secured during the course of a university liberal education. It should be remembered that the amount of time prospective teachers study within departments and schools of education prior to professional certification is very small—on the order of 15 percent of their courses taken are in education. In any case, the skills I am describing as relevant to humanities are best exemplified, practiced, and developed within history, literature, art, and other such courses. Helping students understand, for example, the historical context within which scientific discovery occurs is or should be a concern of departments of science. Put in more general terms, to teach the humanities well requires an undergraduate education in which the kinds of intellectual processes relevant to humanistic learning are cultivated. These processes are, in my view, best developed by faculties outside of schools and departments of education. It is not likely that professors of education will be able to develop skills that have been neglected in 85 percent of the undergraduate courses in which prospective teachers have been enrolled.

The implication of the foregoing is that without the support of the university faculty as a whole, it is unlikely that subjects will be studied by elementary and secondary school students in ways that make them humanistic in character. How teaching and learning take place in the college curriculum needs attention. Whether faculties outside of education will be willing to examine their own courses with respect to the manner in which they are taught remains to be seen. Since on many university campuses the department or school of education has low status, it might very well be the case that change must start elsewhere. The office of the president of the university is often a good place to begin.[13]

USING EVALUATION APPROPRIATELY

Another area that needs attention in schools if humanistic learning is to be cultivated, deals with the ways in which students are evaluated. In standard curriculum theories, evaluation procedures are to follow from the objectives that have been formulated for the curriculum. Evaluation is the means through which one determines if the objectives that have been set are achieved. This approach to evaluation is, of course, the standard means-ends model of curriculum planning: one first formulates ends, then implements means to achieve those ends, and finally evaluates to determine if the ends have been achieved.

In the real world, however, it is often the evaluation method that determines which ends students will pay attention to. Students can afford to neglect lofty goal statements, but they cannot afford to neglect the ways in which they will be evaluated. When evaluation procedures reward forms of study that contradict what the humanities prize—the ability to make rational judgments, the ability to critique incisively, the ability to see things in context, the ability to recognize and appreciate nuance, and so forth—such procedures diminish humanistic learning. When evaluation procedures give students the idea that meaningful humanistic learning consists of remembering bits and pieces of disconnected information in order to meet the demands of those who write test items, the evaluation interferes with what the humanities have to contribute to students. Unfortunately, much of testing has such consequences. To ameliorate our discomfort with subjectivity, we employ assessment methods that are characterized by precision, certainty, and attention to fragmented content.

On the positive side, we need to create evaluation tasks that do ask students to recognize and appreciate nuance, that ask them to evaluate relationships within and between the fields they study, that ask them to use their own subjectivity to interpret the material they read, see, and hear. In short, we need to move in a direction that is virtually 180 degrees away from the direction in which evaluation in the schools has been moving during the past decade.

Alas, it is much easier to describe our educational needs than to meet them through planned educational change. The schools are fettered to a social ecology that supports their existing practices. When those practices are antithetical to the humanities, the future of the humanities in the schools cannot look promising. Yet some goals are worth fighting for even when the odds of winning are small. Surely the contribution the humanities might make to the education of the young is one of them.

Footnotes

1. Commission on the Humanities, *The Humanities in American Life: Report of the Commission on the Humanities* (Berkeley: University of California Press, 1980).

2. Ibid., p. 3.

3. When Aristotle wrote his *Ethics* he said: "Our discussion will be adequate if it has as much clearness as the subject matter admits of, for precision is not to be sought for alike in all discussions, any more than in all the products of the crafts . . . for it is the mark of an educated man to look for precision in each class of things just so far as the nature of the subject admits; it is evidently equally foolish to accept probable reasoning

from a mathematician and to demand from a rhetorician scientific proofs." Aristotle, *Nicomachean Ethics*, Book I, Part III.

4. For a lucid discussion of the context of scientific discovery, see Arthur Koestler, *The Act of Creation* (New York: Macmillan, 1964).

5. For a discussion of the human drama surrounding the discovery of DNA, see James D. Watson, *The Double Helix* (New York: Atheneum, 1968).

6. Commission on the Humanities, *The Humanities in American Life*, p. 2.

7. For many in American culture, artistic productivity is the offspring of talent, not intelligence. It is illuminating to note what John Dewey had to say about this issue as far back as 1934. See John Dewey, *Art as Experience* (New York: G. P. Putnam's Sons, 1934, reprinted 1958), p. 46, and Elliot W. Eisner, *Cognition and Curriculum: A Basis for Deciding What to Teach* (New York: Longman, 1982).

8. For example, see Samuel Bowles and Herbert Gintis, *Schooling in Capitalist America* (New York: Basic Books, 1976).

9. Johnan Galtung, "On Peace Education," in *Handbook on Peace Education*, ed. Christopher Wolf (Frankfurt am Main: International Peace Research Association, 1974).

10. Phillip C. Schlechty and Victor S. Nance, "Do Academically Able Teachers Leave Education? The North Carolina Case," *Phi Delta Kappan* 63 (October 1981): 106-112.

11. For a review of research on time on task, see Barak V. Rosenshine, "Content, Time, and Direct Instruction," in *Research on Teaching: Concepts, Findings, and Implications*, ed. Penelope L. Peterson and Herbert J. Walberg (Berkeley, Calif.: McCutchan Publishing Corp., 1979), pp. 26-56.

12. Herbert A. Thelen, *Education and the Human Quest* (New York: Harper, 1960).

13. I am pleased to say that at Stanford University, President Donald Kennedy has led the way to engage faculty in the systematic study of education at the secondary school level. Such engagement could have a ripple effect with respect to the analysis of pedagogical activity within the University. In addition, at Stanford there is a center for faculty opportunities to make video tapes of faculty teaching.

Part Three
HUMANITIES IN SCHOOL PROGRAMS

CHAPTER VIII

The Humanities and the Summoning Reader

BENJAMIN DEMOTT

My thinking about the role of the humanities in secondary schools focuses on the teaching of literature, and can be summarized, in credo form, as follows:

1. I believe that the proper goal for introductory humanities/literature teaching is the development and refinement of the constructive imagination.

2. I believe that the soundness of this goal flows partly from the special character of literature itself, partly from our nature as knowers—our manner of arriving at understanding of the *x* we call the world. "We animate what we see," said Emerson; "we see only what we animate." Whether concentrating on a scene of a Shakespeare play or on a hummingbird above a geranium pot or on a political debate or on a mechanic replacing a tailpipe or on a pianist committing two-handed octave thunder at the climax of a concerto, we attend feelingly and comprehendingly only if we bring off the necessary deeds of animation. Texts *or* events become appreciable when awakened to life in time: when they are drawn near, that is, registered as moment-to-moment continuums of action and response. And the quality of the human performance in summoning-to-life depends on the subtlety and force of the individual constructive imagination.

3. I believe that the humanities/literature classroom is a uniquely favorable environment in which to practice the arts of animating, the skills of summoning-to-life. Granted, the classroom is merely one of numberless settings in which deeds of animation can occur. Survival for our kind requires frequent movement, in a variety of circumstances, from states of self-enclosure to states of recognition and engagement.

But in the humanities/literature classroom the movement in question is disciplined. A standard of relevant imagining can be maintained. The texts with which the student collaborates—words in their order on the page—can be shown to repay responsible witness. Membership in the classroom community carries with it the expectation that summonings and imaginings will be turned out for public assessment. Students are free both to criticize each other's deeds of animation and to borrow from them. And they are aided by the example of a teacher—a more or less experienced and knowledgeable elder whose performance as animator can be imitated.

4. I believe that, although risks are run when the classroom work described as summoning, constructing, evoking, or animating is separated from other readerly functions, such a separation is necessary. As students advance they can be introduced to the general ecology of imagining—the network of relationships (moral, political, historical, semantic, aesthetic) in which every act of evocation is necessarily embedded. But it is wise, initially, to keep to the center and avoid the margins. Concern with literary conventions, the history of language, stylistic comparison and evaluation, biographical or theoretical problems leads to evasion of the first obligation of teacher and learner, that of developing and refining the constructive imagination.

5. I believe that a flexible concept of texts is appropriate in the humanities/literature classroom. That classroom is busy chiefly with the close imagining of texts as the latter term is commonly understood; from day to day teacher and student work at strengthening awareness of the actions (rational, intuitive, sympathetic) by which summoners create experience in time from black parts on printed pages. "A poem is an act; you have to get into the act." But learning to animate-in-order-to-see means learning to see oneself as animator across the board, as a person essential not alone to the act of reading stories and poems but to the act of reading any experience. It is no mistake, therefore, to widen the angle of vision occasionally for the purpose of noticing the broader implications of the venture of imaginative summoning. One of those implications is that time unimagined equals time relatively blank; another is that truisms and clichés about life being what one makes it, carry a substantial core of meaning. The matter treated in the humanities/literature classroom cannot be, from hour to hour, life in the large. But when the work of animating goes forward

well, it is instructive about the limits and possibilities of the summoning self both in the interpretation of texts and in the shaping of individual lives. Precisely here resides the moral significance of the enterprise.

Spelling out one's credo in this fashion is embarrassing on several counts, not the least of which is that one is obliged to acknowledge that the beliefs are a shade idiosyncratic—not universally shared by fellow professionals. I am conscious, of course, that many teachers tend, out of defensiveness or vanity, to exaggerate the uniqueness or originality of their approach. And I am also conscious that a good many activities regularly undertaken by literature teachers clearly deserve consideration as means of "developing and refining the constructive imagination." Most literature teachers undertake to read texts aloud, expressively. Many teachers seek to help students visualize notable characters—Falstaff, Micawber, Ahab, the Wife of Bath, and so on. Furthermore, one recent and widely circulated commentary on the teaching of the humanities—the Rockefeller Commission report—spoke up without repugnance for the "time-honored" activity of "identifying." It would be worse than idiosyncratic, in short, to argue that the profession of literature teaching has firmly and explicitly taken a position against the beliefs I set forth above as my own.

Still, I have to record that my experience as an observer of introductory teaching of literature, and as a reader of the examination questions for beginning students that are set by a number of prestigious institutions, leads me to doubt that the goal of educating the imagination currently commands high regard. Frequently the determination to strengthen humanities curricula in secondary schools leads to the offering of courses entitled "World Masterpieces" or "The History of English Literature from the Beginnings to 1900"; usually these courses take shape as transmissions, by the teacher, of bodies of presumed "objective knowledge." (In this respect they resemble many undergraduate introductions to literature.) At the end of term, pupils possess a notebook filled with snippets from the teacher's discourse on the backgrounds of our language, the life of the Venerable Bede, medieval mysticism, courtly love and romance, the Wars of the Roses, scansion and verse form, the Anglican Settlement and the Puritan Revolution, metaphysical and cavalier poetry, the life of

John Milton, and differences between neoclassicism and romanticism. The pupils may also have discharged their duty to memorize a sonnet and the succession of English monarchs. Typically they will have had no practice in close imagining.

Nor will their official examiners, preoccupied with problems of placement, expect them to evidence ability in this area. Examination questions center on style, genre ("Prove whether the play is a comedy"), the meaning of value terms ("Define the terms 'truth' and 'ideal' from Ibsen's perspective"), differences and resemblances between two or more writers, grounds for approving or rejecting this or that critical perspective ("Was Germaine Greer correct in saying that G.B. Shaw failed to grasp the mettle of women's rights and role with any genuine insight or conviction?").

My purpose is not to introduce a note of bad-tempered complaint about present practices into a treatise meant to point in positive directions for the future. I wish simply to make clear that my beliefs about the role of the humanities in the secondary school cannot qualify as representative of the existing consensus. Tolerance is often expressed for the posing of questions about the operations of the imagination as it lives in its collaborative partnership with individual texts. But the standard classroom emphasis falls elsewhere—on the study of literature as a body of objective knowledge or upon the mastery of certain aesthetic, moral, social, or historical vocabularies. I have argued elsewhere, at length, against this emphasis, continue to press for change, and expect that change will come.[1] But the pace is slow and just at the moment there is no general assent to the case I argue, namely that literary training is essential in the secondary schools because it aids in the development of individual powers of summoning and animating the experience of others.

One further embarrassment deserves mention: that arising from the impossibility of including, as part of an article addressed to a general audience, a description of the particulars of the approach to the humanities/literature classroom in which I believe. After thirty-two years of teaching I find myself decreasingly patient with discourse about aims and goals and increasingly eager for details of on-the-line practice—notes on class preparation, on questions worth setting, on answers received, on accounts of the actual sound of classroom hours conducted in accordance with an individual teacher's sense of priorities. But policy planners, administrators, and parents have needs and interests that are not well served by such detail. In an Appendix below I offer a miscellany of such matter—teaching "stuff" that might figure in a portion of a class dealing with a moment in Shakespeare's *Macbeth*: the moment in Act I, Scene iii at which Banquo and Macbeth, returning from battle, come upon the Weird Sisters. Readers who have a Shakespeare handy need only refresh their memory of the first few pages of the play to put themselves in position to deal with this Appendix, and it is conceivable that working through that informal monologue may add concreteness and immediacy to the foregoing abstract statement of beliefs.

But the gist of my argument should be visible even without this exercise. As is doubtless evident, not every statement I have read about the value of the humanities in secondary schools makes complete sense to me. Lovers of literature seem sometimes to speak as though ignorance of Shakespeare or of whatever poet happens to be in fashion were proof of bad manners. (Nice people do not eat with their fingers; nice people have read Keats's Odes.) Lovers of poetry and fiction also speak on occasion as though people should be acquainted with great works of imaginative writing solely for the direct experience of beauty that they provide. And there are enthusiasts who locate the significance of literature for secondary students solely in the ethical lessons it teaches, whether explicitly or obliquely.

It is easy to agree that experience of beauty is invaluable, and that many works of literary art are repositories of truth, noble, practical, disconcerting. And, although the idea that it is a sign of breeding to have read the great writers is offensive, it is plain that the reading of imaginative writing does have a significant social dimension. For generations Jane Austen and Charles Dickens, Chekhov and Wordsworth, Cervantes and Moliere—scores of others—have lived in the minds of intelligent men and women, and held a place in their conversation. One way of connecting our students with the humanity preceding their own, thereby clarifying both their personal location and their identity, is by helping them to know not just the news of the present age, but a portion of what earlier ages regarded as interesting and ponderable. At the level of dress codes and the like, keeping up tradition can be pointless, but knowing what the smart people of an earlier time considered to be worth remembering makes obvious sense.

But in my view the heart of the case for the humanities/literature classroom does rest in the end on the uses of an educated imagination. Adeptness at bringing experience to life, shrewdness at speculating about what is taking place from moment to moment in other creatures, responsiveness to imagined feelings, thoughts, reactions—these are qualities without which most days of most lives are empty. The state of development of our gifts in these areas affects every mode of our behavior—our tastes, ambitions, ability to care about the spectrum of human life from sports to politics, our capacity for learning to love, our readiness to provide leadership and to accept it, our very power to perceive. The great words bear repeating: "We animate what we see; we see only what we animate."

Appendix

Assignment. Read the first act of *Macbeth.* We'll focus on Scene iii, lines 39-47 and 51-61, Macbeth and Banquo encountering the witches. Spend some time over this. You're trying to work up the moment, build up its insides. You're getting into phase with what's happening. Make notes on the thoughts and feelings you sense through the language—whatever's of help in enabling you to grasp how the moment goes for either man: where they are for each other, what they are to themselves. We'll be working through the moment step by step together as we usually do. Let's see some intensity in imagining this time. *Bear down.*

Class preparation for teacher (first stage). The aim is to light the chosen moment in such a way as to make clear the elements that have to figure in any full imagining of the ongoing currents of thought and feeling. "Elements" here include physical movements and gestures, tones of speech, contrasts of tones. Once the class hour is in motion a good deal of dreck will be in the atmosphere. The teacher needs a structure to hang on to and the best way to provide it is by starting with a handy list of key elements for full imagining. Call them The Basics. When one has them clearly in mind one feels confident—and the confidence is the shaping resource for the class hour; it communicates—even in the midst of the necessary passages of wandering and chaos—that a clear, doable job of work is in progress.

Key elements for close imaginings here include:

1) Macbeth's silence, Banquo's quickness of speech.
2) Macbeth's motionlessness, Banquo's movement (shifts toward and away from Macbeth, toward and away from the witches).
3) Banquo's characteristic activities of mind (observing, questioning, classifying, sifting evidence, publicly reporting conclusions).
4) Macbeth's heedlessness of Banquo's questions, deductions, explications.
5) Banquo's comparative inattention—at first—to his comrade's absorption.

Class preparation for the teacher (second stage, deeper into the marrow). One has in mind helping students to summon—in the course of a quarter hour or so—two different kinds of consciousness, two different habitations of time, two different modes of responsiveness to life. Some in the room will make it, some won't. But, when preparing, teachers need to be clear about their highest objectives. Therefore:

It's not wholly accurate to speak of the differences between Macbeth and Banquo as absolute but they surely are real differences. One can say, on the basis of his speech, that Banquo is the kind of man who, when presented with the unknown, is immediately eager to share his puzzlement and curious about the best means of resolving it. For him the unfamiliar *x* presented to the senses becomes, quite quickly, a problem to be framed into publicly utterable questions:

Banquo. How far is 't called to Forres? What are these,
So withered and so wild in their attire
That look not like th' inhabitants o' th' earth
And yet are on 't? Live you, or are you aught
That man may question? You seem to understand me,
By each at once her choppy finger laying
Upon her skinny lips. You should be women,
And yet your beards forbid me to interpret
That you are so.

Can the witches understand human speech? Are they male or

female? The act of asking such questions lends a sense of manageability to the ongoing experience, fitting it to familiar rhythms of anticipation and recognition, proposing and disposing. Banquo is surprised, excited, interested, wary; his surprise and interest are those of a social, commonsensical human being—a creature relatively unacquainted with doubt about customary explanations and evaluations of events and persons, disinclined to raise to himself the possibility that received versions of good, evil, God, man, authority, and rebellion are so much rubbish. Time cannot stop for such a sensibility; the abyss does not open; the briefly tensed frame of this body soon enough resumes its normal condition, its habitually relaxed decency, its expectation that life generally will be pleasing. (One second before he's struck down, later in the play, Banquo passes a completely civil, easygoing, clubable word concerning the weather to the barbarous hit men about to murder him.) Banquo is not a fool, not beamish—but he is a human being who finds the world comprehensible on the usually given terms; exceptions *prove* rules to this mind, they don't overturn them, and the job of the intelligence, as this mind conceives it, is that of seeing into the way in which apparent inexplicables—such as the Sisters—can be folded understandingly into the system; in this case, as creatures who do or don't possess gender, do or don't understand human speech, etc.

While teachers prepare this class they may remember that Shakespeare had a certain condescending relish of minds for whom the standard experience of life is that of confirmation—people who move with wonderful ease from being startled to being in possession of The Answers. (Horatio, for instance, resuming his self-confidence—"so have I seen and do in part believe it"—after the momentarily disarraying sight of the Ghost in *Hamlet*.)

Obviously Macbeth's is a different consciousness and his habitation of time at the moment is quite unlike that of his companion. The accidental and strange—the unknown—*erupt* and hold him fast. His inner being is shaken and the sense of succession, one moment following on from a known *before* to a predictable *after*, is gone. There is the physical stress of concentrated attention—a blotting out of sensation, and the moment possesses intensity greater by far for this mind than for Banquo's. Speech, sequence, capacity for analysis—all are graveled, blocked. The moment is an echo, perhaps, a recurrence of an intimation—and the content it carries is inexpressible, something like: *The world is not what it seems, cannot be understood in smooth sequences, in managed and ordered cycles of time, does not conform to our specifications, will not confirm our "truth."* Ordinarily Macbeth's consciousness isn't pitched so high, but this matters less than that it is *capable* of being pitched high. We say about such a consciousness that it's imaginative, meaning that it has the power to bring to life, to make present, what is absent or invisible. It has the capacity to believe that what is not believed by others may yet be believable, or at least worthy of consideration. Its excitement is profound because it senses the possibility that a rule of large provenance may dwell in the strange and the exceptional.

In a measure this quality of consciousness can be described as an "aptitude." Something akin to a gift for music—or for sport—or even for faith itself. But while the aptitude is in some sense natural, it has experienced cultivation. Macbeth's capacity to be a nondismissive, nonreductive witness of the strange stems in part from his knowledge that the outrageous thought and forbidden feeling that visit him visit elsewhere as well. They are familiar to at least one other soul—the soul who happens to be closer to him than anyone on earth. Moreover, forbidden thoughts are not only, to Macbeth's knowledge, familiar to Lady Macbeth; they are dealt with by her welcomingly, unashamedly, as though this strangeness—their unwontedness—were itself worth but a shrug. Macbeth and his Lady have spoken together of the unthinkable. They have faced the truth of their mutual ambition with trust that neither would perceive that inexpressible yearning as evidence of madness, as ground for suicide, or as so immediately hateful as to provoke shock. The world says that to covet what cannot be won except through an act of hideous brutality is to behave unpardonably. Yet Macbeth knows that he and his Lady have exchanged intimations of their covetousness and have not been struck dead—have not even been revulsed by each other, have in truth drawn closer to each other through implicit experiment with the unthinkable.

Not so Banquo. He has had no occasion to live in tolerant adjacency to thoughts against which the whole weight of custom, country, society, church, and history is counterpoised. He has known no companion of heart whose readiness to consider the unthinkable works to confirm the suggestion that unthinkableness itself is only a convention of the fainthearted—an inert politeness passing itself off as law when what it more closely resembles is a tic. In Banquo's world no evidence exists proving that the common arrangements and hierarchies of value are arbitrary and weightless; in Macbeth's world such evidence is met with every day, in the image of his own ambitions that is reflected in his wife's gaze. The profoundly disordered therefore grips him as an emblem of what may truly be the substance of Out There, the lesson lying at the world's heart. The "weirdness" perceived by Banquo is, for him, at once more and less than weird. The witches cannot be dealt with, then, as objects to be classified and thereafter back-burnered. They are seizing embodiments of the possible truth of a wild intuition.

Well, all this rambling rumination need have no place in class. A summary analysis of differences of consciousness is hardly to be presented, or treated as material upon which notes should be taken. The use of such reflection is simply to remind oneself of the larger frame into which a full imagining of the present moment may ultimately be fitted. Keeping it in mind, together with the "elements" just specified, may aid in the framing of questions that initiate imaginative movement in class.

Questions in class. The standard question is: What's going on here? What's taking place at this moment in these human creatures? What is the content of their thought and feeling? When you speak as fully and directly as you can from the center of being that's called Macbeth or Banquo, what exactly do you say?

The sound of the classroom. The teacher, to repeat, pushes away summary interpretations on which essays concerning the meaning of *Macbeth* would be founded. The job is to intensify concentration on the conditions of feeling—the existent innerness—at this humanly interesting moment. Classroom talk is absorbed in particulars. A few words at the start about the two military men returning from a successful battle, weary, wishing the journey done, bored, impatient. (How much farther? How much longer?) After that, the first limbering up queries—set forth lightly. (Not in this class, after all, will we be probing feelings with any hint of the depth, say, of those shared by Macbeth and his Lady in the seconds following the murder.) Lightly the teacher asks about white space. What happens in the white space between "Forres" and "What?" Exactly, the witches are espied. The two men are surprised? Surely. Mysterious hags, sudden apparitions—

or are they apparitions, who knows? What is Banquo's response? What does he do first? When he spies them what's the first movement of his mind, do you think? What does he do mentally? Comes up with a question, good. Right. What is that over there?—that sort of question. He does this how and why? Sees something odd and it occurs to him right away to ask what it is . . . Yes, but who does he ask? What are the possibilities? He can ask the witches. Or Macbeth. Or himself. When you decide to ask your friend, you're in effect saying, "You see what I see? Am I imagining things?" You're conscious of the witches and of yourself and of your friend and it's to your friend you turn. "What are these? . . . wild in their attire . . ." Banquo is dealing with the witches immediately in the third person, what does that signify? Right, they can be talked about. Let's see what we think here. When you speak this way are you scared? No, I agree, not scared. I'd go with that—not certainly in terror. Not so absorbed that you can't say, Hey, what *is* that over there?

Let's get on to the bodies for a minute. Where do you want your actors to look? Eye movement. How should they address the witches? Banquo puts his first question to Macbeth (. . . yet are on it?) Gets no answer. What's he do then? Check: turns back to the witches (Live you?) Maybe . . .? Right, a glance back at Macbeth—the syntax indicates that, doesn't it, "by each at once." Turns are built right into the grammar. The sentence starts with direct address to "you," then shifts to speaking of the witches in the third person, and at the end Banquo is back at the witches a third or fourth time. How come it goes that way? Right: no answer from his friend so how else could it go?

Now another thing. Who's caught up more intently, would you say? Banquo wants to talk about what he sees, wants to ask questions, place it, exchange ideas . . . But how do we imagine Macbeth at this moment? Doesn't say a thing, right. *Hears* nothing? What makes you say that? I agree, but how come? How *can* he not hear his friend asking questions? Standing too far away? Maybe, maybe . . . Yes, he does find his voice after a minute (Speak if you can—) . . . But the minute he hears the prophecy what happens? Back into the prison, right, I agree. Beyond Banquo's reach. So what's Banquo do? He says, "Good sir, why do you . . . fear / Things that do sound so fair?" —And then? Right, no answer. *Riveted*: You're absolutely right. Riveted's the word. Riveted and there's nothing for it except for Banquo to turn away and go back to the witches once more. Now he's almost talking to them as though to friends, not wholly serious—right—he almost has a joke with himself, you're right. Pretending, complaining . . . Why am *I* left out of this prophecy game?

> *Banquo.* Good sir, why do you start, and seem to fear
> Things that do sound so fair?—I' th' name of truth,
> Are ye fantastical, or that indeed
> Which outwardly ye show? My noble partner
> You greet with present grace, and great prediction
> Of noble having and of royal hope,
> That he seems rapt withal; to me you speak not.
> If you can look into the seeds of time,
> And say which grain will grow, and which will not,
> Speak then to me, who neither beg nor fear
> Your favors nor your hate.

Something like that, for openers. We are working toward a sense of the insidedness of two figures, working for five or ten minutes, maybe, at describing differences in class in the way two men of different nature hold themselves physically, mentally, emotionally. We're taking first steps, reminding ourselves what it is like to be an imagining active reader—one who holds alive a sense of the difference between reactions simultaneously presented *and* a sense of the potential usefulness of such a difference as a guide to the nature of the persons before us. The problems for the engaged imagination here are far simpler than those met in the moments of the play that call up the full energies of realization and evocation:

> A foolish thought to say a sorry sight (II, ii, 19)

> think of this, good peers,
> As but a thing of custom (III, iv, 95-6)

> I would not have such a heart in my bosom for
> the dignity of the whole body (V, ii, 55)

The questions concerning us here don't lead on into depths of moral exhaustion, fear, horror, complexly commingled repugnance and pity. Nor does the moment require anything comparable to the extraordinary imaginative agility that's needed by the reader who evokes the great opening scene of *King Lear* or the second scene of *Hamlet*. The requirement at these moments is for universality of comprehension; the good reader's mind and feelings teem with the pressure of fully realized mentalities sealed into their uniquely configured and conflicting assumptions, each hearing and reading every separate inflection and movement of eye in accordance with his/her individual will.

We know better as teachers than to assume, as a result of this or any other opening wedge into the act of imagining Macbeth, that our students will henceforth be in firm command. The ability to "do" even a simple moment comes slowly; the capacity to meet the major challenges—to hold intact simultaneously the separate consciousnesses of Lear, Kent, Cordelia, Goneril and Regan—or of Claudius, Gertrude, Laertes, Polonius and Hamlet—comes only with some years of practice. The point is merely that we're into the work, into the project of showing forth what the constructive imagination does, what kind of competency we're looking toward. We're edging forward out of passivity toward a glimpse of the truth that "reading" has to do fundamentally with the bringing to life of other minds occupying their felt moments of being.

We could of course begin elsewhere—with a Blake song, or with Emily Dickinson's "I heard a fly buzz—" or with George Herbert's "The Collar" or with Flannery O'Connor's "A Good Man Is Hard to Find".

But as it happens *Macbeth* is our text for today. So let's move along now a page or so, try thinking our way into the King for a bit. That's right, Duncan. Here he is with Banquo close on to Macbeth's castle, talking about the air around the place, liking what he sees:

> *King.* This castle hath a pleasant seat. The air
> Nimbly and sweetly recommends itself
> Unto our gentle senses.

What kind of man is Duncan? With what feelings does he approach his host's house? What would it be like to know that one had murdered such a human being as this?

Let us go on.

FOOTNOTE

1. A book length presentation of the case for change, *The Summoning Reader*, will be published in 1984 by St. Martin's Press.

CHAPTER IX

The Paideia Proposal *and American Education*

EDWIN J. DELATTRE

The recent publication of *The Paideia Proposal*[1] by Mortimer Adler and several colleagues has stirred controversy, as might be expected. Unfortunately, the controversy is less than instructive. We must go beyond it in order to get down to the business of improving American precollegiate education.

The controversy is contrived because critics of the *Proposal* indict it for not answering essential questions which it elected not even to ask about implementing reforms in schooling. Then, oddly enough, the very same critics insist that those questions cannot, in any case, be answered. The first claim misses two main points. They are: (a) that the purpose of the *Proposal* is to describe a realizable, nonutopian, educational ideal, and (b) that it now falls to all of us who know what is possible in teaching and learning to offer specific means of approaching that ideal. The second claim leaves the impression that just because particular critics do not know how the prescriptions of the *Proposal* can be brought to life in practice, nobody knows. This impression is false and wasteful. In this chapter I propose to describe the utility of *The Paideia Proposal* and the methods, particularly for in-service teacher education, which can make this utility most evident.

Professor Hugh Kenner's article, "Please Welcome My Next Idea," is typically critical. He asks,

> What utility, for that matter, have the prescriptions of Adler's other 1982 offering, *The Paideia Proposal*? One more high-minded committee job, it prescribes for the desperate state of American education, grades one through twelve, in terms as difficult to disagree with as they seem impossible to implement. ... Save for one gritty specific—all electives should be abolished ... not a thing in the *Proposal's* eighty-four earnest pages will disquiet any school

administrator. Most will purr, isn't that what I've always said we were doing? . . . It is even safe to pretend that the *Proposal* can help to change a bad world ("truly a manifesto," coos Ruth Love), safe because its potential for igniting anything is slight, educators having coopted its jargon long ago.[2]

Kenner's question about utility is rhetorical; his position is something like "*The Paideia Proposal* is as American as apple pie; but we can't bake an apple pie, because we have no apples. And the *Proposal* is trivial because its sound argument has been trivialized into mere educationist jargon."

Let us try here to take his question more seriously than he does, to treat it as genuine and important rather than as rhetorical and pointless. Let us try to take advantage of this moment's chance to show how to snatch the language back from those in whose mouths it is mere jargon, and offer specific steps for approximating the ideals of the *Proposal* which are well within the present-day capacity of American schools. Let us see whether American education "has the apples to bake this pie."

Among the central claims and prescriptions of *The Paideia Proposal* are these:

1. Universal education and universal suffrage are inseparable.

2. Schooling must prepare all young people for continuation of learning in adult life, during their working years and beyond.

3. It must therefore impart to them skills of learning and give to them the stimulation that will motivate them to keep their minds actively engaged in learning.

4. To impart these skills, education for all (grades one through twelve) must be general and liberal, not specialized or occupational.

5. Schooling must, accordingly, concentrate on three primary modes of teaching and learning for all students:

a. Acquisition of organized knowledge through instruction based on lectures and textbooks in languages, literature, fine arts; mathematics and natural sciences; and history, geography, and social studies.

b. Development of skills of learning based on coached exercises and supervised practice in reading, writing, speaking, listening, calculating, observing, measuring, estimating, and assessing critically.

c. Enlargement of ideas and ideals through Socratic questioning and active discussion of books (not textbooks but seminal books), and works of art; and active participation in music, drama, and the visual arts.

6. To these primary features of schooling should be added physical education and studies of the world of work (not merely of jobs, but of work).[3]

The authors of the *Proposal* assert that there is one major obstacle to implementation of its prescriptions. None of the critics dissents from this observation: "The present teacher-training programs turn out persons who are not sufficiently equipped with the knowledge, the intellectual skills, or the developed understanding needed to guide and help the young in the course of study we have recommended." (p. 60)

Of course, it is clear that not all school teachers are the products of teacher-training programs, and not all who are, are educationally limited to what they have learned in them. The issue here is whether colleges of education can be expected to combat their present limits in the foreseeable future. It is not whether there are, in fact, many wonderful and exemplary teachers in American schools.

The initial questions about implementation, then, are whether very much can be done to overcome these limits to the preservice education (training) of teachers in colleges of education, and whether any possible change at that level would by itself equip school teachers to learn and to teach in the terms of the *Proposal*.

It seems unlikely that the curricula of colleges of education are susceptible to short-term change, and equally unlikely that standards for public school teacher certification set by the various states can be easily altered. The curricula and the certification standards are tied to vested interests of faculty departments within the colleges, departments which are not themselves devoted to the study and practice of the liberal arts, including mathematics and the natural sciences, or the fine arts. The departments are instead geared to the study of teaching about these subjects and to designing curricula for school children and adolescents.

Given this history of deemphasis of the study and practice of the scholarly and scientific disciplines, for colleges of education to prepare prospective teachers to lecture well, with substance as well as style; to write well; to assess arguments with depth and penetration; to engage in Socratic dialogue with the clarity, consistency, irony, self-control, tirelessness, and eloquence it requires; to read seminal books with contemplative power; and to reflect knowledgeably on works in the fine arts—all this would require a near total overhaul of much of their present enterprise. The point is simple: Colleges of education emphasize being a teacher. They do not sufficiently emphasize becoming or being a learner, a practitioner of the subjects one teaches. *The Paideia Proposal*, to the contrary, insists that in order to teach well, in order to motivate students, one must be an advanced learner in the presence of the young and therefore a practitioner of what one teaches.

Until colleges of education transform their vision of teachers, and of teaching itself, the preservice training of prospective teachers will not change. There are, of course, some faculty members and administrators in colleges of education who have this vision and may succeed in leading the way. There may come to be progressive infiltration of colleges of education by practitioners of the arts and sciences, and there may even be the possibility of cooperation between colleges of education and colleges of arts and sciences. But these are not immediate prospects from which we can draw significant encouragement or hope.

Perhaps more important, even if the colleges could change, even if they wanted to change, they could not insure that teachers would for their lifetimes be practitioners of the arts of inquiry and discovery, insure that the teachers would be lifetime learners. For these, more than preservice training and education are required. For these, teachers must come to see themselves as practitioners, as learners. The very best teachers always do that, of course, no matter what their educational backgrounds. The challenge is to find ways to establish this regard for learning on a wide, ideally even universal, scale.

Since contemporary preservice education promises so little toward achievement of these ideals of teaching, the question is whether other means are available. The answer is "Yes." The opportunity to encourage and sustain teachers as practitioners of the arts and sciences rests in the design and support of sound programs of continued education—in-service programs in the schools themselves.

Indeed, the conclusion seems inescapable that if students in our schools are to have widespread opportunities to learn in the company of advanced learners or practitioners, these opportunities must be brought into being by school teachers and administrators themselves, irrespective of the limits of their preservice training. Specifically, they must be made by the work the teachers and administrators do in the interest of their own intellectual maturation while they serve in the schools; that is, they must be made by the in-service programs teachers and administrators build for themselves.

Where, then, can they begin, or continue their venture in active learning? By recognizing that *The Paideia Proposal* emphasizes what we and our children have long been understood to have in common as rational and sensitive learners. The *Proposal* urges a reconstitution of American schooling through teachers who practice the arts of inquiry and discovery for themselves. The *Proposal* therefore has one implication above all for in-service education: *In-service education is first and foremost for the sake of teachers as practitioners of what they teach.* It is not first and foremost for the sake of teachers *as teachers*, for the sake of their teaching skills, or even for the sake of their students, because if these are put first, in-service education is necessarily self-defeating. It is self-defeating because if the teachers neglect themselves *as practitioners*, as advanced learners, they can never become first-rate teachers. *Never.*

If teachers are not respectful of their own learning, for their own sakes as people, if they lack respect for the cultivation of their own minds, they cannot possibly set an honest and motivating example for the young. They cannot, except hypocritically, encourage any student to work at learning.

In view of this fact, it is imperative, right here, to snatch back a bit of the language coopted by educationists and reduced to contentless jargon. Educationists, the teachers of teachers, often invoke Socrates and appeal to his educational ideals and methods, such as dialogue, while at the very same time designing preservice and in-service programs for teachers which ignore their engagement in the arts of learning. Yet Socrates never ignored himself as a philosopher in his dialogues, never engaged in dialogue merely to teach, never treated himself as a mere means to the learning of other people. He understood that without contemplative investment in his own maturation, he was bound to be largely worthless to himself and therefore useless as an exemplar to others. Every educator who ignores these facts has little or no idea what Socrates stood for and, in invoking Socrates, crudely takes his name in vain and degrades being a teacher.

For these reasons, teachers and administrators who design and participate in programs of in-service education must resist the temptations they are constantly taught to succumb to by their preservice training. Of these, the most important is the temptation to ask, not how they can become better learners, more knowledgeable students, more able inquirers and thinkers, but only how they can use this morning's in-service lesson in this afternoon's classes; the temptation to think of truly practical in-service studies as limited to those which are immediately useful with their students. These are temptations to ignore entirely the irreplaceable practicality of teachers becoming progressively powerful learners, temptations to believe that the only investments worth making by teachers in themselves are those which affect their classroom planning in the short-run.

This constant harping on the immediately useful, which is as much a part of every school as the bells that announce the end of classes, and the diminished vision of teachers which inspires shortsightedness, are directly related to the phenomenon known as "teacher burn-out." Teachers burn out, lose interest in teaching, for many specific reasons, such as facing every day droves of unwilling students, working under the shadow of poorly educated administrators, suffering the criticisms of parents who unrealistically expect schools to raise their children, and watching their own financial circumstances deteriorate. And all such considerations take their fullest and most brutal toll when the future promises nothing but more of the same. Surely nothing can make it seem more thoroughly bleak than the prospect of intellectual emptiness of the sort which comes from realizing that one is doing little to advance one's own powers of mind. Exclusive emphasis on the immediately useful, so characteristic of many contemporary preservice and in-service programs for teachers, is, accordingly, the most vicious and destructive feature of American education, not least because the attitude underlying it cannot fail to reach the students and influence them for the worse.

Only when this lesson is learned, that the first goal of all education worthy of the name, and therefore of in-service education, is the improvement of the minds of those who study, will in-service programs that treat teachers as students and practitioners of the arts and the sciences have a chance of success. And only then will the second goal of in-service education be realizable: the improvement of educational opportunities for the students of those teachers.

What, then, might be the model of an excellent in-service program?

Not generally, but specifically, what kinds of form and content must it have? These are the questions which must be answered for any significant portion of *The Paideia Proposal* to be put into practice.

In-service education designed to promote advanced learning among teachers and administrators, and also to bring this learning into play for their students, must be based on a vision of an intellectual community of teachers and administrators. "Intellectual community" means a group of people who think together—not alike, but together, and who do so across subject area barriers. It is a community that avows the importance of mathematics and the sciences as well as literature and sculpture, one which prizes integrity or wholeness of mind. It is united by the highest kind of friendship in the sense that Aristotle meant when he spoke of it as consisting in activities of shared contemplation rather than, as in the case of cattle, eating in the same place. Or in the sense that Socrates had in mind when he explained that participants in dialogue who in cooperation pursue the truth have to be candid, to understand how to inquire reasonably, and must be convinced of their own capacity to err—that is, to be open and intellectually humble with their companions.

Every such intellectual community is brought to life in practice by shared study of works that can be expected to improve the mind. Such shared study provides the common background and knowledge which make pointed discourse possible. This is true of the great historic correspondences such as that of Madison and Jefferson or of Abigail and John Adams, of the scientific and philosophic communities, as well as of all memorable dialogues, of cultural institutions, of family life, and of every educational institution ever to achieve distinction. Thus, in-service programs based on this kind of study are uniquely grounded in the highest traditions of human accomplishment.

But what might this involve in particular settings? Well, suppose that a group of teachers and administrators decides that it is important for them to begin by coming to understand the life of teachers as practitioners. They might start by reading and discussing together Gilbert Highet's *The Art of Teaching*; Moses Hadas's *Old Wine, New Bottles*; Robert Ulich's *Three Thousand Years of Educational Wisdom*, which includes writings by practitioner-teachers such as Augustine, Loyola, and Agassiz. They might consider Plato's *Meno*, where Socrates is at once a practicing philosopher and a teacher of several levels of students, or Aristotle's *Nicomachean Ethics*, especially Books VIII and IX on friendship. In reading and discussing such works, reflecting on them, and (dare one hope) even corresponding about them (imagine what joy to have a *letter* in one's mailbox at school from a colleague, a letter of ideas and questions, and not just one more memo in the endless stream of mimeographed announcements), teachers and administrators work as real learners. They can, by such efforts, acquire the knowledge, develop the skills, and engage in genuine dialogue that will enable them to reach the pedagogical standards urged by *The Paideia Proposal*. Indeed, once the intellectual community has a past, its future can be very full. The participants can design ongoing programs of learning for themselves in whatever directions they wish. By participating in a real curriculum, a program of study of their own, they become true colleagues with shared aspirations for their future.

Or suppose, as is the case in many schools, that teachers are concerned about the quality of their students' thinking. The first in-service step would be a program of reading, conversation, and writing for teachers and administrators that would instruct them in sound reasoning. They could start with Book III of Thucydides' *Peloponnesian War*, discussing the claim of Mitylene's envoys to Athens that "There can never be any solid friendship between individuals, or union between communities that is worth the name, unless the parties be persuaded of each other's honesty," and with Plato's *Gorgias* where it becomes clear that discovering the truth through reasoning requires not only honesty, but also standards of reason. They could supplement these readings with a decent textbook in logic, such as Copi's *Introduction to Logic*, and go on to examine the reasoning, for example of Euclid, the Federalists, Charles Darwin, Abraham Lincoln, Galileo, and so on. They ought to emphasize study of technical and nontechnical reasoning, including the methods of philosophy, science, and mathematics. Lewis Carroll and A. Conan Doyle would be instructive and fun as part of such a program. Vast worlds are open to any intellectual community whose members understand and appeal in discourse to criteria of consistency and relevance, to the adequacy of evidence for conclusions.

Or, finally, suppose a group of teachers and administrators decides that it wants to design a comprehensive in-service program which incoming teachers could join and which established teachers also could do in segments over a period of years. One model is the kind of program offered in the Graduate Institute for teachers at the St. John's College campuses in Santa Fe, New Mexico, and Annapolis, Maryland. This sort of program takes teachers seriously as learners. The Graduate Institute is divided into four segments—Literature, Mathematics and Natural Science, Philosophy and Technology, and Politics and Society. The principle for selection of readings is that once a person has grasped the work in the program, then he or she should be able to study virtually anything in the arts and sciences and so go on to learn well for a lifetime.

The four segments include seminars, small discussion groups, lectures, and preparation of papers. It should be understood that particular readings need not be treated as the only ones which would do, but they are illustrative of the *kinds* of works that contribute to teachers becoming practitioners. For example, in Mathematics and Natural Science, teachers read selections from Euclid, Plato, Lucretius, Aristotle, Bacon, Descartes, Galileo, Hume, Darwin, Freud, and Lobachevsky. In Literature, authors include Homer, Plato, Aeschylus, Sophocles, Euripides, Chaucer, and Shakespeare. In Politics and Society, readings are included from Plutarch, Machiavelli, Hobbes, Locke, Rousseau, Marx, Aquinas, the Federalists, and de Tocqueville. Teachers and administrators in schools can set up their own ongoing programs of seminars, perhaps conjoined with potluck suppers, presentation of papers, correspondence, and so on.

Again, the point is not that these readings in particular have been selected, but that these readings, like others, are important and instructive, and joint thinking about them leads to fertility and rigor of mind. They are the works of practitioners, and they invite dialogue between readers and author. Moreover, they constitute a program of study that leads to a future of learning. That is, no one can truly grasp such works without thinking as a practitioner. Designing a coherent, six-month or longer in-service program such as this one promises continuing opportunity to teachers and administrators. It tends to eliminate the *ad hoc*, episodic character of so much shallow, putatively useful in-service work now typically done.

A further word is necessary here about in-service education as it is frequently practiced in the schools, because the prescriptions of *The Paideia Proposal* imply a dramatic change. Much present in-service is dominated by visiting consultants whose panaceas for all school problems are completely unrelated to the relevant circumstances of the individual school. Many such programs contain no study whatsoever of primary sources, but focus exclusively on the same pedagogical and curricular matters addressed by preservice training. They consist largely of introductions to fads such as "values clarification," "back to basics," and the like, none of which does anything to advance teacher learning in arts and sciences. This fact is doubly dangerous because it is impossible to treat questions of value in classrooms without some grasp of the nature of reasoned discourse about normative issues, and it is impossible to teach basics without a solid understanding of critical thinking. The studies prescribed for teachers by *The Paideia Proposal* are one main and irreplaceable means of overcoming such pernicious shallowness.

When teachers armed with such studies think of their own maturation in choosing materials, making assignments, conducting classes, and assessing performance for their students, they quickly recognize how dramatically their powers are increased.[4] Their in-service work as practitioners comes to have long-range utility for their service as teachers. In-service programs that promote intellectual community are the principal means of approximating the ideals of *The Paideia Proposal*. Only lack of respect for the abilities of teachers can even suggest that such steps are beyond American schools.

Several practical points about implementation must be made in conclusion. For intellectual communities to take root in schools, administrative support and participation are essential. Teachers and administrators alike must be given released time for preparatory study in solitude and for subsequent reflection together; schools must include released time as a priority line item in their budget. In short, schools must be willing to spend time and money on their ultimate resource—individual teachers and administrators. If schools and their surrounding communities view this practice as financially prohibitive, then they had better prepare themselves to accept American schooling in its present condition: high likelihood of teacher burn-out and inadequate opportunity for students to learn in the company of truly able teachers.

It cannot be overestimated here how central is the participation of administrators in the intellectual community. The daily responsibilities of administrators tend to pull them farther and farther away from study of scholarly or scientific subjects. It is all too easy for administrators to indulge in the idle fancy that such studies can be forsaken without harm to themselves or their schools. Add that many administrators are neither scholars nor accomplished teachers in the first place, and the necessity of their participation—if they are to lead the faculty, design coherent schedules of classes, and budget intelligently—is clear. Participation in the intellectual community is their only hope of providing good and credible leadership.

So, to conclude with our original questions posed by Kenner: What is the utility of *The Paideia Proposal* and how could its prescriptions ever be put into practice? Its utility is that it shows clearly the standards teachers and administrators should set for themselves and, in turn, for their students, and what our basic educational aspirations ought to be for ourselves and for our students. Its prescriptions can be put into practice through commitment to sound and ongoing in-service educational programs more plausibly than in any other way. Such programs take time, effort, money, and a vision of teachers and administrators as practitioners of the arts of learning. The vision, finally, is a sense of ourselves as maturing, learning adults, a sense which makes us fit to accept responsibility for the instruction of the young and which makes it appropriate for them to trust us as we teach.

Footnotes

1. Mortimer J. Adler, *The Paideia Proposal: An Educational Manifesto* (New York: Macmillan, 1982).

2. Hugh Kenner, "Please Welcome My Next Idea," *Harper's* 265 (December 1982): 56-58.

3. For the distinction, see Edwin J. Delattre, "Real Career Education Comes from the Liberal Arts," *Chronicle of Higher Education*, 5 January 1983, p. 80.

4. See, for example, Edwin J. Delattre, "The Art of In-service Education," *American Educator* 6 (Winter 1982): 14-17.

CHAPTER X

Precollegiate Humanities: Leadership and Curriculum Issues

FRANCIS ROBERTS

Factors Affecting Humanities in the Schools

"We don't have any humanities program in our school right now, although we are thinking about starting one," says the principal.

"But don't you offer courses in English, history, and languages?" I ask.

"Oh, sure, but we don't have any interdisciplinary courses, or any that blend in the arts, etc."

In one form or another, I have had that conversation a hundred times with school principals, department chairs, and superintendents of schools. There are many curriculum and leadership issues, but clearly a major one in precollegiate humanities is the lack of a common meaning for the term itself. This is not surprising. As we have seen in the preceding essays, the term has varied meanings even among professional humanists. Although this variability makes little difference in most discussions, it is a critical factor when turning attention to school improvement. Schools, unlike the more separate settings of universities, exist in communities and under the close supervision of lay school boards. The language of the school must be one that is clear to the community. The term "humanities" is not now a part of that common language.

If one has doubts, attend the next meeting of the local school board and ask for a report on the humanities curriculum. Depending on the school superintendent or board member, your answer will vary from a full and thoughtful reply to a comment about a new interdisciplinary course for gifted seniors. In many communities the question will trigger a very guarded reply and some anxious glances—indicating the board's fears of charges of "secular humanism." It is the awkward truth that in this book we offer a series of essays on a topic that is not clear to the people who are to carry out the work: teachers, principals, superintendents, and school board members. Nor does the term mean much to students.

So into the complex life of the contemporary school system is thrust a call for improving an aspect of the curriculum which is imprecisely defined, irregularly used, and often regarded with suspicion. The first step in strengthening the humanities in the schools therefore must be to talk about the humanities in a clearer way. There are two common ways of handling such troublesome terms: try to tell people the "correct" meaning, or use other words. During the early months of my service as director of the elementary and secondary humanities programs at the National Endowment for the Humanities, I tried the first approach. I went to great lengths to define the humanities and place them in their proper intellectual context. The harder I tried, the more often I failed. There seemed endless confusion about the difference between humanities and humanistic, between the humanities and the social sciences or the arts. The modifier "secular" sometimes seemed nearby, ready to jump into the conversation. The word "interdisciplinary" was always thrust into the conversation.

For me, a turning point came at the national convention of school superintendents, the American Association of School Administrators, where I was to make a presentation. The badge given me at the registration desk announced to all that I worked at the "N. Endow. for Humans." At that moment I decided that the best way to describe the part of the curriculum of concern to me was simply to say to school people and school boards, "My work centers on history, foreign languages, literature, writing, and the other disciplines of the humanities." One may quarrel with my answer, but I have found it helps focus discussion with school leaders. In any case, one must not dwell too long on definitions, fascinating as they are to academics.

The second issue, unfortunately, is also one of ambiguity. It is this: to what extent is it possible to talk in general terms about 100,000 separate schools located in 16,000 school districts? Here we confront a fascinating paradox—enormous similarity that masks equally great variety. Schools, in this sense, are like people—one has no difficulty spotting a human animal or, in most circumstances, predicting its behavior, yet each is different. Similarly, anyone led blindfolded into any American high school would, upon removal of the blind, unfailingly identify the institution. Schools are rarely mistaken for something else. They have common sounds, sights, and smells. Despite the fact that each is designed by a different architect and built in a different place, the structures offer only marginal differences in layout. They function in remarkably similar fashion, too. Class sizes vary quite widely from the small groups in favored public and selective private schools to packed classes in poorer districts, but what seems to go on in the classes varies far less.

This overt similarity in appearance and daily operation beguiles occupants, leaders, and critics alike into generalizing about the state of the schools, or, in this case, about the condition of the humanities in the schools. The schools are complex institutions. Although one may strive for a slogan or single concept that explains the current condition of the schools, they defy such simple descriptions. "Back-to-basics" is no more adequate a tag than the "relevance" of an earlier period. And each school seems able to sustain simultaneously many different sets of goals and many different characteristics. Recently, for example, I visited a large suburban high school. From my perspective as a former secondary principal, the school seemed pretty casual. Some of the classes were poorly taught, many students appeared to have minimal interest in what was going on, and much of the student work appeared sloppy. Yet the school leads its region in academic awards, test scores, and so forth, and has national recognition in college admissions circles. In contrast, many other schools I have studied give a stronger appearance of success, while accomplishing little more than instilling military discipline.

It is widely held, for example, that most schools are pathologically resistant to change, that their creaking bureaucracies are headed by former coaches, that new ideas flow into the system at the rate of cold molasses. It is said that it takes decades to accept an improvement. To an extent, these views are true. Schools are very conservative social institutions. The school I attended in New England and from which I graduated in 1949 is remarkably unchanged today. When I visit, I am not uncomfortable there or unfamiliar with course content, routines, or the school's problems. As chance would have it, the school is the same one my mother graduated from decades earlier. During her long life we had many chances to compare notes on an institution which she, too, always found familiar. In one sense, the pervasive sameness is astounding. How can such schools survive? What can be the curriculum that bridges those many decades?

Sometimes schools do not change much because they have chanced upon a style and a curriculum that looks beyond the moment, or they have a faculty that keeps new ideas bubbling up within the same old structure. Sometimes, the school should change but does not, as in the case of many urban schools. There the population changed, even the language changed, but the schools did not—until nearly too late. Such schools are washed over by social change and become factories for failure.

Whatever the reasons why schools appear resistant to change, there is another side. The very same schools that appear not to change, the administrators who are resistant to new ideas, the teachers who are said to be "burned out" and in professional ruts—these same people in the same schools are also on occasion given to accepting and even initiating changes so abruptly as to appear mindless. In the 1970s, sequential curricula and year-long courses in social studies and English were cast out in favor of a bizarre conglomerate of mini-courses, short courses, casual electives, and even educational happenings. These changes did not erupt just in Southern California or the upper West Side in New York. The curriculum seemed everywhere to fly apart. In the 1970s, if there was resistance to change, it was nearly invisible. Conventional thinking about the curriculum was overturned so fast and so generally that "change" became the central and only subject matter, and "change agents" littered the educational landscape. Everything, you may recall, was declared irrelevant.

Now, in the mid 1980s, our schools are caught in what is called a computer revolution. The invention itself is radical. Its educational possibilities are enormous. The velocity of change is that of a whirlwind. The path is, unfortunately, as directionless as a whirlwind. It is a powerful and erratic force that is commanding the attention of key staff in nearly every district in the nation. Schools, for good or bad, are subjected to the most heated sales pitch in educational history. Despite otherwise austere budgets, schools that a decade ago carefully weighed the purchase of a new typewriter have scooped up computers like peanuts. The purchases may be wise, even prudent. Surely those school leaders who followed or led the earlier fads must have believed they were helping improve education. In a curious way, changes of large scale or highly visible form seem easier for the innovators to introduce. The wholesale introduction of the junior high school movement in the first third of this century and its rapid conversion to a middle school in the last quarter of the century are but examples. Others include introduction of large-scale competitive sports (with huge gyms and Roman stadia) and the school centralization movement. When people say schools change only with glue-like speed, how many realize that from 1931 to 1982 the number of local school districts (each with its own school board) plummeted from 128,000 to 16,000? That was by far the most radical reorganization of government in the history of any democracy; it transformed the American school by concentrating its leadership, its government, and the center of curriculum. It is in the midst of this remarkable pattern of extreme institutional conservation on the one hand and revolutionary change on the other that one asks the quiet question, "How can teaching be improved in history, languages, and English"?

Part of the reason for the irregular image presented by the American school is the lack of agreement on its job. There is, to use Walter Lippmann's term, no "public philosophy" for education, no commonly held set of purposes that translate into action. This is not to say that school boards have any trouble adopting agreeable sets of goals to be listed in the front of their policy books or that almost anyone's five, seven, or twenty "cardinal principles" of education would not be adopted by acclamation at the next national meeting. But when one peels off the sticker of idealistic prose, one discovers conflict. Part of the conflict is due to the varied patterns of ownership of the curriculum.

Should the curriculum in English be determined mainly by the teacher who is to teach it? That would certainly make sense. Indeed, it is one of the main assumptions in some of the earlier essays in this volume. Yet few teachers I meet believe this is now the case. Perhaps more revealing, few administrators believe it *should* be the case. Although such freedom to decide what to teach is more common to independent schools, most public schools are part of those 16,000 centralized school districts, and most of the school districts are organized on an authority model more similar to business or to general government than to the more diffused authority model in a college or university. Many of the would-be helpful critics from the universities do not fully appreciate this distinction in control. Because schools and college faculty members and administrators seldom have much contact with one another, and rarely have occasion to compare notes on the consequences of their sharply different work context, there has been little discussion of what may be one of the central explanations for the weaknesses of the humanities curriculum in the schools. That weakness is caused in large part by the single fact that the faculty member in a school does not actually "own" the curriculum in the sense that a faculty member does in a college. Having had the uncommon experience of serving six years each as a high school principal, superintendent of schools, and president of a small college, I am struck by this contrast in ownership. Neither state legislatures, state commissioners of education, boards of trustees, college presidents, or any dean would be taken seriously if they chose to prescribe the structure or content of a *college* curriculum—the curriculum belongs to the faculty—yet this is far from the case in precollegiate education.

True, at the college level there are many artful ways that a college administration influences the decisions the faculty makes—allocation of faculty time, research funds, space, and so forth. Nevertheless, the faculty generally retains responsibility for the curriculum. Contrast this to the circumstances within which curriculum choices are determined for schools. Although it is common to speak of decentralized administration of the public schools, the decentralization is at best partial and often stops short of the individual school where the teaching takes place. Depending on the jurisdiction, the scope of the curriculum is determined in part by state education laws, by policies and regulations governing testing practices and state examinations, by state-mandated curricula, by state textbook adoption procedures, district-level curriculum mandates, district-wide exams, uniform textbook selection, and grading policies.

Woven through this web of oversight is the political process of choosing state legislators, state boards of education, local boards, and all of the officials appointed by these bodies. The political process inevitably incorporates and reflects ideological outlooks from left, right, and center, as well as the personal views and education of the participating officials. Together, these factors are part of the basis on which curriculum decisions are made. Censorship of school books is but one reminder of the vulnerability of the curriculum and teacher to the interests and decisions of those who oversee the schools. (The absence of such controversy should be equally disturbing, for it often suggests that only one viewpoint dominates curriculum decisions.)

To this burden of supervision and oversight is added the influence and often conflicting counsel of the professional groups. The administrator organizations, often influenced by what they perceive to be business models for running organizations, talk of "management of learning," goals and objectives, and various measures of process and outcome. Members of these groups tend to think of teachers as employees rather than as independently practicing professionals—a crucial distinction. They also are locked in struggle with teachers' unions for control of instructional decisions. The curriculum content is often said by administrators to be the prerogative of "management." Schools are conceived of as businesses.

The professional groups representing specific areas of the curriculum such as English, history, social studies, and languages devote large sections of their publications and significant portions of their conventions and meetings to discussion of school curriculum. By means of this discussion, these organizations make important contributions to the shape, extent, and direction of humanities curricula. They also carve out their own areas of interest.

What takes place, then, in a tenth-grade English class or is offered in ninth-grade social studies or in the fifth grade is the distillate of a pot-boiler of educational, economic, political, and administrative decisions. Some of the decisions contribute to stronger programs; some weaken the program. Few of those broader curriculum decisions are made by the teachers.

The Problem of Determining Content

But the problems of the school curriculum can hardly be thought of only in terms of a power struggle between teachers and administrators or between greater and lesser central control. Although I favor a much larger role for teachers, I also know from close experience that such political control in no way insures a more substantive curriculum. There needs to be more serious discussion of the intellectual structure and content of the curriculum. Much of the substantive discourse and debate evidenced in the earlier essays in this book are examples of what is missing in curriculum discussion. Such discussion is not easy to promulgate, in part because of the tendency of critics within and outside the schools to offer simplistic prescriptions for content of the curriculum. The recent deluge of such presentations from prominent and often well-funded commissions and committees shows the problem: it is arrogant and futile to prescribe the specific content or core of the curriculum. There is just too much knowledge. This is not the Middle Ages.

For example, if someone issues a list of books all high school students should read, you may be sure it includes only the books that person knows, not any of the thousands of other possibilities. Similarly, the history we mandate is the history we know. This is perfectly sensible if we admit to the modest basis for our choice. When we propose to choose humanities curricula for everybody else it is well to remind ourselves of the limits of our own knowledge. President Eliot of Harvard had his own famous five-foot shelf, and full exploration of his Harvard Classics could consume a lifetime. But full exploration of nearly *any* five feet of books in your study or mine might also merit the attention of a lifetime.

Unless one has the iron will of an Edwin Delattre and his colleagues at St. John's College and can choose a few great books and then make this choice stick, one is forced to admit that the range of curriculum content is vast. One hundred secondary school departments of English could each make up a solid four-year curriculum in literature without ever duplicating their choices of fiction, drama, poems, and essays. In history, the problem at first appears to be simpler. All one needs to do is identify sufficiently large categories so as to gain the agreement of one's colleagues on the curriculum committee or the school board or whomever else is to have a say. Thus, a school may require American History, World History, and perhaps Far Eastern History (on the often accurate assumption that that field is virtually ignored in the World History course.) Yet the choices often border on the absurd. What can be the realistic expectations of a tenth-grade study of the history of the *whole* world, or even a large part of it? College faculties with much fuller academic preparation than most secondary school teachers know better than to offer to cover the history of *anybody's* world in one year. And the flow of scholarship informing us of the extent and complexity of the many early civilizations of human kind only adds each year to the absurdity.

At the 1907 meeting of the Council of the American Historical Association a committee was appointed to consider and report on the study of history in secondary schools. The five members wrestled for nearly four years with what was then a far smaller quantity of scholarship and a much simpler kind of high school, but nonetheless found themselves forever tripping over the central questions of how much of *which* history. In their 1911 report, the *Study of History in Secondary Schools*,[1] they recommended a four-year course in history, far more history than most schools today offer within the social studies. They then recognized that not all schools would require four years of history, but they could offer only the following guidance on selecting what should be taught in three years, not four. "It would be inappropriate," they reported,

> to attempt here any ample illustration of the process of condensation and elimination that might be suitable for a three-years' course. That process can be accomplished only by the skillful text-writer or by the wise teacher in the classroom. We do suggest, however, that if it seems wise to omit any detailed study of ancient history and to give the three years substantially to the other three blocks, the teacher, while omitting all detail, may still attempt to give his pupils some idea of the growth of the ancient nations, and some idea of their achievements and their qualities.[2]

The distinguished panel concluded with their own touch of absurdity by acknowledging that such treatment must be "hurried and unsatisfactory" but that "it need not be profitless."

It is this sort of compulsion to jam information into the curriculum that has contributed to the present sad state of the humanities curriculum. Often the richness of the curriculum has been replaced by outlines and summaries of the content. Our students, in turn, may not be taught history, for example, but are taught to become experts at list making.

How, then, is a decision made about what is to be taught in history, languages, and literature? Jacob Burckhardt, the famous historian, suggested an answer for history when he described history as "what one age finds worthy of note in another."[3] In this, he allows for a good deal of room for judgment and for differences of opinion. The school curriculum, one might suggest following Burckhardt, is what one generation of teachers finds worthy of note for another generation of students.

If the goal is more scholarly teaching, the curriculum choices should be guided by two criteria: (a) what the teachers themselves know best and think important, and (b) what they can be helped to learn. I suggest this would be a radical departure from the current practices in which state authorities, test makers, district curriculum experts, and all the others "above" the teachers or outside the individual schools decide what is to be taught. Deciding what every student should learn in history in 16,000 school districts makes no sense at all if one disregards the competence and preparation of individual teachers.

To strengthen the humanities curricula, one must study the local faculty, and find out what they know and have enthusiasm for. This may mean that the curriculum catalogue of a particular school or district will not have all of the courses or topics that the college professors would like. One school may offer a course in Latin American studies because it has the trained faculty. Another school may offer more European history. One does not toughen up the curriculum in English or history merely by requiring a new set of courses. Those who have majored in English may be reminded of Alexander Pope's *Dunciad*, in which ignorance is crowned king. This is just what happens when a school system or a state requires a new curriculum without consideration of the competence of the staff. I hold a permanent teachers certificate in Social Studies, but my main training falls within American history and the social sciences. It would not be wise to assign me a course in Far Eastern history, just because it is a "neglected" area of the curriculum.

Teachers must teach what they know and what they care deeply about. It is recognized that administrators, school boards, and state authorities are reluctant to delegate this large responsibility to teachers, and in reality, not all teachers are ready. The key, then, to improving the teaching of history, literature, and language is to begin with the faculty.

There is no education subject on which more nonsense has been offered than teacher education. Piles of research studies seek to establish one teaching technique as superior to another; volumes are written on testing methods and procedures; magazines and books are filled with descriptions of processes, goals, and objectives. The results of this trivialization of teaching have been that many of the best minds in many of the best people—teachers and students—have been ill-used. But what is the *cause* of the trivialization? It is this: there has been a failure to recognize that teaching is not what one is trained to do; it is a natural act. *All humans are teachers.*

Teaching is part of the biology of the human race. At the point where our ancestors became articulate, the teaching profession was born. Mark Hopkins did not invent it, nor did John Dewey, Jesus Christ, or Socrates. Teaching is programmed into the genes. It has been the essential feature of human survival, the means of transmitting that which is important, useful, and stimulating from one generation to another. To test this contention, observe any group of humans over the age of three, assembled for any purpose. Whether the gathering is mandated, voluntary, or accidental makes no difference. Nor does the array of ages, cultures, or experience. Assuming conversation is permitted, teaching begins immediately. People begin to ask each other questions, exchange information, skills and opinions, measure each other's minds, and enlarge each other's experience. They teach.

The task of teacher education or faculty development is to develop or improve the natural ability of the teacher. Teaching, like loving, *is* complex, but it is also part of our nature. Neither loving nor teaching is well described in state certification requirements. State certification rules may rationalize hiring and firing and offer a means of deciding on pay scales, but most have little bearing on the quality of teaching. If there is a problem in the humanities curriculum, it is a problem in teaching. The failure of the schools—where they are failing—is a failure not of teachers, but a failure of teaching—a failure to recognize and honor the power of teaching.

Ways to Improve Teaching

To strengthen the humanities, one must improve the competence of teachers and they must be permitted a much larger role in the school. To consider how this might be facilitated, attention is directed to the role of universities, to state and federal agencies and policies, and ultimately to the leadership in the local schools and districts. I turn first to the colleges. It is a favorite activity of critics to heap scorn and ridicule on the "educationists" in the teachers colleges. Whatever the weaknesses of such parts of the university, the point missed by the critics is that the criticism is largely misplaced. In citing the colleges and departments of education as the cause of academic depression and poor teaching in the schools is to send the hounds barking up the wrong tree. The problem has less to do with the shortcomings of the "educationists" than with the indifference of the "liberal artists," if I may link one pejorative term with another. Until recently, very few graduate schools of arts and sciences, very few graduate faculty in English, history, or languages expressed serious interest in the in-service education of school teachers.

For some years, I was superintendent of schools in a community in which was located a large, first-rate university. Teachers in the local schools wanted to study part-time to strengthen their academic preparation in their teaching fields. English teachers wanted graduate courses and seminars in English, history teachers in history. They were, with few exceptions, told to go elsewhere. The university did not at that time welcome them and made no provision for their need to study on a part-time basis. Ironically, they were forced to drive past the local university and enroll many miles away in other colleges. Even there, it was only the education faculty who welcomed them. What most teachers wanted was not a master's degree in guidance or school administration, but a master's degree in history or biology or languages. Only when the teachers themselves threatened through their union to boycott the university's student-teacher program which was carried out in their classrooms did the university ease its rules. The message long remained, however, that teachers need not apply. Declining graduate school enrollment, among other things, is causing things to change. Teachers are now welcomed.

College faculty members in the humanities have not, until recently, expressed any enthusiasm for direct work with teachers in the schools. Except for the active role of the National Humanities Faculty, and occasional leaders of summer institutes and special projects, rare indeed is the liberal arts faculty member who has spent any time in the nearby public schools, except perhaps as a complaining parent. Before going to Washington, I served six years as president of Bank Street College of Education. As one of those "educationists" I spent a good share of my time helping teachers. I worked with them in their classrooms in the South Bronx, in Bedford-Stuyvesant, in Macon County, Alabama, and in Stamford, Connecticut. These teachers appreciated whatever help one could offer. In hundreds of hours in the schools I seldom heard of (and rarely met) a professor from the liberal arts faculties of universities, great or ordinary.

More bridges must be built between the scholars and the schools. Following several experimental grants to Dartmouth, Wesleyan, St. John's, and Johns Hopkins, the National Endowment for the Humanities has tried to respond by setting up a program of teacher institutes in which leading scholars work intensively with groups of humanities teachers to increase the teachers' competence in their field and to help them develop stronger curricula. The National Humanities Faculty, also with support from the National Endowment for the Humanities, began in 1982 a series of cooperative school-university programs which built on earlier successful experience in which National Humanities Faculty scholars worked in schools across the nation. As I write, William Bennett, Chairman of the Endowment, has just announced a major new Summer Seminar program on specific humanities topics of importance to the schools. More initiatives are planned at the National Endowment. But colleges need not wait for federal dollars. Teachers want more training in their academic fields; parents and students recognize this need. College departments of languages, history, and English must develop summer and part-time master's programs and doctoral programs with school teachers in mind. In addition to formal degree programs, the colleges should offer colloquia, seminars, lectures, and similar programs. Some may find it appealing to establish centers for the teaching of English or history. Others may find that faculty can join forces with the teachers in the schools to develop collaborative projects in the humanities disciplines. Georgetown University's department of English has successfully operated such a joint venture with the Washington, D.C. schools, and for several years Yale University has run the Yale-New Haven Teachers Institute, a year-round collaborative effort with the New Haven, Connecticut, school system. Many colleges find the graduate liberal arts programs and degrees an appropriate means for building bridges to the schools. In some cases, the programs are the common cause of professors of education and liberal arts—rare, happy truces in the wars of academe.

Many of the states can do what the federal government has been doing through the National Endowment for the Humanities: sponsor institutes, workshops, and projects in the academic subjects. I would hope more states would also return to their staff positions of leadership in each of the academic fields—not general curriculum supervisors, but specialists with an interest in teaching and with solid graduate training in their disciplines. Their commitment should be to scholarly teaching in the subject fields, not endless stirring of curriculum stews.

Perhaps the most important step the states can take is to look very carefully at their state testing and state regulations. As I noted earlier, there is a growing but mistaken belief that the best way to strengthen teaching is to narrow the scope of the curriculum, require teachers to teach what others order, then test pupils on their mastery of this prescribed subject matter. State leaders must be persuaded that this approach, although leading to a temporary rise in test scores, in the longer run weakens the schools by weakening the teacher's role in deciding what is to be taught and how it is to be evaluated. More state tests mean fewer class discussions of important ideas, fewer and shorter papers written by students. By sticking close to the black heading in the state-approved courses of study and the standard textbooks, teachers will mass-produce higher scores on standardized tests, but this will be accomplished at a high price for the humanities.

School boards and superintendents must be careful that they do not replicate at the local level the excessive testing and continued fascination with prescribed district-wide curricula. One can see why school board members admire the symmetry of such prescriptive arrangements, but these officials must be mindful that students go to school in a schoolhouse, not a school system. They live in a *general* community and are part of its economics, sociology, and culture. But they attend a *particular* school. It is in the individual schoolhouse where teachers work. One finds few teachers in the central offices or state education offices. Let me, then, turn to the individual school as the focus of my concluding remarks.

Teaching and How It Is Supported

In a quarter century of educational experimentation, accompanied by the distractions of large-scale school construction and widespread school closures, financial stresses, narrow measures of achievement, and sweeping social changes, the one topic that has been given little attention is *teaching*—plain old classroom teaching. Having looked at every other conceivable aspect of education, it is now time to recognize the teacher, and to move that indispensable individual out from the shadow of computers, television, state-wide testing, standardized textbooks, and away from the clutches of all those forces of good and ill will, left and right, who would use the schools to further their own purposes.

The goals of education in a democracy are not obscure—they are to develop the minds and sensibilities of free and responsible people. There are many places where this education goes forward—in museums, libraries, churches, on playing fields, in fast-food joints, movie houses, camping trips, before TV sets, and under the hood of an old car. But the center for learning, the only place designed, built, and staffed for that purpose is the schoolhouse. The principal place to concentrate attention is on that building. It is only there that the long lists of issues in curriculum, leadership, finance, social reform, and intellectual development are sorted out and weighed for value and importance. If the humanities are to be strengthened, it is to the schoolhouse we must look.

There are, ultimately, two primary issues. The first is whether school authorities will recognize and support the faculty in greatly expanded responsibility for the curriculum. The second issue, related to the first, is whether the individual school can be rediscovered as the center for learning in the humanities. I confess I am not too hopeful on either.

In my study there are two books to which I frequently turn when I ask myself what has gone wrong in our schools. Neither is explicitly about schools. The first is Burton R. Clark's *The Distinctive College*.[4] Clark, formerly on the faculties at Yale and Harvard, and now teaching at the University of California, Los Angeles, examined a number of liberal arts colleges. He asks what is it that leads to distinction? In each institution so characterized, Clark found these elements: first, a significant leader, who in his own way mobilized the human and other resources of the institution, and helped chart fresh initiatives; second, a distinctive curriculum, one designed for that institution, not for colleges in general, and clearly not one easily transferred elsewhere merely by exchanging syllabi. The curriculum, or in a larger sense the program of the college, is interwoven with the symbols and rituals of the college, the beliefs and approaches of the faculty, and the patterns of courses. One knows as a student that one is at a particular institution, not just any college.

The third characteristic noted by Clark is what he calls the "organizational saga." This is the oral history of the institution. Clark writes:

> The most important characteristic and consequence of an organizational saga is the capturing of allegiance, the committing of staff to the institution. Emotion is invested to the point where many participants significantly define themselves by the central theme of the organization. The organizational motif becomes individual motive, much more than a statement of purpose, a cogent theme, a doctrine of administration, or a logical set of ideas. Deep emotional investment binds participants—as comrades in a cause. Indications of an organizational legend are pride and exaggeration: the most telling symptom is an intense sense of the unique.[5]

If Clark's characteristics were applied to schools it is clear they would be different from those bland, test-wise, branch offices of the local school systems one often finds.[6] Nor are they to be created by mandating a state-wide curriculum in the humanities or in any other subjects. Their rarity is not due to the over-influence of the "educationists," nor will they even be shaped up in Washington and shipped out as "models." The absence of large numbers of distinctive elementary and secondary schools among the nation's nearly 100,000 schools shows how timid and conforming is our education, and ultimately how lacking in the kind of academic power that only a faculty and its leaders can develop and sustain.

And the question of leadership? For some answers, I turn to my second book, Plato's *Republic*.[7] In Francis Cornford's rich and compelling introduction, he explores Plato's continuing concern for what Cornford calls "the rival claims of the contemplative and the active life."[8] My thoughts drift back to my years as a high school principal; I think of the pressured lives of my fellow principals, the books unread by busy school leaders. In my heavily-marked copy of the *Republic* is one passage that seems central to our present discussion:

> Unless either philosophers become kings in their countries or those who are now called kings and rulers come to be sufficiently inspired with a genuine desire for wisdom; unless, that is to say, political power and philosophy meet

together, while the many natures who now go their several ways in the one or the other direction are forcibly debarred from doing so, there can be no rest from troubles, my dear Glaucon, for states, nor yet, as I believe, for all mankind; nor can this commonwealth which we have imagined ever till then see the light of day and grow to its full stature. This it was that I have so long hung back from saying.[9]

When I reread the passage substituting the word "principal" for "kings and rulers," and the word "school" for "country," the issues of curriculum and leadership in our schools, the problems of achieving excellence in the humanities are clearer. Yet the paradox remains.

To me, the issues of curriculum and leadership in the humanities boil down to this single question: *To what extent are we willing in the years ahead to help each school become a distinctive, individual institution where the faculty and its leaders talk frequently together about books and ideas, and select those that they think important enough and interesting enough to teach to our children?*

Footnotes

1. Andrew C. McLaughlin, chairman, *The Study of History in Secondary Schools*, Report to the American Historical Association by a Committee of Five (New York: Macmillan, 1911).

2. Ibid., pp. 22-23.

3. Jacob Burckhardt, cited in Henry S. Commager, *The Nature and Study of History* (Columbus, Ohio: Charles E. Merrill, 1965), p. 1.

4. Burton R. Clark, *The Distinctive College* (Chicago: Aldine Publishing Co., 1970).

5. Ibid., p. 235.

6. See Francis J. Roberts, "School Principal: Minor Bureaucrat or Educational Leader," *Urban Review* 8 (Winter 1975): 243-50.

7. Plato, *The Republic*, trans. Francis M. Cornford (New York: Oxford University Press, 1945).

8. Ibid., p. xix.

9. Ibid., p. 178-79. See also, Roberts, "School Principal."

CHAPTER XI

Implementing Successful Humanities Courses and Programs

BENJAMIN LADNER

Whatever else one learns from the variety of perspectives presented in the essays in this volume, it is certainly clear that the humanities cannot be reduced to a single category, approach, or activity. The human enterprises of talking, reading, thinking, and writing generate a variety of imaginative expressions which are worthy of understanding and are appropriate for the work of such disciplines as history, English, foreign languages, philosophy, religious studies, and the like. Simply put, the humanities are our disciplined efforts of reflection and discourse which deal with what matters in human experience. Therefore, the work of the humanities follows the innumerable contours of what goes on and how we make sense of what goes on in our individual and collective lives.

The key to moving successfully from an abstract and theoretical consideration of humanities subjects to the practical implementation of work in a humanities classroom is this: the *method* of teaching must be consistent with and an extension of the *content* of what is being taught. Humanities subjects themselves must be recognized as resources for determining how they can best be approached and communicated effectively.

This does not mean simply using history textbooks to teach history or a novel to teach literature. Nor does it imply the artificial dramatization of "dull" material in order to make it "interesting." The teaching-learning process in the humanities can never be reduced to the mere exchange of information. Instead, the process always demands the serious engagement of the inquirer's mind and imagination with ideas, events, and perspectives which ultimately affect the person of the inquirer—teacher or student. This is why the humanities historically have been so volatile and, from Socrates to the present, have often been labeled as dangerous. In studying them there is always the possibility—indeed, the assumption—that one's understanding and perspective on life will be altered.

It is crucial that humanities teachers recognize the extent to which they are themselves at stake in the process—"at stake" in the sense that the treatment of profound ideas with third graders, graduate students, or in the privacy of one's study requires an uncommon vulnerability to unanticipated meanings. It is the pursuit of these new meanings that leads to discovery and to the satisfaction of understanding. What is disarming and sometimes frightening about this process is the way in which these meanings also *pursue you* as reader, listener, speaker, viewer, or teacher. Nevertheless, the hallmark of work in the humanities is this process of reciprocal movement, back and forth, from person to text or idea and back again to the inquiring person.

Successful humanities courses and programs continually devise ways to insure that this process takes place. Moments of successful teaching in the classroom are grounded both in the teacher's previous vulnerability to what is being taught and in his or her openness to the inherent power of the subject matter to lead the joint efforts of teacher and student to understand. There is no substitute for the willingness of teachers to lend themselves imaginatively and sympathetically to the unique framework established by the text or issue being studied.[1]

Moreover, unlike the process of thinking, which is necessarily restricted to the silence and privacy of one's ideas, teaching is an act. It is something that is done, not just thought about. Human action requires human community and is predicated upon human intention. Therefore, those who would teach successfully have first to ask themselves what they intend to *do* with their students in the classroom. Teaching in the humanities is inescapably the unification of theory and practice, even if what is taught is itself theoretical in nature.

Therefore, the practice of teaching, if it is to be successful, must reflect a direct concern with human purposes and actions since it is itself the prime example of the unified relationship of thought and action, of theory and practice. As Kliebard has noted:

> The rescue of humanistic study from its present state of decay in elementary and secondary schools . . . lies primarily in reconstructing all the studies that

comprise the curriculum so that their origins in human purposes and activity are restored and made the focal point of study. . . . The problem . . . is one of restoring the subjects of study to their place *in* experience.[2]

Connecting "subjects of study to their place *in* experience" must begin in the experience of the teacher. The teacher must act in such a way as to demonstrate how thinking achieves human purpose *through the act of teaching*. Knowledge and understanding must be recognized not as neutral ends in themselves but as instruments of human inquiry which contribute to the fulfillment of what human beings intend and enact.

What has been suggested in various ways by writers in this book is that effective teaching of the humanities implies a radical alteration of the priorities of both schools and colleges. We do not need to produce another round of new curriculum designs, teaching strategies, or behavioral objectives. We do not need newer, more costly, or more technically efficient materials and resources. We do not need longer school days or school years. We do not need a return to "basic skills," as if reading, writing, and figuring were void of content and unrelated to the meaning of what is written or read. These subjects, under whatever course title, have, after all, been the staples of American school curriculums for decades. What is desperately needed is a change in the structure and climate of schools and classrooms, and a change in the preparation and expectation of what teachers actually do—with texts, with students, and with each other as colleagues.

After working with thousands of teachers in hundreds of schools during the past fifteen years, the National Humanities Faculty (NHF) has been able to identify patterns and features of humanities courses and programs that have contributed to successful teaching-learning experiences. The NHF emphasizes substantive knowledge and excellent teaching as prerequisites for effective humanities education in our nation's schools. By utilizing the resources of its distinguished members, who are appointed for the express purpose of working directly with elementary and secondary teachers, the NHF has served a unique role in American education. It has helped to overcome the unfortunate fragmentation in education between teachers in schools and colleges. The false separation of persons at different institutions who nonetheless work in the same disciplinary areas diminishes the potential richness that invariably emerges from serious intellectual collaboration. It is this academic depth and richness that the National Humanities Faculty seeks to develop in America's elementary and secondary schools.

From this experience in every conceivable school setting the following elements have repeatedly appeared as crucial to the development of successful humanities courses and programs.

1. *Teaching and learning take place in a school climate which is sustained by an active community of inquiry.*

If there is a single prerequisite for the successful implementation of humanities courses and programs it is that they emerge from the activities of thinking, writing, reading, and talking which animate humanities disciplines and topics. Humanities education can only flourish where the humanities are daily enacted and in the process establish a context for schooling that is enlivened by their practice.

Where no such context exists, one must be established. However intransigent are the factors that mitigate against the shared public enactment of the humanities—bureaucratic obdurateness, administrative resistance, parental anxiety, collegial lethargy, the schedule—it is important that a group of persons be actively involved in intellectual investigation and conversation outside of specific teaching assignments. In its work in the schools the National Humanities Faculty requires that a project team be formally constituted not only to be responsible for a range of project activities but more importantly to engage in shared inquiry on a regular basis so that teaching is rooted in a community of learning. Ideally the group is comprised of persons from a range of disciplines, and has as its chief concern not building the humanities as disciplines or departments but engaging in the activities of shared inquiry. It is important that a respected teacher be designated as the leader-coordinator of the group.

I need hardly observe that the typical elementary or secondary school in this country does not easily accommodate the establishment and activities of such intellectual communities. However, if we are serious about reforming and improving not only humanities courses but schools and school systems as well, ways must be found to engage teachers regularly with each other as intellectual colleagues and with profound texts and ideas so that the school becomes an extension of this enterprise.

In a typical school day teachers do most of the talking most of the day while they are apart from colleagues who are involved in the same task. The entrenched and rigid schedules in which teaching occurs encourage approaches to content that are mechanistic and disconnected. There is little doubt that a major restructuring of both the curriculum and the schedule is needed. Times must be set aside during the day as a regular part of what goes on in school—not as an additional after-school activity—for teachers to work together intellectually. This cannot be accomplished by planning meetings, faculty meetings, or an occasional in-service day. Small groups of teachers must collaborate regularly, paralleling student classes, in order to maintain the intellectual life and quality of the learning community which every school ought to be.

The study of subject matter and texts in the humanities must precede and inform curriculum development. Even as the lockstep schedule of schools imposes a similar rigidity upon teaching methods and curriculum content, the initiation of collegial discussions of intellectually substantive matters will lead to the necessity of developing different curriculum structures that are commensurate with the vitality and imaginative force of profound ideas. The curriculum soon becomes an expression of the deliberations of a community of inquiry rather than an imposed and inflexible framework. Administrators are often concerned that the results of this kind of process for curriculum development will result in a loose conglomeration of materials, methods, and activities. The experience of NHF has been that, on the contrary, there emerges a common set of understandings that lead to sound learning activities in which both teachers and students have an important stake. Building into the curriculum sensible accommodations for a plurality of needs and abilities increases the likelihood of successful learning experiences.

Where the radical alterations of teacher, class, and curriculum schedules which I am proposing are not likely to occur, small groups of teachers can at least arrange to have simultaneous free periods for purposes of shared intellectual inquiry. Also, special projects can be developed with the assistance of the National Humanities Faculty in which the primary aim of the project is the development of a serious learning community inside the school.

2. *The teacher is recognized as the central person in the educational process.*

The humanities teacher is not primarily a "learning facilitator," a counselor, a club sponsor, a "talking book," or a conduit for data. Teachers matter because of the value of their knowledge and their ability to teach. Despite our penchant for precision, quantification, and statistical formulation, increased access to computers and learning machines does not increase our children's education. The teacher is someone who knows something worth knowing and who knows how, where, and when to lead someone else into the truth of that knowledge. The teacher is not a substitute for library books, for a machine that is too expensive to buy, or for a parent in need of daytime child care. The teacher is a teacher because he or she stands in a particular relation to truth and to knowledge, and embodies an appropriate understanding of an approach to these realities. Although their salaries suggest otherwise, teachers are not just cheap labor.

As indicated earlier, the humanities teacher is someone engaged in a transaction that places both teacher and student in a direct, sometimes ambiguous, sometimes precarious, relation to a text, a tradition of thought or belief, or a profound issue or problem. He or she is a bridge between past and future. Through the act of publicly approaching what is under study, the teacher enables students to achieve this same access through the immediacy of the teacher's own approach. If the teacher is not constantly vulnerable to the possibility of being changed—in one's understanding or in one's very soul—by the truth of what is being taught, no real humanities teaching has occurred.

No humanities course or program that does not take seriously the pivotal role of the teacher and does not take steps to insure the support of the teaching act will have a chance of consistent educational success.

3. *Teachers "own" the courses they teach.*

Two factors are important here: the involvement of teachers in planning, both before and during the course or program, and the freedom and authority of teachers to execute what is planned. Standardized curriculums and program formats which are mandated "from the top down" (that is, from administrators who are removed from the classroom) or whole educational programs which have been devised elsewhere and adopted without the involvement of those who must teach the materials, are ultimately prescriptions for teacher resentment and student boredom. Genuine ownership of courses by teachers requires both involvement and responsibility. Not only must the teacher be involved in planning, he or she must also be responsible for "summoning-to-life," as Benjamin DeMott describes it, the poem, novel, idea, language, or event which is being taught.

4. *Administrators provide strong support for teachers and activities in humanities courses and programs.*

One of the most unfortunate divisions in elementary and secondary schools is the separation of administrators from teachers and from teaching-learning settings. The consequences of this division have bred misunderstanding, isolation, and distrust on both sides. A prominent feature of successful humanities programs is the reintegration of principals, curriculum supervisors, and superintendents into the teaching-learning process.

NHF projects require that administrators be members of the core group of persons on the project team and that they become involved with texts and ideas in the humanities, whether or not these have previously been a part of their academic and professional background. This has the effect not only of establishing peer relationships between teachers and administrators but also of resetting the focus for many administrators who have not undertaken serious intellectual inquiry in years, least of all in a truly collegial setting. Given the opportunity, they often rediscover themselves as educators first and as administrators second.

By reading novels, critical essays, historical documents, and working with forms of art, administrators are enabled to imagine the task of administration itself in a different light. Despite nearly universal acknowledgement of the contrary, administration need not be assumed to be mechanistic and bureaucratic in nature. In fact, of course, administrators—like artists, novelists, and philosophers—are called upon to give shape and direction to living entities—in this case schools. "Form," said Francis Bacon, "is the freeing of a direction." The formative (and often formidable) task facing the artist, writer, thinker, and teacher can be instructive for administrators. No less creative and imaginative energy is required for "freeing the direction" of persons who teach and learn than is required for those who shape words, thoughts, or lumps of clay into powerful and compelling forms. The questions of how one achieves balance and harmony with living forms so that the structures themselves enhance our life-space—interior and exterior—is as relevant for the administrator as it is for the sculptor, writer, or architect. Educational administration is primarily an imaginative undertaking rather than a managerial one.

Personal presence and involvement by administrators are strong expressions of support for work in the humanities. But other forms of support are also significant. Teachers need to be rewarded in visible and tangible ways for their achievements in teaching. Salary increases, involvement in special projects and public presentations, and assignment to leadership roles are some of the ways in which administrators can both recognize and support good teachers in humanities programs.

The general concern about teachers' salaries and the specific problem of whether they should be tied to teaching effectiveness are difficult issues. Nonetheless, they are worthy of comment in a discussion about humanities teaching because humanities teachers, more than others, are recognized as having to deal with ambiguous subjects which are difficult to communicate or assess.

However, making responsible judgments for which one can give plausible accounts in the context of one's peers is precisely what education in the humanities aims to achieve. For teachers and administrators to shy from or flatly reject this responsibility for themselves undermines the integrity and insight of our human responsibility for knowledge and its bearing upon human experience.

Of course there must be agreed upon standards for excellent teaching. It is simply not true that these cannot be developed or that we cannot recognize good teaching. In addition to a long tradition of ideas and subjects against which to compare the quality of the content of teaching, we also have our own experience of those few powerful and effective teachers from our personal past who, by their enduring impact upon us, clearly define what we now know: good teachers know their subjects, care about their students, share their insights with colleagues, deal insightfully with important ideas, demand large investments of mind, imagination, and energy from themselves and their students, and they embody in their lives the value of what they know and teach. They can be recognized and rewarded.

Successful humanities courses and programs rest on the consistent involvement of excellent teachers. Invariably these are persons who are recognized and rewarded by administrators for the quality of their work. Beyond the rewards of higher salaries for first-rate teaching, administrative support must also be forthcoming at the end of courses or projects when new ideas and approaches may demand administrative assistance in order to alter schedules, curriculum, or textbooks. Teachers cannot be expected to improve their courses if the changes that emerge from their planning are not likely to be implemented because of administrative indifference or resistance.

5. *In addition to books, teachers use other "texts" and resources in the local community.*

In teaching the humanities there can be no compromising the central place of close textual study of important books and essays. However, such "texts" as local or family histories, unique community records, or architecture can serve as subjects for fruitful inquiry. Effective humanities courses also draw upon such local resources as civic leaders, parents, museums, community theatres, service organizations, and other schools to enrich their teaching.

Colleges and universities have traditionally had little formal relation with nearby elementary and secondary schools. In recent years, National Humanities Faculty collaborative projects, which pair schools and colleges in order to work on humanities projects, have demonstrated the extraordinary benefits of these educational partnerships. They are not always easily forged. Early suspicions and preconceptions must be overcome as school teachers and college professors discover that they are professional colleagues engaged in a common task that is mutually beneficial. Once this happens, however, the combined resources of the faculties and institutions can have a direct effect upon those who teach and upon the quality of humanities courses.

It is certainly true that college and university professors have a great deal to offer their colleagues in the schools. And when they work alongside them as peers in a common task, through such endeavors as National Humanities Faculty programs, the teachers are direct beneficiaries of scholarly expertise which would otherwise be inaccessible. What is less well known, but just as consistently true, is that school teachers have a great deal to teach college faculty. For one thing, teachers know their students as persons in ways that college professors rarely do. School students are known by neighborhood and family affiliations, and are regarded in light of this wider, local community. The school as well as the act of teaching are set within the community in ways that have a direct bearing on the approach to and impact of knowledge, especially in the humanities. College faculty have much to learn from school teachers about the dynamics of the relationship between the personal histories of students and the possibilities for effective humanities teaching in light of these histories.

Furthermore, although teachers in schools are criticized for perpetuating the very teaching methods by which they were taught in college, the fact is that many of them are more lively, varied, and creative in their approach to the teaching task than their counterparts in higher education. College faculty can learn about teaching from elementary and secondary teachers.

Finally, college faculty usually have no idea what is actually being taught in the schools. School faculty can provide them with a realistic understanding of the preparation students are receiving for becoming students of college faculty. Faculty members of the National Humanities Faculty have revised their own courses, and, in some cases, the direction of their research, in light of what they have learned from their school-level colleagues in this regard.

6. *The activities of reading, thinking, writing, and talking are regularly practiced by students.*

Doing the work of the humanities means that students are regularly reading engaging materials, thinking about profound issues, writing thoughtfully, and talking to teachers and their peers about substantive matters. It was noted earlier that teachers must also be doing these same things. These activities are not the special responsibility of a single discipline, course, or teacher. They are the glue of all successful humanities courses and programs.

Perhaps this is an obvious feature of humanities courses that can simply be assumed. Yet it is surprising how often the lack of consistency and regularity in the use of these skills defeats the best intentions of well-meaning teachers.

For students to engage in these activities in humanities courses does not simply develop these skills as tools for learning. They also become the basis for the development of an informed citizenry. These fundamental humanities endeavors, even in the early grades of school, begin to shape within students a sense of the rhythm and balance of public discussion, the demand for informed judgment, the patience of collective deliberation, the weight and significance of tradition, and the personal responsibility for truth. In other words, education for civility, for the care and transmission of humane culture, is rooted in the unique abilities cultivated by humanities teaching and learning. These abilities can only emerge in the continued practice by students of reading, thinking, writing, and talking.

* * *

"But one can quite easily teach without educating," says Hannah Arendt in her famous essay on "The Crisis in Education," "and one can go on learning to the end of one's days without for that reason becoming educated."[3] The current concern about the condition of our schools is that there are hours and days and years of teaching, but "without educating."

If teaching is to become educating, the work of the humanities must take place at the crucial junctures of human experience where meaning joins with the contours of our lives. The humanities are concerned with those stories, objects, shapes, events, words that fit our lives, that give us the world as home. But here is the key for teaching the humanities: these stories, words, and events must be spoken by one who is himself at home in the world. The enterprise of humanities education in the schools rests unavoidably, irreplaceably on the individual teacher who judges, authorizes, chooses, sets limits, and who is at home with the meanings he or she considers. There is no substitute for these meanings cutting deeply into one's own life and issuing in passionate thought for and with one's students. There is no real teaching in the humanities that is not by example. It is not so simple, I know, but neither is it as complex and difficult as we sometimes suppose.

Teaching the humanities at the precollegiate level is the profoundly serious business of taking responsibility for oneself and for the world against the background of what has been known and thought and said and done for the sake of what can yet be discovered and achieved. "Education," Arendt concludes,

> is the point at which we decide whether we love the world enough to assume responsibility for it and by the same token save it from that ruin which, except for renewal, except for the coming of the new and young, would be inevitable. And education, too, is where we decide whether we love our children enough not to expel them from our world and leave them to their own devices, nor to strike from their hands their chance of undertaking something new, something

unforeseen by us, but to prepare them in advance for the task of renewing a common world.[4]

Footnotes

1. For examples of how this works see the essays in this volume by Benjamin Demott and John McDermott.

2. See chapter 2 in this volume.

3. Hannah Arendt, *Between Past and Future* (New York: Viking Press, 1968), p. 196.

4. Ibid.

Name Index

Subject Index

INFORMATION ABOUT MEMBERSHIP IN THE SOCIETY

From its small beginnings in the early 1900s, the National Society for the Study of Education has grown to a major educational organization with more than 3,000 members in the United States, Canada, and overseas. Members include professors, researchers, graduate students, and administrators in colleges and universities; teachers, supervisors, curriculum specialists, and administrators in elementary and secondary schools; and a considerable number of persons who are not formally connected with an educational institution. Membership in the Society is open to all persons who desire to receive its publications.

Since its establishment the Society has sought to promote its central purpose—the stimulation of investigations and discussions of important educational issues—through regular publication of a two-volume yearbook that is sent to all members. Many of these volumes have been so well received throughout the profession that they have gone into several printings. A recently inaugurated series of substantial paperbacks on Contemporary Educational Issues supplements the series of yearbooks and allows for treatment of a wider range of educational topics than can be addressed each year through the yearbooks alone.

Through membership in the Society one can add regularly to one's professional library at a very reasonable cost. Members also help to sustain a publication program that is widely recognized for its unique contributions to the literature of education.

The categories of membership, and the current dues in each category, are as follows:

Regular. The member receives a clothbound copy of each part of the two-volume yearbook (approximately 300 pages per volume). Annual dues, $20.

Comprehensive. The member receives clothbound copies of the two-volume yearbook and the two volumes in the current paperback series. Annual dues, $35.

Retirees and Graduate Students. Reduced dues—Regular, $16; Comprehensive, $31.
The above reduced dues are available to (a) those who have retired or are over sixty-five years of age and who have been members of the Society for at least ten years, and (b) graduate students in their first year of membership.

Life Membership. Persons sixty years of age or over may hold a Regular Membership for life upon payment of a lump sum based upon the life expectancy for their age group. Consult the Secretary-Treasurer for further details.

New members are required to pay an entrance fee of $1, in addition to the dues, in their first year of membership.

Membership is for the calendar year and dues are payable on or before January 1. A reinstatement fee of $.50 must be added to dues payments made after January 1.

In addition to receiving the publications of the Society as described above, members participate in the nomination and election of the six-member Board of Directors, which is responsible for managing the business and affairs of the Society, including the authorization of volumes to appear in the yearbook series. Two members of the Board are elected each year for three-year terms. Members of the Society who have contributed to its publications and who indicate a willingness to serve are eligible for election to the Board.

Members are urged to attend the one or more meetings of the Society that are arranged each year in conjunction with the annual meetings of major educational organizations. The purpose of such meetings is to present, discuss, and critique volumes in the current yearbook series. Announcements of meetings for the ensuing year are sent to members in December.

Upon written request from a member, the Secretary-Treasurer will send the current directory of members, synopses of meetings of the Board of Directors, and the annual financial report.

Persons desiring further information about membership may write to

KENNETH J. REHAGE, Secretary-Treasurer
National Society for the Study of Education

5835 Kimbark Ave.
Chicago, Ill. 60637

PUBLICATIONS OF THE NATIONAL SOCIETY FOR THE STUDY OF EDUCATION

1. The Yearbooks

NOTICE: Many of the early yearbooks of this series are now out of print. In the following list, those titles to which an asterisk is prefixed are not available for purchase.

*First Yearbook, 1902, Part I—*Some Principles in the Teaching of History.* Lucy M. Salmon.
*First Yearbook, 1902, Part II—*The Progress of Geography in the Schools.* W. M. Davis and H. M. Wilson.
*Second Yearbook, 1903, Part I—*The Course of Study in History in the Common School.* Isabel Lawrence, C. A. McMurry, Frank McMurry, E. C. Page, and E. J. Rice.
*Second Yearbook, 1903, Part II—*The Relation of Theory to Practice in Education.* M. J. Holmes, J. A. Keith, and Levi Seeley.
*Third Yearbook, 1904, Part I—*The Relation of Theory to Practice in the Education of Teachers.* John Dewey, Sarah C. Brooks, F. M. McMurry, *et al.*
*Third Yearbook, 1904, Part II—*Nature Study.* W. S. Jackman.
*Fourth Yearbook, 1905, Part I—*The Education and Training of Secondary Teachers.* E. C. Elliott, E. G. Dexter, M. J. Holmes, *et al.*
*Fourth Yearbook, 1905, Part II—*The Place of Vocational Subjects in the High-School Curriculum.* J. S. Brown, G. B. Morrison, and Ellen Richards.
*Fifth Yearbook, 1906, Part I—*On the Teaching of English in Elementary and High Schools.* G. P. Brown and Emerson Davis.
*Fifth Yearbook, 1906, Part II—*The Certification of Teachers.* E. P. Cubberley.
*Sixth Yearbook, 1907, Part I—*Vocational Studies for College Entrance.* C. A. Herrick, H. W. Holmes, T. deLaguna, V. Prettyman, and W. J. S. Bryan.
*Sixth Yearbook, 1907, Part II—*The Kindergarten and Its Relation to Elementary Education.* Ada Van Stone Harris, E. A. Kirkpatrick, Marie Kraus-Boelté, Patty S. Hill, Harriette M. Mills, and Nina Vandewalker.
*Seventh Yearbook, 1908, Part I—*The Relation of Superintendents and Principals to the Training and Professional Improvement of Their Teachers.* Charles D. Lowry.
*Seventh Yearbook, 1908, Part II—*The Co-ordination of the Kindergarten and the Elementary School.* B. C. Gregory, Jennie B. Merrill, Bertha Payne, and Margaret Giddings.
*Eighth Yearbook, 1909, Part I—*Education with Reference to Sex: Pathological, Economic, and Social Aspects.* C. R. Henderson.
*Eighth Yearbook, 1909, Part II—*Education with Reference to Sex: Agencies and Methods.* C. R. Henderson and Helen C. Putnam.
*Ninth Yearbook, 1910, Part I—*Health and Education.* T. D. Wood.
*Ninth Yearbook, 1910, Part II—*The Nurses in Education.* T. D. Wood, *et al.*.
*Tenth Yearbook, 1911, Part I—*The City School as a Community Center.* H. C. Leipziger, Sarah E. Hyre, R. D. Warden, C. Ward Crampton, E. W. Stitt, E. J. Ward, Mrs. E. C. Grice, and C. A. Perry.
*Tenth Yearbook, 1911, Part II—*The Rural School as a Community Center.* B. H. Crocheron, Jessie Field, F. W. Howe, E. C. Bishop, A. B. Graham, O. J. Kern, M. T. Scudder, and B. M. Davis.
*Eleventh Yearbook, 1912, Part I—*Industrial Education: Typical Experiments Described and Interpreted.* J. F. Barker, M. Bloomfield, B. W. Johnson, P. Johnston, L. M. Leavitt, G. A. Mirick, M. W. Murray, C. F. Perry, A. L. Safford, and H. B. Wilson.
*Eleventh Yearbook, 1912, Part II—*Agricultural Education in Secondary Schools.* A. C. Monahan, R. W. Stimson, D. J. Crosby, W. H. French, H. F. Button, F. R. Crane, W. R. Hart, and G. F. Warren.
*Twelfth Yearbook, 1913, Part I—*The Supervision of City Schools,* Franklin Bobbitt, J. W. Hall, and J. D. Wolcott.
*Twelfth Yearbook, 1913, Part II—*The Supervision of Rural Schools.* A. C. Monahan, L. J. Hanifan, J. E. Warren, Wallace Lund, U. J. Hoffman, A. S. Cook, E. M. Rapp, Jackson Davis, J. D. Wolcott.
*Thirteenth Yearbook, 1914, Part I—*Some Aspects of High-School Instruction and Administration.* H. C. Morrison, E. R. Breslich, W. A. Jessup, and L. D. Coffman.
*Thirteenth Yearbook, 1914, Part II—*Plans for Organizing School Surveys, with a Summary of Typical School Surveys.* Charles H. Judd and Henry L. Smith.
*Fourteenth Yearbook, 1915, Part I—*Minimum Essentials in Elementary School Subjects—Standards and Current Practices.* H. B. Wilson, H. W. Holmes, F. E. Thompson, R. G. Jones, S. A. Courtis, W. S. Gray, F. N. Freeman, H. C. Pryor, J. F. Hosic, W. A. Jessup, and W. C. Bagley.
*Fourteenth Yearbook, 1915, Part II—*Methods for Measuring Teachers' Efficiency.* Arthur C. Boyce.

*Fifteenth Yearbook, 1916, Part I—*Standards and Tests for the Measurement of the Efficiency of Schools and School Systems.* G. D. Strayer, Bird T. Baldwin, B. R. Buckingham, F. W. Ballou, D. C. Bliss, H. G. Childs, S. A. Courtis, E. P. Cubberley, C. H. Judd, George Melcher, E. E. Oberholtzer, J. B. Sears, Daniel Starch, M. R. Trabue, and G. M. Whipple.

*Fifteenth Yearbook, 1916, Part II—*The Relationship between Persistence in School and Home Conditions.* Charles E. Holley.

*Fifteenth Yearbook, 1916, Part III—*The Junior High School.* Aubrey A. Douglass.

*Sixteenth Yearbook, 1917, Part I—*Second Report of the Committee on Minimum Essentials in Elementary-School Subjects.* W. C. Bagley, W. W. Charters, F. N. Freeman, W. S. Gray, Ernest Horn, J. H. Hoskinson, W. S. Monroe, C. F. Munson, H. C. Pryor, L. W. Rapeer, G. M. Wilson, and H. B. Wilson.

*Sixteenth Yearbook, 1917, Part II—*The Efficiency of College Students as Conditioned by Age at Entrance and Size of High School.* B. F. Pittenger.

*Seventeenth Yearbook, 1918, Part I—*Third Report of the Committee on Economy of Time in Education.* W. C. Bagley, B. B. Bassett, M. E. Branom, Alice Camerer, J. E. Dealey, C. A. Ellwood, E. B. Greene, A. B. Hart, J. F. Hosic, E. T. Housh, W. H. Mace, L. R. Marston, H. C. McKown, A. E. Mitchell, W. C. Reavis, D. Snedden, and H. B. Wilson.

*Seventeenth Yearbook, 1918, Part II—*The Measurement of Educational Products.* E. J. Ashbaugh, W. A. Averill, L. P. Ayers, F. W. Ballou, Edna Bryner, B. R. Buckingham, S. A. Courtis, M. E. Haggerty, C. H. Judd, George Melcher, W. S. Monroe, E. A. Nifenecker, and E. L. Thorndike.

*Eighteenth Yearbook, 1919, Part I—*The Professional Preparation of High-School Teachers.* G. N. Cade, S. S. Colvin, Charles Fordyce, H. H. Foster, T. S. Gosling, W. S. Gray, L. V. Koos, A. R. Mead, H. L. Miller, F. C. Whitcomb, and Clifford Woody.

*Eighteenth Yearbook, 1919, Part II—*Fourth Report of Committee on Economy of Time in Education.* F. C. Ayer, F. N. Freeman, W. S. Gray, Ernest Horn, W. S. Monroe, and C. E. Seashore.

*Nineteenth Yearbook, 1920, Part I—*New Materials of Instruction.* Prepared by the Society's Committee on Materials of Instruction.

*Nineteenth Yearbook, 1920, Part II—*Classroom Problems in the Education of Gifted Children.* T. S. Henry.

*Twentieth Yearbook, 1921, Part I—*New Materials of Instruction.* Second Report by Society's Committee.

*Twentieth Yearbook, 1921, Part II—*Report of the Society's Committee on Silent Reading.* M. A. Burgess, S. A. Courtis, C. E. Germane, W. S. Gray, H. A. Greene, Reginia R. Heller, J. H. Hoover, J. A. O'Brien, J. L. Packer, Daniel Starch, W. W. Theisen, G. A. Yoakum, and representatives of other school systems.

*Twenty-first Yearbook, 1922, Parts I and II—*Intelligence Tests and Their Use,* Part I—*The Nature, History, and General Principles of Intelligence Testing.* E. L. Thorndike, S. S. Colvin, Harold Rugg, G. M. Whipple, Part II—*The Administrative Use of Intelligence Tests.* H. W. Holmes, W. K. Layton, Helen Davis, Agnes L. Rogers, Rudolf Pintner, M. R. Trabue, W. S. Miller, Bessie L. Gambrill, and others. The two parts are bound together.

*Twenty-second Yearbook, 1923, Part I—*English Composition: Its Aims, Methods and Measurements.* Earl Hudelson.

*Twenty-second Yearbook, 1923, Part II—*The Social Studies in the Elementary and Secondary School.* A. S. Barr, J. J. Coss, Henry Harap, R. W. Hatch, H. C. Hill, Ernest Horn, C. H. Judd, L. C. Marshall, F. M. McMurry, Earle Rugg, H. O. Rugg, Emma Schweppe, Mabel Snedaker, and C. W. Washburne.

*Twenty-third Yearbook, 1924, Part I—*The Education of Gifted Children.* Report of the Society's Committee, Guy M. Whipple, Chairman.

*Twenty-third Yearbook, 1924, Part II—*Vocational Guidance and Vocational Education for Industries.* A. H. Edgerton and others.

*Twenty-fourth Yearbook, 1925, Part I—*Report of the National Committee on Reading.* W. S. Gray, Chairman, F. W. Ballou, Rose L. Hardy, Ernest Horn, Francis Jenkins, S. A. Leonard, Estaline Wilson, and Laura Zirbes.

*Twenty-fourth Yearbook, 1925, Part II—*Adapting the Schools to Individual Differences.* Report of the Society's Committee. Carleton W. Washburne, Chairman.

*Twenty-fifth Yearbook, 1926, Part I—*The Present Status of Safety Education.* Report of the Society's Committee. Guy M. Whipple, Chairman.

*Twenty-fifth Yearbook, 1926, Part II—*Extra-Curricular Activities.* Report of the Society's Committee. Leonard V. Koos, Chairman.

*Twenty-sixth Yearbook, 1927, Part I—*Curriculum-making: Past and Present.* Report of the Society's Committee. Harold O. Rugg, Chairman.

*Twenty-sixth Yearbook, 1927, Part II—*The Foundations of Curriculum-making.* Prepared by individual members of the Society's Committee. Harold O. Rugg, Chairman.

*Twenty-seventh Yearbook, 1928, Part I—*Nature and Nurture: Their Influence upon Intelligence.* Prepared by the Society's Committee. Lewis M. Terman, Chairman.

*Twenty-seventh Yearbook, 1928, Part II—*Nature and Nurture: Their Influence upon Achievement.* Prepared by the Society's Committee. Lewis M. Terman, Chairman.

*Twenty-eighth Yearbook, 1929, Parts I and II—*Preschool and Parental Education.* Part I—*Organization and Development.* Part II—*Research and Method.* Prepared by the Society's Committee. Lois H. Meek, Chairman. Bound in one volume. Cloth.

*Twenty-ninth Yearbook, 1930, Parts I and II—*Report of the Society's Committee on Arithmetic.* Part I—*Some Aspects of Modern Thought on Arithmetic.* Part II—*Research in Arithmetic.* Prepared by the Society's Committee. F. B. Knight, Chairman. Bound in one volume.

*Thirtieth Yearbook, 1931, Part I—*The Status of Rural Education.* First Report of the Society's Committee on Rural Education. Orville G. Brim, Chairman.

Thirtieth Yearbook, 1931, Part II—*The Textbook in American Education.* Report of the Society's Committee on the Textbook. J. B. Edmonson, Chairman. Cloth. Paper.

*Thirty-first Yearbook, 1932, Part I—*A Program for Teaching Science.* Prepared by the Society's Committee on the Teaching of Science. S. Ralph Powers, Chairman.

*Thirty-first Yearbook, 1932, Part II—*Changes and Experiments in Liberal-Arts Education.* Prepared by Kathryn McHale, with numerous collaborators.

*Thirty-second Yearbook, 1933—*The Teaching of Geography.* Prepared by the Society's Committee on the Teaching of Geography. A. E. Parkins, Chairman.

*Thirty-third Yearbook, 1934, Part I—*The Planning and Construction of School Buildings.* Prepared by the Society's Committee on School Buildings. N. L. Engelhardt, Chairman.

*Thirty-third Yearbook, 1934, Part II—*The Activity Movement.* Prepared by the Society's Committee on the Activity Movement, Lois Coffey Mossman, Chairman.

Thirty-fourth Yearbook, 1935—*Educational Diagnosis.* Prepared by the Society's Committee on Educational Diagnosis. L. J. Brueckner, Chairman. Paper.

*Thirty-fifth Yearbook, 1936, Part I—*The Grouping of Pupils.* Prepared by the Society's Committee. W. W. Coxe, Chairman.

*Thirty-fifth Yearbook, 1936, Part II—*Music Education.* Prepared by the Society's Committee. W. L. Uhl, Chairman.

*Thirty-sixth Yearbook, 1937, Part I—*The Teaching of Reading.* Prepared by the Society's Committee. W. S. Gray, Chairman.

*Thirty-sixth Yearbook, 1937, Part II—*International Understanding through the Public-School Curriculum.* Prepared by the Society's Committee. I. L. Kandel, Chairman.

*Thirty-seventh Yearbook, 1938, Part I—*Guidance in Educational Institutions.* Prepared by the Society's Committee. G. N. Kefauver, Chairman.

*Thirty-seventh Yearbook, 1938, Part II—*The Scientific Movement in Education.* Prepared by the Society's Committee. F. N. Freeman, Chairman.

*Thirty-eighth Yearbook, 1939, Part I—*Child Development and the Curriculum.* Prepared by the Society's Committee. Carleton Washburne, Chairman.

*Thirty-eighth Yearbook, 1939, Part II—*General Education in the American College.* Prepared by the Society's Committee. Alvin Eurich, Chairman. Cloth.

*Thirty-ninth Yearbook, 1940, Part I—*Intelligence: Its Nature and Nurture. Comparative and Critical Exposition.* Prepared by the Society's Committee. G. D. Stoddard, Chairman.

*Thirty-ninth Yearbook, 1940, Part II—*Intelligence: Its Nature and Nurture. Original Studies and Experiments.* Prepared by the Society's Committee. G. D. Stoddard, Chairman.

*Fortieth Yearbook, 1941—*Art in American Life and Education.* Prepared by the Society's Committee. Thomas Munro, Chairman.

Forty-first Yearbook, 1942, Part I—*Philosophies of Education.* Prepared by the Society's Committee. John S. Brubacher, Chairman. Paper.

Forty-first Yearbook, 1942, Part II—*The Psychology of Learning.* Prepared by the Society's Committee. T. R. McConnell, Chairman. Cloth.

*Forty-second Yearbook, 1943, Part I—*Vocational Education.* Prepared by the Society's Committee. F. J. Keller, Chairman.

*Forty-second Yearbook, 1943, Part II—*The Library in General Education.* Prepared by the Society's Committee. L. R. Wilson, Chairman.

Forty-third Yearbook, 1944, Part I—*Adolescence.* Prepared by the Society's Committee. Harold E. Jones, Chairman. Paper.

*Forty-third Yearbook, 1944, Part II—*Teaching Language in the Elementary School.* Prepared by the Society's Committee. M. R. Trabue, Chairman.

*Forty-fourth Yearbook, 1945, Part I—*American Education in the Postwar Period: Curriculum Reconstruction.* Prepared by the Society's Committee. Ralph W. Tyler, Chairman.

*Forty-fourth Yearbook, 1945, Part II—*American Education in the Postwar Period: Structural Reorganization.* Prepared by the Society's Committee. Bess Goodykoontz, Chairman. Paper.

*Forty-fifth Yearbook, 1946, Part I—*The Measurement of Understanding.* Prepared by the Society's Committee. William A. Brownell, Chairman.

*Forty-fifth Yearbook, 1946, Part II—*Changing Conceptions in Educational Administration.* Prepared by the Society's Committee. Alonzo G. Grace, Chairman.

*Forty-sixth Yearbook, 1947, Part I—*Science Education in American Schools.* Prepared by the Society's Committee. Victor H. Noll, Chairman.

*Forty-sixth Yearbook, 1947, Part II—*Early Childhood Education.* Prepared by the Society's Committee. N. Searle Light, Chairman. Paper.

Forty-seventh Yearbook, 1948, Part I—*Juvenile Delinquency and the Schools.* Prepared by the Society's Committee. Ruth Strang, Chairman. Cloth.

Forty-seventh Yearbook, 1948, Part II—*Reading in the High School and College.* Prepared by the Society's Committee. William S. Gray, Chairman. Cloth. Paper.

*Forty-eighth Yearbook, 1949, Part I—*Audio-visual Materials of Instruction.* Prepared by the Society's Committee. Stephen M. Corey, Chairman. Cloth.

*Forty-eighth Yearbook, 1949, Part II—*Reading in the Elementary School.* Prepared by the Society's Committee. Arthur I. Gates, Chairman.

*Forty-ninth Yearbook, 1950, Part I—*Learning and Instruction.* Prepared by the Society's Committee. G. Lester Anderson, Chairman.

*Forty-ninth Yearbook, 1950, Part II—*The Education of Exceptional Children.* Prepared by the Society's Committee. Samuel A. Kirk, Chairman.

Fiftieth Yearbook, 1951, Part I—*Graduate Study in Education.* Prepared by the Society's Board of Directors. Ralph W. Tyler, Chairman. Paper.

Fiftieth Yearbook, 1951, Part II—*The Teaching of Arithmetic.* Prepared by the Society's Committee. G. T. Buswell, Chairman. Cloth, Paper.

Fifty-first Yearbook, 1952, Part I—*General Education.* Prepared by the Society's Committee. T. R. McConnell, Chairman. Cloth, Paper.

Fifty-first Yearbook, 1952, Part II—*Education in Rural Communities.* Prepared by the Society's Committee. Ruth Strang, Chairman. Cloth, Paper.

*Fifty-second Yearbook, 1953, Part I—*Adapting the Secondary-School Program to the Needs of Youth.* Prepared by the Society's Committee: William G. Brink, Chairman.

Fifty-second Yearbook, 1953, Part II—*The Community School.* Prepared by the Society's Committee. Maurice F. Seay, Chairman. Cloth.

Fifty-third Yearbook, 1954, Part I—*Citizen Cooperation for Better Public Schools.* Prepared by the Society's Committee. Edgar L. Morphet, Chairman. Cloth, Paper.

*Fifty-third Yearbook, 1954, Part II—*Mass Media and Education.* Prepared by the Society's Committee. Edgar Dale, Chairman.

*Fifty-fourth Yearbook, 1955, Part I—*Modern Philosophies and Education.* Prepared by the Society's Committee. John S. Brubacher, Chairman.

Fifty-fourth Yearbook, 1955, Part II—*Mental Health in Modern Education.* Prepared by the Society's Committee. Paul A. Witty, Chairman. Paper.

*Fifty-fifth Yearbook, 1956, Part I—*The Public Junior College.* Prepared by the Society's Committee. B. Lamar Johnson, Chairman.

*Fifty-fifth Yearbook, 1956, Part II—*Adult Reading.* Prepared by the Society's Committee. David H. Clift, Chairman.

*Fifty-sixth Yearbook, 1957, Part I—*In-service Education of Teachers, Supervisors, and Administrators.* Prepared by the Society's Committee. Stephen M. Corey, Chairman. Cloth.

Fifty-sixth Yearbook, 1957, Part II—*Social Studies in the Elementary School.* Prepared by the Society's Committee. Ralph C. Preston, Chairman. Cloth, Paper.

*Fifty-seventh Yearbook, 1958, Part I—*Basic Concepts in Music Education.* Prepared by the Society's Committee. Thurber H. Madison, Chairman. Cloth.

*Fifty-seventh Yearbook, 1958, Part II—*Education for the Gifted.* Prepared by the Society's Committee. Robert J. Havighurst, Chairman.

*Fifty-seventh Yearbook, 1958, Part III—*The Integration of Educational Experiences.* Prepared by the Society's Committee. Paul L. Dressel, Chairman. Cloth.

Fifty-eighth Yearbook, 1959, Part I—*Community Education: Principles and Practices from World-wide Experience.* Prepared by the Society's Committee. C. O. Arndt, Chairman. Cloth, Paper.

Fifty-eighth Yearbook, 1959, Part II—*Personnel Services in Education.* Prepared by the Society's Committee. Melvene D. Hardee, Chairman. Paper.

*Fifty-ninth Yearbook, 1960, Part I—*Rethinking Science Education.* Prepared by the Society's Committee. J. Darrell Barnard, Chairman.

*Fifty-ninth Yearbook, 1960, Part II—*The Dynamics of Instructional Groups.* Prepared by the Society's Committee. Gale E. Jensen, Chairman.

Sixtieth Yearbook, 1961, Part I—*Development in and through Reading.* Prepared by the Society's Committee. Paul A. Witty, Chairman. Cloth.

Sixtieth Yearbook, 1961, Part II—*Social Forces Influencing American Education.* Prepared by the Society's Committee. Ralph W. Tyler, Chairman. Cloth, Paper.

Sixty-first Yearbook, 1962, Part I—*Individualizing Instruction.* Prepared by the Society's Committee. Fred T. Tyler, Chairman. Cloth.

Sixty-first Yearbook, 1962, Part II—*Education for the Professions.* Prepared by the Society's Committee. G. Lester Anderson, Chairman. Cloth.

Sixty-second Yearbook, 1963, Part I—*Child Psychology.* Prepared by the Society's Committee. Harold W. Stevenson, Editor. Cloth.

Sixty-second Yearbook, 1963, Part II—*The Impact and Improvement of School Testing Programs.* Prepared by the Society's Committee. Warren G. Findley, Editor. Cloth.

Sixty-third Yearbook, 1964, Part I—*Theories of Learning and Instruction.* Prepared by the Society's Committee. Ernest R. Hilgard, Editor. Paper, Cloth.

Sixty-third Yearbook, 1964, Part II—*Behavioral Science and Educational Administration.* Prepared by the Society's Committee. Daniel E. Griffiths, Editor. Paper.

Sixty-fourth Yearbook, 1965, Part I—*Vocational Education.* Prepared by the Society's Committee. Melvin L. Barlow, Editor. Cloth.

*Sixty-fourth Yearbook, 1965, Part II—*Art Education.* Prepared by the Society's Committee. W. Reid Hastie, Editor.

Sixty-fifth Yearbook, 1966, Part I—*Social Deviancy among Youth.* Prepared by the Society's Committee. William W. Wattenberg, Editor. Cloth.

Sixty-fifth Yearbook, 1966, Part II—*The Changing American School.* Prepared by the Society's Committee. John I. Goodlad, Editor. Cloth.

*Sixty-sixth Yearbook, 1967, Part I—*The Educationally Retarded and Disadvantaged.* Prepared by the Society's Committee. Paul A. Witty, Editor. Cloth.

*Sixty-sixth Yearbook, 1967, Part II—*Programed Instruction.* Prepared by the Society's Committee. Phil C. Lange, Editor. Cloth.

Sixty-seventh Yearbook, 1968, Part I—*Metropolitanism: Its Challenge to Education.* Prepared by the Society's Committee. Robert J. Havighurst, Editor. Cloth.

Sixty-seventh Yearbook, 1968, Part II—*Innovation and Change in Reading Instruction.* Prepared by the Society's Committee. Helen M. Robinson, Editor. Cloth.

Sixty-eighth Yearbook, 1969, Part I—*The United States and International Education.* Prepared by the Society's Committee. Harold G. Shane, Editor. Cloth.

Sixty-eighth Yearbook, 1969, Part II—*Educational Evaluation: New Roles, New Means.* Prepared by the Society's Committee. Ralph W. Tyler, Editor. Paper.

*Sixty-ninth Yearbook, 1970, Part I—*Mathematics Education.* Prepared by the Society's Committee. Edward G. Begle, Editor. Cloth.

Sixty-ninth Yearbook, 1970, Part II—*Linguistics in School Programs.* Prepared by the Society's Committee. Albert H. Marckwardt, Editor. Cloth.

*Seventieth Yearbook, 1971, Part I—*The Curriculum: Retrospect and Prospect.* Prepared by the Society's Committee. Robert M. McClure, Editor. Paper.

Seventieth Yearbook, 1971, Part II—*Leaders in American Education.* Prepared by the Society's Committee. Robert J. Havighurst, Editor. Cloth.

Seventy-first Yearbook, 1972, Part I—*Philosophical Redirection of Educational Research.* Prepared by the Society's Committee. Lawrence G. Thomas, Editor. Cloth.

Seventy-first Yearbook, 1972, Part II—*Early Childhood Education.* Prepared by the Society's Committee. Ira J. Gordon, Editor. Paper.

Seventy-second Yearbook, 1973, Part I—*Behavior Modification in Education.* Prepared by the Society's Committee. Carl E. Thoresen, Editor. Cloth.

Seventy-second Yearbook, 1973, Part II—*The Elementary School in the United States.* Prepared by the Society's Committee. John I. Goodlad and Harold G. Shane, Editors. Cloth.

Seventy-third Yearbook, 1974, Part I—*Media and Symbols: The Forms of Expression, Communication and Education.* Prepared by the Society's Committee. David R. Olson, Editor. Cloth.

Seventy-third Yearbook, 1974, Part II—*Uses of the Sociology of Education.* Prepared by the Society's Committee. C. Wayne Gordon, Editor. Cloth.

Seventy-fourth Yearbook, 1975, Part I—*Youth.* Prepared by the Society's Committee. Robert J. Havighurst and Phillip H. Dreyer, Editors. Cloth.

Seventy-fourth Yearbook, 1975, Part II—*Teacher Education.* Prepared by the Society's Committee. Kevin Ryan, Editor. Cloth.

Seventy-fifth Yearbook, 1976, Part I—*Psychology of Teaching Methods.* Prepared by the Society's Committee. N. L. Gage, Editor. Paper.

*Seventy-fifth Yearbook, 1976, Part II—*Issues in Secondary Education.* Prepared by the Society's Committee. William Van Til, Editor. Cloth.

Seventy-sixth Yearbook, 1977, Part I—*The Teaching of English.* Prepared by the Society's Committee. James R. Squire, Editor. Cloth.

Seventy-sixth Yearbook, 1977, Part II—*The Politics of Education.* Prepared by the Society's Committee. Jay D. Scribner, Editor. Paper.

Seventy-seventh Yearbook, 1978, Part I—*The Courts and Education,* Clifford P. Hooker, Editor. Cloth.

Seventy-seventh Yearbook, 1978, Part II—*Education and the Brain,* Jeanne Chall and Allan F. Mirsky, Editors. Paper.

Seventy-eighth Yearbook, 1979, Part I—*The Gifted and the Talented: Their Education and Development,* A. Harry Passow, Editor. Paper.

Seventy-eighth Yearbook, 1979, Part II—*Classroom Management,* Daniel L. Duke, Editor, Paper.

Seventy-ninth Yearbook, 1980, Part I—*Toward Adolescence: The Middle School Years.* Mauritz Johnson, Editor. Cloth.

Seventy-ninth Yearbook, 1980, Part II—*Learning a Second Language,* Frank M. Grittner, Editor. Cloth.

Eightieth Yearbook, 1981, Part I—*Philosophy and Education*, Jonas F. Soltis, Editor. Cloth.
Eightieth Yearbook, 1981, Part II—*The Social Studies*, Howard D. Mehlinger and O. L. Davis, Jr., Editors. Cloth.
Eighty-first Yearbook, 1982, Part I—*Policy Making in Education*, Ann Lieberman and Milbrey W. McLaughlin, Editors. Cloth.
Eighty-first Yearbook, 1982, Part II—*Education and Work*, Harry F. Silberman, Editor. Cloth.
Eighty-second Yearbook, 1983, Part I—*Individual Differences and the Common Curriculum*, Gary D Fenstermacher and John I. Goodlad, Editors. Cloth.
Eighty-second Yearbook, 1983, Part II—*Staff Development*, Gary Griffin, Editor. Cloth.
Eighty-third Yearbook, 1984, Part I—*Becoming Readers in a Complex Society*, Alan C. Purves and Olive S. Niles, Editors. Cloth.
Eighty-third Yearbook, 1984, Part II—*The Humanities in Precollegiate Education*, Benjamin Ladner, Editor. Cloth.

Yearbooks of the National Society are distributed by

UNIVERSITY OF CHICAGO PRESS, 5801 ELLIS AVE., CHICAGO, ILLINOIS 60637

Please direct inquiries regarding prices of volumes still available to the University of Chicago Press. Orders for these volumes should be sent to the University of Chicago Press, not to the offices of the National Society.

2. The Series on Contemporary Educational Issues

In addition to its Yearbooks the Society now publishes volumes in a series on Contemporary Educational Issues. These volumes are prepared under the supervision of the Society's Commission on an Expanded Publication Program.

The 1984 Titles

Women and Education: Equity or Equality? (Elizabeth Fennema and M. Jane Ayer, eds.)

Curriculum Development: Problems, Processes, and Programs (Glenys G. Unruh and Adolph Unruh)

The 1983 Titles

The Hidden Curriculum and Moral Education (Henry A. Giroux and David Purpel, eds.)

The Dynamics of Organizational Change in Education (J. Victor Baldridge and Terrance Deal, eds.)

The 1982 Titles

Improving Educational Standards and Productivity: The Research Basis for Policy (Herbert J. Walberg, ed.)

Schools in Conflict: The Politics of Education (Frederick M. Wirt and Michael W. Kirst)

The 1981 Titles

Psychology and Education: The State of the Union (Frank H. Farley and Neal J. Gordon, eds.)

Selected Issues in Mathematics Education (Mary M. Lindquist, ed.)

The 1980 Titles

Minimum Competency Achievement Testing: Motives, Models, Measures, and Consequences (Richard M. Jaeger and Carol K. Tittle, eds.)

Collective Bargaining in Public Education (Anthony M. Cresswell, Michael J. Murphy, with Charles T. Kerchner)

The 1979 Titles

Educational Environments and Effects: Evaluation, Policy, and Productivity (Herbert J. Walberg, ed.)

Research on Teaching: Concepts, Findings, and Implications (Penelope L. Peterson and Herbert J. Walberg, eds.)

The Principal in Metropolitan Schools (Donald A. Erickson and Theodore L. Reller, eds.)

The 1978 Titles

Aspects of Reading Education (Susanna Pflaum-Connor, ed.)

History, Education, and Public Policy: Recovering the American Educational Past (Donald R. Warren, ed.)

From Youth to Constructive Adult Life: The Role of the Public School (Ralph W. Tyler, ed.)

The 1977 Titles

Early Childhood Education: Issues and Insights (Bernard Spodek and Herbert J. Walberg, eds.)

The Future of Big City Schools: Desegregation Policies and Magnet Alternatives (Daniel U. Levine and Robert J. Havighurst, eds.)

Educational Administration: The Developing Decades (Luvern L. Cunningham, Walter G. Hack, and Raphael O. Nystrand, eds.)

The 1976 Titles

Prospects for Research and Development in Education (Ralph W. Tyler, ed.)

Public Testimony on Public Schools (Commission on Educational Governance)

Counseling Children and Adolescents (William M. Walsh, ed.)

The 1975 Titles

Schooling and the Rights of Children (Vernon Haubrich and Michael Apple, eds.)

Systems of Individualized Education (Harriet Talmage, ed.)

Educational Policy and International Assessment: Implications of the IEA Assessment of Achievement (Alan Purves and Daniel U. Levine, eds.)

The 1974 Titles

Crucial Issues in Testing (Ralph W. Tyler and Richard M. Wolf, eds.)

Conflicting Conceptions of Curriculum (Elliott Eisner and Elizabeth Vallance, eds.)

Cultural Pluralism (Edgar G. Epps, ed.)

Rethinking Educational Equality (Andrew T. Kopan and Herbert J. Walberg, eds.)

All of the preceding volumes may be ordered from

McCutchan Publishing Corporation
2526 Grove Street
Berkeley, California 94704

The 1972 Titles

Black Students in White Schools (Edgar G. Epps, ed.)

Flexibility in School Programs (W. J. Congreve and G. L. Rinehart, eds.)

Performance Contracting—1969-1971 (J. A. Mecklenburger)

The Potential of Educational Futures (Michael Marien and W. L. Ziegler, eds.)

Sex Differences and Discrimination in Education (Scarvia Anderson, ed.)

The 1971 Titles

Accountability in Education (Leon M. Lessinger and Ralph W. Tyler, eds.)

Farewell to Schools??? (D. U. Levine and R. J. Havighurst, eds.)

Models for Integrated Education (D. U. Levine, ed.)

PYGMALION *Reconsidered* (J. D. Elashoff and R. E. Snow)

Reactions to Silberman's CRISIS IN THE CLASSROOM (A. Harry Passow, ed.)

The 1971 and 1972 titles in this series are now out of print.